Entrepreneurs of Profit and Pride

MEDIA AND SOCIETY SERIES
J. Fred MacDonald, General Editor

Television Studies: Textual Analysis
  Gary Burns and Robert J. Thompson
Enduring Values
  June Sochen
Australian Movies and the American Dream
  Glen Lewis
Who Shot the Sheriff?
  J. Fred MacDonald

Entrepreneurs of Profit and Pride
From Black-Appeal to Radio Soul

LIBRARY

Mark Newman

PRAEGER

New York
Westport, Connecticut
London

Library of Congress Cataloging-in-Publication Data

Newman, Mark.
    Entrepreneurs of profit and pride: from Black-appeal to radio
soul / Mark Newman.
       p.   cm.
    Bibliography: p.
    Includes index.
    ISBN 0-275-92888-8
    1. Afro-Americans in radio broadcasting. 2. Afro-Americans—
Social life and customs. 3. Radio audiences—United States.
4. Afro-American radio stations. 5. Radio advertising—United
States. 6. Entrepreneurship—United States. I. Title.
PN1991.8.A35N49   1988
305.8'96073—dc19   88-5887

Library of Congress Catalog Card Number: 88-5887
ISBN: 0-275-92888-8

First published in 1988

Praeger Publishers, One Madison Avenue, New York, NY 10010
A division of Greenwood Press, Inc.

Printed in the United States of America

The paper used in this book complies with the
Permanent Paper Standard issued by the National
Information Standards Organization (Z39.48-1984).

10 9 8 7 6 5 4 3 2 1

*This book is dedicated to
the memory of my father*

CONTENTS

PREFACE

"Radio Days," Woody Allen's 1987 film tribute to the medium's golden years, nostalgically and lovingly recaptures America's fascination with radio. The screen image centers family life around the radio. Through the eyes of the narrator, a small boy, we see how each family member responds individually to his or her favorite show. The boy's aunt cannot help but sing and dance when her favorite songs are played. He imagines he sees a Nazi submarine off the coast after the radio sounds the alarm. And his imagination conjures up a strikingly different fearless Masked Avenger from the short, bald actor who plays the role.

During radio's first three decades, from approximately 1920 to 1950, it went from the wonder of the age to a familiar member of the family, a welcome facet of everyday life. There are many factors behind radio's appeal and the willingness of Americans to have it intrude so heavily upon their lives, as it still does today though in a different way. It was the first medium to bring the world into the home. More important was the way in which the world entered—through sound. The listener had to fill in the missing dimensions; the face of the Masked Avenger, the appearance of a Nazi submarine, the movements that accompanied Frank Sinatra's singing, or boxer Joe Louis uppercutting German heavyweight Max Schmeling.

One of the more novel techniques devised by radio to compensate for its limitations was used for the appearance of dancer Bill Robinson on the "Rudy Vallee Show." An elaborate stage was built so that microphones could capture and broadcast the sounds of his famous tap and soft-shoe dances.

In all these ways and more, radio engaged the listener's imagination. Sound coming over the speaker served as the amorphous, incomplete image that each listener filled in to suit an individual need or fancy. Radio was an anomaly, a mass medium whose appeal was to the individual. It affected people intimately by opening up a personal communications dialogue between the listener and the voices coming over the speaker.

But sometimes this dialogue was flawed. Black writer William Branch recalled that as a child he would sit with his family in front of the radio set laughing wildly at the antics of Amos and Andy, black characters played by white actors Freeman Gosden and Charles Correll. But Branch also remembered that his father never laughed. Later he learned why. Amos and Andy were supposedly "us." Branch's father apparently did not experience the feeling of sharing something special that stands at the center of radio's appeal, at least with "Amos 'n' Andy." As was true for many blacks, radio provided an ambivalent experience. The shows were entertaining and informative, but they could also prove embarrassing. Or they could entertain, inform, and serve, evoking feelings of pride and solidarity. It all depended on a turn of the dial.

Radio was a microcosm of society. During the years 1920 to 1954, it was also divided by a color line. On one side of the line was network broadcasting; on the other independent, black-appeal narrowcasting. The result was that blacks had two very distinct and different radio experiences. At the same time William Branch's father was gritting his teeth over the black image Amos and Andy presented to the world via network broadcasting, listeners in Chicago received an opposite black image via Jack L. Cooper's pioneering black-appeal programs narrowcast on station WSBC.

Assessing how blacks fared in radio or ascertaining why they fared as they did is difficult because the literature on the subject is spotty at best. The few existing treatments of the black experiences deal in the context of larger themes, using either tangential discussions or separate chapters to focus primarily on the negative influence race exerted in broadcasting. No work distinguishes between the two separate and very different experiences of broadcasting and narrowcasting. Nor do any gauge radio's influence on the black audience. Basically the field is wide open, particularly regarding black-appeal radio, for which no published books exist.

Black-appeal radio, very simply, is programming and advertising designed specifically for black audiences and black consumers. Black-appeal shows and commercials create that special shared feeling of personal, private communication. The only mass medium with an established and integral black-appeal component is radio. And in varying degrees it has had such a component since 1929.

This books fills the void in black-appeal scholarship. Focusing on the seminal period from approximately 1920 to 1954, it combines historical and communications methods of inquiry to examine black-appeal's origins, development, and impact on the black listening audience. It also expands the scholarship on blacks in broadcasting, because the conditions here instigated black-appeal programming.

By applying the basic, 1940s communications inquiry—who says what in which channel to whom with what effect, and how, where, when, and why—the foundation upon which radio generally and black-appeal programming specifically developed is uncovered. Radio is a communications medium that combines business and culture. In part, the emphasis on business is the result of the commercialization of the medium, as the very term *commercial radio* implies. The interaction between business and culture translated into the sale of airtime to advertisers to finance programming, that is, culture. The shows lured listeners, allowing sponsors to pitch their goods and services efficiently and effectively to masses of potential consumers. Thus, radio is a business, first and foremost, for profits determine what kinds of communications go on the air.

Advertising, then, is not only the financial basis of radio, it also is a determinant of programming. The size of the viewing audience often determines whether a show continues to be aired or not. This interplay of advertising and programming along with the phsyical attributes of the radio station, primarily the power of the signal, are the determining factors in the development of the broadcast and narrowcast strategies. The larger stations with strong signals could reach more people in more localities. These stations often gravitated to broadcasting by becoming affiliates of a national network that beamed universal programming coast-to-coast to the one big audience. The object was to air something for everyone over a network connection that reached a potential audience of millions so that large ad revenues could be earned to put into star quality shows.

The so-called golden age of radio remembered in "Radio Days" and so many other books and movies represented the ultimate realization of the broadcast strategy. Radio became the medium of big stars and big shows featuring wide-ranging entertainment. Mystery, adventure, comedy, music, science fiction, drama, and soap opera; Bob Hope, Bing Crosby, Paul Robeson, Duke Ellington, Jack Benny, and Gracie Allen—all could be brought into the American home with a touch of the dial. Network broadcasting was the radio that entertained, but usually embarrassed, blacks.

Narrowcasting was developed by stations with weaker signals that frequently covered only a small area. WSBC in Chicago, for example, was a part-time station sharing a frequency with two other similarly fixed outlets. Its signal did not even cover the entire city. The station's programming/marketing strategy was, and is today, a classic example of narrowcasting. It segmented its airtime to appeal to different ethnic groups with foreign language programming, thus building an advertising base among the merchants who catered to these groups. Where broadcasting was the expansive radio of power, narrowcasting was the tightly focused radio of numbers.

Whether in broadcasting or narrowcasting, the development of black-appeal radio and, where present, black-appeal programming depended upon the other primary business influence—entrepreneurship. For instance, Westinghouse executive Harry P. Davis's recognition of radio's potential as a mass medium was a classic, innovative response to change, or, in other words, a textbook entrepreneurial exercise. In 1920, he founded the first radio station, KDKA, in Pittsburgh. Two years later, in 1922, AT & T's innovative idea to open the airwaves to the public produced the first commercial, placing radio on the road to commercialization.

Programming, too, benefited from entrepreneurship, which is not restricted to the economic realm. In the mid-1920s, Chicago *Tribune* executive Ben McGanna launched a programming idea that transferred the newspaper comic strip to the airwaves, eventually producing radio's first big hit. "Amos 'n' Andy." Similarly, black entertainer Jack L. Cooper responded to a situation he likened to taxation without representation—blacks could sing but not talk on the air—by producing the first black-appeal show in Chicago in 1929.

Entrepreneurship provided a rationale and an opportunity to respond innovatively to change—societal, technological, and racial. It served as a wedge to open the eyes and the office doors of white executives who could not see the possibilities of appealing to blacks. Like athletics, entertainment, and religion, entrepreneurship provided blacks with a means of subverting the color line. As a result, it played a special role in black life. This is particularly true regarding the media, as shown in the Introduction.

In radio, entrepreneurship served as the linchpin linking the interaction of business and culture to a profits-and-pride formula. This book postulates that entrepreneurship provided the economic opportunity for black-appeal programming to appear and evolve and that it was the determining factor in the potent influence that radio exerted on the germination, development, and spread of the post–World War II black consciousness and culture known as "soul."

How black-appeal developed locally and nationally was determined by the relationship between entrepreneurial initiative and narrowcasting. Since the market niche was local and entrepreneurship was geared toward individual innovation (at least in this aspect of radio), black-appeal radio emerged individually and independently in cities and towns throughout the United States as conditions and recognition merited. The concept of black-appeal radio first appeared in 1929, but the coming of economic depression retarded its growth until the 1940s, when black-appeal boomed. Where a handful of stations beamed shows at blacks before 1940, 400 were doing so in 1954. Together these stations blanketed the country with black-appeal programming that was similar in format but individually tailored to the needs of local audiences. Black-appeal was not a national network in the broadcasting mold; it was more a loose confederation of independent operations engaged in similar pursuits.

This book examines the reasons behind the creation of black-appeal, its development, and its impact on the black audience. It is divided into three sections. Part I identifies the three major forces influencing broadcasting's treatment of blacks and black-appeal's development: opportunity, imagery, and communication. Chapters 1 and 2 discuss the reasons behind the negative imagery and faulty communication, which blocked opportunities for blacks in broadcasting, creating the need for black-appeal narrowcasting. Part II, Chapters 3 through 6, analyzes the various patterns of development of black-appeal ventures focusing on three representative, yet different, local examples and the national boom itself. Part III assesses the impact of black-appeal radio on soul consciousness in Chapter 7 and soul culture, that is, music, in Chapter 8. A short Coda discusses the role of the media in society as a purveyor of business and culture, drawing upon the black-appeal example.

Regarding the selection of case studies and the use of research data further discussion is needed. The viability of black-appeal as a field of study has been little recognized by scholars because no data base or literature exists, except for sporadic and sometimes hard-to-find articles and an M.A. thesis or two.

My recognition of black-appeal as a subject of study illuminates the problems surrounding its study. The idea for this book came to me while I was filming a documentary on a black radio show in Helena, Arkansas, and Memphis, Tennessee. Actually, the star of "King Biscuit Time," blues singer Sonny Boy Williamson, had been the inspiration for the movie. We wanted to do a film on blues but needed a subject that allowed the music to be showcased, as in a radio program.

The more interviews we conducted and the more people we met and the more photographs we collected, the greater my interest grew in black-appeal radio. That Helena and Memphis provided very different but extremely significant examples of this phenomenon and that I had already conducted valuable research on the subject contributed to my fascination. When production on the film moved to another black-appeal center, Chicago, where as a teenager I had tuned in the black station WVON, the decision was made. I would write a book on black-appeal radio, not blues—though a blues component would be included for reasons enumerated below.

Chance and fortune, to a great extent, produced the idea for this book. But the selection of Helena, Memphis, and Chicago as case studies, though in part fortuitous, was actually a very calculated decision. Taken separately each city stands alone as a very important part of the black-appeal story. Together they exemplify the general pattern of development.

The concept originated in Chicago with Jack L. Cooper's pioneering work in the late 1920s and 1930s. Cooper innovated many of the programming ideas and practices that became standard in most black-appeal ventures coast to coast, in part because he set the example that others followed. Cooper's story illuminates the vital interaction between advertising and programming under the entrepreneurial initiative present in all enterprises but so predominant in Chicago as to make it the likely example to study.

Chicago was the capital of black-appeal in the late 1940s and 1950s. The

experience of the midwestern city also exemplified development in large northern and western metropolises, where ethnic narrowcasting supplied a friendly
programming niche for black-appeal programming. The coming of the boom to
Chicago provides a good transition to the analysis of the nationwide black-
appeal explosion that took place after 1945.

Helena is a small southern town located fifty miles south of Memphis, Tennessee, on the Arkansas side of the Mississippi River. Here the impetus was
the revolution in southern agriculture that produced a new black consumer class
in the area. This revolution also initiated the massive black migration to cities
throughout the United States that helped to precipitate the boom nationwide.
The black-appeal focus here is on "King Biscuit Time," which is still on the
air.

Memphis experienced a different pattern of development. Both in the 1930s
and after World War II, black-appeal's emergence centered around conditions
in the local radio industry. Initially, it was the inability to attract a white audience tuned into network shows that produced black programs. In the 1940s,
a failed effort at a theme station (the new programming format developed at
that time partially in response to television) led to the first all-black station.
This later venture involved personnel with black-appeal experience, a unique
situation. Most important however was the institution of a service component
that integrated radio station WDIA into the black community. It became the
most powerful and prominent black-appeal station in the 1950s, receiving the
plum of radio transmission—a clear 50,000-watt channel.

Beyond the difference in patterns of development, these three cities had other
qualities that made them good candidates for selection. In terms of size, they
represent a logical progression from small town to medium-size city to large
metropolis. Similarly, all are inland ports. All had established black populations and black cultural traditions, particularly regarding blues. Chicago had
the largest black community in the U.S. Geographically these cities are aligned
along a primary black migration route. A straight line can be drawn from the
starting point in the countryside around Helena to Memphis, which served as a
depot and terminus, to the ultimate destination, Chicago.

All these attributes make Chicago, Helena, and Memphis good matches for
individual and comparative analysis. They epitomize and exemplify black-appeal development.

Researching black-appeal ventures means going to the cities and the stations
to conduct interviews and gather print and visual materials. I found hard data
difficult to obtain because radio stations are notoriously lax in keeping records.
Photos are plentiful and very illuminating, providing visual proof of statements
made in interviews. But only Jack L. Cooper retained and maintained files of
any size: newspaper clippings, letters, telegrams, advertising communications
and contracts, and the ubiquitous photos. His widow, Gertrude, kindly allowed
me access to these materials, without which the Chicago analysis would have

been woefully inadequate. This book is, as a result, based largely on new research data.

As for published data, the only hard body to be found is in the black-radio annuals of *Sponsor* magazine, a defunct trade journal. Its articles, surveys, and profiles supplied a valuable cross-checking reference. They also provided a national perspective on the boom.

The difficulties of researching this subject demonstrate that the very study of black-appeal radio requires as much innovative response to situations as black-appeal radio itself did. The same is true of analysis. How does one gauge effects on consciousness? What had the most impact on black consciousness? Programming? Advertising? The hiring of black announcers and disc jockeys? What process of communication occurred to change consciousness?

Analyzing the rise of soul consciousness, I found that the business aspects came to the fore. Basically, consciousness raising and change revolved around two dialogues. The white-black dialogue centered on meeting mutual needs with advertising acting as the channel of communication, because black-appeal sponsors were overwhelmingly white. To gain the appropriate black response at the dial and the cash register, whites had to appeal to black consumers as equals, deserving the same respectful solicitation accorded white consumers. This appeal included the types of goods and services advertised, the content of the commercials, and the ad campaigns themselves. Blacks, in turn, had to respond by supporting sponsor products and services.

The black-black dialogue was between audience members and the black air personalities. The communication included the way blacks on the air symbolized progress as well as how they talked to the audience, forging bonds of solidarity and friendship, and, of course, how they influenced program development. Another area of importance was the involvement of black radio personalities in the black community. Together these dialogues added new terms to black consciousness that instilled self-respect, pride, and solidarity. Being black was positive, not negative.

As will be seen from this discussion, race pervaded the black-appeal experience. But it acted as a two-edged sword, both a negative and a positive force. Race was a given that black-appeal entrepreneurs of both races had to overcome and manipulate to achieve their desired ends.

Another ever-present factor was blues. It is used here as an example and symbol of appeal and change. It was a proven money maker. In black-appeal media ventures in music and records, as well as radio, blues was the lure that attracted listeners and consumers. But as black-appeal developed and black consciousness changed, blues lost much of its appeal. Blues had always suffered from an image problem in the black community: it was considered "devil's music" that appealed to the lower classes. Its message did not contain the idea of progress so essential to soul. Nor did its lack of musical sophistication or rural imagery appeal to young, urban blacks. As such, in analyzing the decline of blues and its replacement by soul music, we can illuminate the ways radio influenced black culture.

This book, then, fills many gaps in black-appeal scholarship and expands the literature both on the development of local radio and the role of the media in society. It does this thematically rather than encyclopedically by following what is best described as a spherical mode of interdisciplinary analysis. The use of primary source materials and the focus on business and culture indicate many other possibilities for future works.

The successful conclusion of this study, not surprisingly, owes many debts to many people too numerous to name. I would like to thank UCLA professors Alex Saxton, Richard Weiss, and Michael Jones, who read the many versions and whose comments greatly improved the quality of this effort. I would like to thank Northeastern Illinois University professor J. Fred MacDonald, who early on saw the possibilities of this subject and offered much help and encouragement. To all those people who submitted to my questioning, particularly Gertrude Cooper, Nat D. Williams, and Robert Thomas, thanks are also due. But most of all, to my wife Kim and my family whose unwavering support and cooperation contributed so much to my finishing this work, my love and gratitude.

INTRODUCTION: FOR PROFITS AND PRIDE

Black-appeal radio, indeed any black-appeal media, is the product of entrepreneurial activity by blacks and whites. A term much bandied about in the 1980s, *entrepreneurship* always has been an integral component of the American economy. In black-appeal efforts, it dictated that a formula combining profits and pride would, on one hand, allow for the exploitation of available opportunities. On the other hand, it determined that business success would influence black consciousness and black culture.

To understand how and why *entrepreneurship* influenced black-appeal media development, the meaning of the term itself must be understood. A difficult task, since, as Peter F. Drucker writes, "there has been total confusion over the definitions of *entrepreneur* and *entrepreneurship* since the term was first coined almost two hundred years ago."[1] Regarding the black entrepreneur, an added complication is the race factor.

In the early 1800s, French economist J. B. Say wrote, "The entrepreneur shifts economic resources out of an area of lower and into an area of higher productivity and greater yield."[2] According to Drucker, Say's intent was to issue a manifesto,

a declaration of dissent: the entrepreneur upsets and disorganizes. As Joseph Schumpeter formulated it, his task is "creative destruction."[3]

While providing insight into the workings of entrepreneurship, such descriptions depict little of the excitement surrounding entrepreneurship. "Who are these entrepreneurs?'' asks the Conference Board. ''Are they bolder, smarter, hungrier than the rest of us? Mad geniuses? Gamblers? What makes them lay their talent on the line time after time?''[4]

In *Entrepreneurial Megabucks,* A. David Silver is even more boosterish in his praise. ''Without entrepreneurs, there would be no economy,'' he proclaims, calling them the ''new American heroes.'' Silver compares the entrepreneur-as-hero to Abraham Lincoln and Franklin Roosevelt. He enthusiastically, but very inaccurately, asserts,

Being an entrepreneur is like being the builder of civilization; like the pioneers who opened the Far West, after America inherited the land from Mexico in 1821. . . . The entrepreneurs who began around 1960 have transformed the American economy in much the same way as the frontiersmen built the Far West.[5]

After trimming away the hyperbole and bravado of this image, one thing is evident. The entrepreneur is more than someone ''who organizes and manages a business undertaking, assuming the risk for the sake of profits''; or, ''one who starts his own, new small business.''[6]

Drucker deflates the extravagant claims of the boosters and points out the inaccuracies of the generally accepted definitions. He notes that not all new small businesses are entrepreneurial. Large, established corporations, such as General Electric, have long engaged in entrepreneurship. Though they need capital, entrepreneurs are neither capitalists nor investors. And they may be employers, employees, or people working entirely alone. Regarding gambling and risk, Drucker writes, ''They take risks, of course, but so does anyone engaged in any kind of economic activity. . . . The commitment of present resources to future expectations . . . means . . . uncertainty and risk.''[7] Drucker adds that entrepreneurs often assume less risk than other business people because they operate in areas where competition is less intense. Lastly, he states that ''entrepreneurship is by no means confined solely to economic institutions.''[8] The modern American university and the hospital stand as textbook examples. In other words, entrepreneurs and entrepreneurship defy strict pigeon-holing.

The concept and practice of entrepreneurship extends into every facet of society. Entrepreneurship is an integral aspect of human social relations and rests on a theory that change is normal and healthy. The goal, particularly in the economy, is ''doing something different rather than better.''[9] This description explains J. B. Say's definition. By shifting economic resources to areas where opportunities are more plentiful, the entrepreneur innovates.

Drucker, in fact, sees innovation as ''the specific tool of entrepreneurs; . . . the means by which they exploit change.'' They are not so much actors producing change as reactors to it. ''The entrepreneur always searches for change, responds to it, and exploits it as an opportunity.''[10] In the economy, two entrepreneurial motivations are evident: profits, of course, but equally important is the ability to respond to change, to innovate, and to pursue an idea.

THE BLACK ENTREPRENEUR AND RACE

Defining the black entrepreneur involves taking into account another dimension—the race factor. Race pervades every aspect of black entrepreneurship, working for and against black entrepreneurial ventures. It can negatively influence activities by retarding change, obstructing responses, and limiting opportunity. Or it can provide the motivation for the entrepreneurial activity and favorable black response in the marketplace. It can insure success and limit risk. Equally important, race has shaped things so that successful black entrepreneurship symbolizes progress, thereby enhancing race pride and consciousness. In the media, it can also influence the development of black culture. All of these negative and positive aspects were integral to the development of black-appeal radio.

Race raised black entrepreneurship to a higher level because it added a powerful motivation to profits and innovation, namely, pride of progress. In this regard, Silver is accurate. Black entrepreneurs were, and are, race heroes. Each instance in which they successfully searched out change and responded innovatively to exploit opportunity represented a stride in racial progress that instilled pride. They were champions of the black cause. In fact, the term *entrepreneur* also means champion.[11] Entrepreneurial success in the very visible and pervasive media, where imagery and symbolism are so important, had even greater impact.

But as is true of *entrepreneurship* generally, the terms *race* and *championship* have been defined differently in different undertakings. The above mentioned influences could appear in strikingly different combinations, depending upon the situation and the medium.

For example, after the Civil War, blacks found entertainment a means of subverting the color line. They also discovered that subversion necessitated performance in venues acceptable to whites. This largely meant adherence to the stereotypical and degrading blackface minstrelsy tradition. In *Harlem Renaissance,* Nathan Huggins recounts that, "Black performers accommodated themselves to the [minstrelsy] tradition, while at the same time they tried to innovate and find more room for their talents within the convention; they moved to the musical review."[12]

The action of the black performers certainly fits within the entrepreneurial sphere. They recognized change and responded to it innovatively creating something different, achieving greater opportunity and obviously earnings. But they also responded to a racial image and convention, creating a venue that downplayed negative images while stressing positive attributes. Their actions championed a change in the black image that enhanced feelings of pride rather than embarrassment.

W. C. Handy's entrepreneurship in music composition and publishing earned him the title "Father of the Blues," acknowledging his contributions to the development of American popular music. His career further illuminates the role of the black entrepreneur in media and the black community.

Handy did not sire the blues. It was, he explains, "a common medium through which any individual might express his personal feelings in a sort of musical sociology. My part in their history was to introduce the 'blues' form [the twelve-bar, three-chord structure that defines it] to the general public." [13]

This introduction was partly based on a strong commitment to individual and racial progress. In his autobiography, *Father of the Blues* (originally titled "Fight It Out"), Handy writes, "I had read *The Black Phalanx, The Rising Sun,* and other books which told of the achievements of our race. Young as I was, I knew we were limited and proscribed." He drew inspiration from McGuffey's Fifth Reader, which contained a declamation by former Attorney General William Wirt entitled, "There Is No Excellence without Great Labor." Handy adopted the declamation as "a governing factor in all my subsequent undertakings," particularly, the maxim "What man has done, man can do." [14]

Handy launched his career as a musician in 1896, at the age of twenty-three. In 1903, he accepted the directorship of a black band in Clarksdale, Mississippi. A concert in Cleveland, Mississippi, showed him the change taking place in black music tastes. After relinquishing the bandstand to a trio of country players, Handy stood amazed as "More money than my nine musicians were being paid for the entire engagement" showered down at their feet. [15]

Handy's eyes opened to the possibility of blues. "Folks would pay money for it." He incorporated blues into his band's repertoire increasing "the popularity of our orchestra by leaps and bounds." When a song he composed for a Memphis mayoral candidate proved popular, he had it published. [16] Though bilked out of the copyright to "Memphis Blues," Handy recognized that song publishing was a viable way to profit from the blues. He formed Pace & Handy Music Company—Publishers, with Harry A. Pace around 1913. The firm flourished, precipitating a blues craze among blacks and whites. In 1918, Handy moved the business to New York City, the center of music publishing. [17]

Handy's entrepreneurial innovation was not as a pioneer black composer or music publisher. Blacks already had made a foothold in these areas. His innovation revolved around composing and publishing blues. Having recognized that black music tastes were changing and embracing blues and having maximized his opportunities in performance, Handy moved the blues out of an area of low yield and into one of greater productivity and yield: song publishing. He did not create change so much as upset and disorganize the publishing industry. He accomplished Joseph Schumpeter's "creative destruction," first by exploiting the appeal of the blues through his company, and second, by succeeding as a black man in the highly competitive music publishing industry.

Handy's accomplishments extended beyond the music industry. Recalling the inspiration of Wirt's declamation and his recognition of proscribed racial opportunity, he wrote of the fulfillment he experienced at the 1939 New York World's Fair: "There on the American Commons, tablets were erected containing the names of six hundred men and women from all races who had contributed to some degree to American culture, and among those names I saw mine." [18]

Handy's contributions had a strong impact on race pride, consciousness, and black culture. Handy demonstrated that a purely racial music form could capture the hearts of all Americans, and that it could successfully compete with white music. He stressed this racial connection, writing: "It is my contention that all real work in typical Negro music can come only from one to the manner born. It's his mother tongue. The art of writing blues . . . can be assumed but cannot be delegated outside of the blood." [19]

The integration of the blues into the popular music mainstream was a potent symbol of progress during a period of increasing racial segregation. Handy also showed that a black man could successfully compete with whites and win the praise of both races. In this fashion, the black entrepreneur was a champion.

Perry Bradford's experience in the record industry adds another perspective to the study of black media entrepreneurship. He innovated the concept of having black musicians make records for the black consumer market. Like Handy, Bradford was a seasoned performer who used the appeal of the blues as the basis of his innovative response to change. But in almost every other aspect the experiences of the two men differed profoundly.

Bradford's response was to the socioeconomic changes in the black community after World War I. In 1920, Bradford was living in New York City. He witnessed the massive migration of southern blacks into New York, part of a large exodus that brought hundreds of thousands of blacks to northern cities. Not only was the nation's racial demography changing but a new, burgeoning black urban consumer class was being created by this influx. The coming of peace brought a return of prosperity in which blacks shared, enhancing their consumer status. The 1920s also saw a tremendous rise in race pride and solidarity epitomized by the concept of the New Negro. [20]

These changes, combined with the acknowledged popularity of blues and jazz and the ongoing expansion in the phonograph industry, provided Bradford an entrepreneurial opportunity. "There's fourteen million Negroes in our great country," he reasoned, "and they will buy something if recorded by one of their own because we are the only folks that can sing and interpret hot jazz songs just off the griddle correctly." [21]

Appeals to race pride, solidarity, and progress are evident throughout Bradford's assertion. He played on pride and solidarity, claiming that such an approach would prove profitable, particularly as a sales pitch to black consumers. There was no question as to whether blacks could afford records, Bradford claimed, drawing upon the progress he saw in New York.

Bradford's idea differed sharply from Handy's. Where he targeted a new market—the black consumer—with a new medium, Handy aimed at an existing middle or wholesale market, using a familiar medium to sell a new song form. Handy's customers passed on the blues songs to consumers. And they did so in a traditional way, through performance—though records did play some role. But Handy came up against a stone wall when he proposed recording blacks, and he had to give up the attempt.[22] His efforts aimed at both races; Bradford focused solely on blacks, W. C. Handy was more a black media entrepreneur, whereas Perry Bradford was a black-appeal media entrepreneur, with their respective customers defining the difference.

Because of his emphasis on appealing to blacks with a new medium, Bradford discovered that race was a two-edged sword. For months, he pounded unsuccessfully on record company doors, trying to convince white executives that blacks could and would buy records by their own artists. The white image of blacks was a retarding factor here because these executives couldn't believe blacks owned enough phonographs or were viable enough consumers to respond to the same appeal as whites.[23] Black-appeal radio faced similar difficulties with images that skewed reality.

As happened later in radio, white recording executives pointed to some prominent failures to bolster their views of the black consumer's lack of buying power and responsiveness. Before World War I, attempts had been made to market records to blacks. None of these was in the black-appeal vein and none involved blues. Instead they were tailored along white and black-middle-class perceptions of what blacks wanted to or should hear. But the mass of blacks interested in the latest popular sounds, like blues, were uninterested "in 'humorous' shows, comic monologues, 'plantation airs,' and choral versions of religious music heard at Negro colleges." Nor did they respond to recordings by black classical performers.[24] As part of a well-rounded catalog of records these discs may have met some success, but material in the blackface tradition and high culture alone had little sales appeal.

Bradford, of course, had the proven ability of the blues as a selling point. Finally, he found a friendly ear, that of Fred Hager, the white recording manager of OKeh Records.[25] The first recording featured black vaudeville singer Mamie Smith backed by a white band. It sold well enough to merit another session again with Smith doing vocals but this time accompanied by a black jazz band. Titled "Crazy Blues," it became a major hit.[26] Blues scholar Derrick Stewart-Baxter called it a "sales blockbuster."[27] Again the blues had shown its ability as a money maker and blacks had amply demonstrated their growing consumer power.

The color line may have blinded recording executives and made them deaf to black appeals for discs, but the sight and sound of money quickly opened their eyes and ears. Record companies began setting up separate race record catalogs, as the discs marketed to blacks were called.[28] This term reflects growing racial solidarity and pride: "The Race" was what blacks called themselves.

Race records quickly became the one bright spot in the recording industry as a severe depression hit in the early 1920s. In 1923, Columbia, a major label, lost 2 million dollars and fell into receivership. Between 1921 and 1925, Victor's sales dropped by $25 million. The introduction of commercial radio caused this decline. Not only did radio provide better sound quality, but it also was cheaper to buy a radio and listen to music virtually for free than to purchase a phonograph and continually buy discs. And there was the excitement that surrounded this new technological advance that brought the world into the home.[29]

Blacks both did and did not share in radio mania during the 1920s. Certainly, the radio had some appeal, but blacks were not considered a viable audience by radio executives or advertisers. The programming contained little that appealed exclusively to them, as is shown in Chapters 1 and 2. For racially defined entertainment and marketing, records remained the black medium of choice. It assumed a role that radio would play up until the advent of television, for very similar reasons.[30]

By 1927, reports Jeff Titon in *Early Downhome Blues,* an estimated 10 million records were purchased annually by blacks, a figure, he notes, almost "equal to the black American population counted by the census-takers."[31] Obviously not every black person bought a record, but the total sales volume shows that the black response to race records was phenomenally high. No doubts could remain as to their status as a mass consumer market worthy of media appeal.

Like Handy, Bradford based his entrepreneurship on music publishing, founding his own firm. His activities, however, extended beyond composing and performing to record production. But where Handy succeeded, even overcoming a brush with bankruptcy, Bradford's business failed miserably after a few years.[32] He became another casualty, one more statistic proving that entrepreneurship is risky.

Bradford blamed his misfortune on racism. When he railed that "I've been blocked by an armful of Broadway music publishers," undoubtedly he was right.[33] But his situation was analogous to that of Handy. Being black had been more of a help than a handicap. His original sales pitch proves that being black was one of his greatest assets. Profits do not remove prejudice but, as will be shown throughout these pages, they can overcome it.

Bradford failed because he paid no attention to the business side of entrepreneurship, of which he was woefully ignorant. A chapter in his autobiography states his credo: "We Never Let No Business Interfere With Our Pleasure."[34] He also describes several instances of his ignorance. For example, in *Born With the Blues,* he writes of receiving his first royalty payment and the panic that ensued because he found no money in the envelope, only a bank draft. Bradford had to rush over to OKeh's office, where the treasurer explained the workings of bank drafts to him.[35] He never made the switch from entertainment to business, making him an easy mark for shrewd businessmen.

For these reasons, the industry he launched soon passed Perry Bradford by without giving him either the financial rewards or the recognition he desired and deserved. Unlike W. C. Handy, Bradford does not have a park named after him. Nor does the public know him as the father of race records. Perry Bradford is not recognized as a race hero or champion.

The irony is that the race record industry followed in the path Bradford proposed. A look at the Columbia catalog of releases between November 1923 and May 1931 shows the course of black-appeal record development. Of the 689 discs released, 328 were blues.[36] This reflected market demand. W. C. Handy writes, "The market was definitely there . . . In Clarence Williams' place and in Thomas' Music Store in Chicago I had seen cooks and Pullman porters buying a dozen or two dozen records at a time. Not sophisticated music, of course, but oddities that appealed to them, and blues—always blues."[37] The tastes of the public as identified by Bradford dictated the releases by the record companies.

Blues became even more integrated into American popular music and life while black-appeal records became a permanent part of black life, black culture, and the record industry. The innovation Bradford championed survived even though the champion himself wound up working at a race track in the 1940s.[38]

FOR PROFITS AND PRIDE

In all the above examples, the intricate and sometimes complex workings of the profits-and-pride formula are shown. Though the two complemented each other, black entrepreneurship in the media was a business venture first and a stride for racial progress second. Individual and business profits produced the racial benefits because, after all, success was based on the dollar. Handy became a race hero because his blues song sheets proved popular and band leaders and vaudeville performers of both races bought them. The same was true of race records. Bradford's business failure and resulting lack of recognition further demonstrates the primacy of profits, particularly in regard to the entrepreneur as race hero.

Pride was also a potent marketing tool in the pursuit of profits. It helped identify and consolidate the consumer market. Blacks bought records because the discs featured their own musicians performing black music. Enjoyment and pride were the twin sales appeals. Pride provided record companies with an effective promotional device to increase sales and was used as such in their advertising campaigns. "Paramount is devoted to the interests of the Race, and it owes its steady growth to this fact," stated a Paramount records ad that also touted its black manager, J. Mayo Williams.[39] Promoting race pride was good business. The solicitude of companies such as Paramount had the added effect of increasing race pride and consciousness. Unstated though certainly understood was the warning that the success of such appeals to pride depended upon blacks responding at the cash register.

In conclusion, the profits-and-pride formula allowed successful exploitation of the opportunity the entrepreneurial initiative opened to blacks. The two factors stood as symbols of the economic and racial motivations of the black entrepreneur. Because of the kind of medium it was, black-appeal radio represented the culmination, the natural progression, of this formula. It exerted a major influence on blacks, much greater than that of sheet music or records. The roles radio played—as a channel of communication, a purveyor of imagery, an integral part of everyday American life—made it a primary force in the development of soul consciousness and its cultural expression in music. Another factor was that a turn of the radio dial offered black entrepreneurship opportunities of an almost diametrically opposed nature.

NOTES

1. Peter F. Drucker, *Innovation and Entrepreneurship: Practice and Principles* (New York: Harper & Row Publishers, 1985), p. 21.

2. Ibid.

3. Ibid., p. 26.

4. "The Entrepreneur in You," *Across the Board,* vol. 21, nos. 7, 8 (July-August 1984), p. 1.

5. A. David Silver, *Entrepreneurial Megabucks: The 100 Greatest Entrepreneurs of the Last Twenty-Five Years* (New York: John Wiley & Sons, 1985), p. 451.

6. Drucker, *Innovation and Entrepreneurship,* p. 21.

7. Ibid., p. 25.

8. Ibid., p. 23.

9. Ibid., p. 26.

10. Ibid., pp. 27–28.

11. It is derived from the French *entreprenour.*

12. Nathan Huggins, *Harlem Renaissance* (New York: Oxford University Press, 1971), p. 274.

13. W. C. Handy, *Father of the Blues: An Autobiography,* ed. Arna Bontemps (New York: The Macmillan Company, 1941), p. 99.

14. Ibid., p. 273.

15. Ibid., p. 77.

16. Ibid., p. 78.

17. Ibid., pp. 169–177.

18. Ibid., p. 273.

19. Ibid., p. 231.

20. See Alain Locke, ed., *The New Negro: An Interpretation* (New York: Albert & Charles Boni, 1925).

21. Perry Bradford, *Born with the Blues* (New York: Oak Publications, 1965), p. 117.

22. Handy, *Father of the Blues,* p. 20.

23. Even today, in radio, this attitude persists. See "Radio's Wacky Road to Profit," *Newsweek,* vol. 105, no. 12 (March 25, 1985).

24. Ronald C. Foreman, Jr., "Jazz and Race Records, 1920–1933: Their Origins and Their Significance for the Race Record Industry and Society," (unpublished Ph.D. diss., University of Illinois, 1968), pp. 15, 35–37.

25. Bradford, *Born with the Blues,* p. 13.

26. Ibid., p. 115.

27. Derrick Stewart-Baxter, *Ma Rainey and the Classic Blues Singers* (New York: Stein & Day, 1970), p. 12.

28. Apparently Ralph Peer of OKeh records coined the term *race records. Colliers,* vol. 101, no. 18 (April 30, 1938), p. 24.

29. See Chapter 3 for a brief profile of the Black Metropolis concept.

30. See Chapter 2.

31. Jeff Titon, *Early Downhome Blues* (Urbana: University of Illinois Press, 1977), p. 205.

32. In this case, the risk lay not with the entrepreneurial idea but with the entrepreneur.

33. Bradford, *Born with the Blues,* p. 155.

34. Ibid., pp. 130–49.

35. Ibid., pp. 138–39.

36. Dan Mahoney, comp., *The Columbia 13/14000-D Series: A Numerical Listing* (Stanhope, N. J.: Walter C. Allen, 1961), p. 12.

37. Handy, *Father of the Blues,* p. 201.

38. Bradford, *Born with the Blues,* p. 172.

39. Paul Oliver, *The Story of the Blues* (New York: Chilton Book Company, 1969), p. 97.

PART I

IMAGERY, COMMUNICATION, AND OPPORTUNITY

INTRODUCTION

AMOS: Andy I don't know what I going to do. The lawyer's getting un-couraged about it.
ANDY: Amos . . . That ain't "uncouraged"—it's "decouraged."

T. Luke you ain't never gon to be to understand what I tells you wit no degree o'delinquency . . .
L. Timber what you is tryin to say is destitute.[1]

On the surface these two radio program excerpts seem much alike. Both employ the comic malapropisms, black dialect, and one-upmanship that were the stock and trade of radio writers in the 1920s and 1930s. The format is the comic strip serial radio adapted from the newspaper funny pages while the style of humor is group caricature.

The premise of the shows was similar, too. Each followed the misadventures of a pair of black migrants newly arrived in the North. "The boys hail from Atlanta and have come to the big city to make fame and fortune," explain Freeman Gosden and Charles Correll in *All About Amos 'n' Andy*.[2] Jack L. Cooper's Luke and Timber left Memphis for Chicago also to make their fortunes. Each week the fun began as listeners laughed at the antics of these hapless fellows unable to fulfill their dreams. After one year in Chicago, Amos and Andy had "one broken-down topless automobile, one business enterprise—the Fresh-Air Taxicab Company of America, Incorpulated—one desk (not paid for), one swivel chair for the president to rest and sit in. . . ."[3] As for the Chicago restaurant, Luke complains that "It's bout to close up."[4]

The shows seem strikingly similar to each other, one the clone of the other. Was this the case? "Amos 'n' Andy" was a very popular program that paved the way for the golden age of radio comedy. Debuting on NBC in 1928, it took the country by storm, at its peak drawing 40 million listeners to their sets. Success led to imitations like "The Goldbergs" and "Life with Luigi," which lampooned the Jewish and Italian experiences.[5]

But "Luke and Timber" was different. A by-product of the "Amos 'n' Andy" craze, it was a black-inspired rebuttal rather than a copy. Veteran black entertainer Jack L. Cooper saw Gosden and Correll as white men in blackface derogatorily satirizing the black experience primarily for white audiences. His "Luke and Timber" was a humorous look at the black life and times beamed to black audiences. Each serial projected an image, another likeness. But where Gosden and Correll presented the white imitation of blacks, Cooper countered with a black self-likeness. Obviously, who was projecting—or communicating—the image was the pivotal question regarding effect. Together the two serials exemplify and symbolize the two black radio experiences that were molded out of the interplay between imagery, communication, and opportunity.

What the media do is communicate imagery. A slice of life is captured and imitated. Technology's ability to reproduce reality combines with the shared perceptions of the presenters and receivers to project an image. Television, for example, presents a composite picture of what the camera eye and microphone capture. Comprised first of raw footage and then creatively transformed into an acceptable format, the final image is projected as dots and lines on the video screen, which by its very size can only reproduce a miniaturized picture of what was originally shot. In context and appearance what we see and hear at home may look and sound very different from the original scene filmed or videotaped. This original view, in turn, can only capture part of what transpired, limited as it is by what the camera focused on and the microphone recorded.

The television image is not an objective picture of reality but a subjective one influenced by human perceptions and technology. So is that of radio, only more so. What is aired on radio is limited to sound. The listeners either imagine the visual scene or ignore it. In this respect Marshall McLuhan was right: the medium can be the message. What is imitated and then presented is determined by the medium of presentation, which in turn is influenced by the symbiotic relationship between man and machine. The technological aspects of the medium and human perceptions reinforce one another, either certifying an existing image as reality or altering our conceptions by projecting one different from that commonly held to be true. The crux of the matter is who is saying what in which channel to whom with what effect and why.[6]

Opportunity fills in the specifics of the above formula, if the medium is commercial. Since advertising is the foundation of commercial radio, marketing for profits is its raison d'etre. The return comes from communicating images that draw listeners, and to do this the fickle pulse of the public must be kept. The opportunity to respond innovatively to change is therefore integral to radio's history, development, and practice. But this entrepreneurial response itself is influenced by the images the entrepreneur and the business community have of the audience and the consumer market that affect opportunity. The interplay between imagery, communication, and opportunity, as a result, is less linear than spherical in construct. It posits a multidimensional dialogue between blacks and whites on varying subjects and in diverse contexts, reflecting their changing relationships.

For now, the focus is on how and why imagery inhibited communication and later combined with other factors to block opportunity. Did shows like "Amos 'n' Andy" and "Fibber McGee and Molly", whose cast included a black character named Silly, faithfully imitate black life or not? If not, why not? These questions produce two answers determined, not surprisingly, by race and influenced by a century-long entertainment tradition. The answers focus on how whites perceived blacks and how blacks perceived themselves. Further they prompt other questions. How did whites perceive blacks responding to their efforts? How did blacks respond to the white image presented by the media? What factors contributed to the image dilemma?

NOTES

1. The "Amos 'n' Andy" excerpt comes from Jim Harmon, *The Great Radio Comedians* (Garden City, N.Y.: Doubleday & Company, Inc., 1970), p. 74. The "Luke and Timber" excerpt is from a radio script in the Jack L. Cooper Files, Chicago Historical Society, Chicago, Ill. (hereafter referred to as JLC Files).

2. Charles J. Correll and Freeman F. Gosden, *All about Amos 'n' Andy* (New York: Rand McNally, 1929), pp. 43–44.

3. Ibid.

4. "Luke and Timber" radio script, JLC Files.

5. J. Fred MacDonald, *Don't Touch That Dial: Radio Programming in American Life from 1920 to 1960* (Chicago: Nelson-Hall, 1979), pp. 27–28, 98.

6. See Preface.

1

JUMPING
JIM CROW

In the 1930s, "the Negro was played to be laughed at, if not derided," writes veteran radio executive Lester Weinrott. "Amos 'n' Andy," he says, "was as, if not more popular among Blacks than it was among white listeners." The proof, Weinrott says, is that "no voice was heard to protest."[1]

Critics of radio's treatment of blacks and the "Amos 'n' Andy" show had an opposing view. Summarizing 30 years of radio history, in 1950, Dr. E. I. Robinson of the Los Angeles NAACP complained, "Radio points to one side of the Negro, the worst side most frequently." From the 1930s to the 1950s, other blacks also attacked the medium. A 1931 critic declared, "The radio should not be prostituted to the teaching of race inferiority or spreading mischievous propaganda between the races." Black radio performer Canada Lee argued as late as 1949 that "A virtual Iron Curtain exists against the entire Negro people as far as radio is concerned. . . . Who would know us only by listening to Amos and Andy, Beulah, Rochester, and minstrel shows."[2]

These critics attacked radio for its pervasive airing of "the stereotyped conception of the Negro as a simpleton, or a 'bad actor,' or a doglike creature with unbounded devotion to his master or mistress."[3] Obviously playing blacks to be laughed at and derided did not meet with as much black—and white—acceptance and approval as Weinrott claimed.

Shows like "Amos 'n' Andy" that lampooned blacks did attract black audiences. Jazz musician Milton "Mezz" Mezzrow writes in his autobiography, *Really the Blues,* that "Amos 'n' Andy" was "a program all Harlem listened to."[4] J. Fred MacDonald, in his history of radio programming, notes that even after "Amos 'n' Andy" peaked in popularity among the total audience, its ratings in the heavily black populated South remained very high.[5]

In part, black support of radio, even with its racial bias, was both natural and logical. The radio mania that swept America in the 1920s was color-blind. The medium was the marvel of the age. Representing a zenith of this trend, Gosden and Correll's imitation of black life captured the attention of the entire nation. The show was so popular that the New York Telephone Company reported in March 1930 that its operators sat idle during the time it was aired.[6] For blacks not to listen to radio, or "Amos 'n' Andy" in particular, would have meant they did not constitute a media market; that they were so totally isolated from the American mainstream as to be immune to trends all others responded to enthusiastically. Besides, the show was funny and there was little else about blacks being broadcast.

But listening did not mean acquiescence. Protests against "Amos 'n' Andy" were also prevalent. The year 1931 was a high point, featuring a crusade against the program, a scathing indictment in the *Negro Year Book,* and the first petition to the Federal Radio Commission asking for the show's cancellation. Sponsored by the black newspaper, the Pittsburgh *Courier,* this petition's three major points aptly summed up black dissatisfaction: the show exploited blacks to their detriment and for white financial benefit. It obstructed the instilling of black self-respect while hindering race progress. And it negatively stereotyped black business activities.[7]

How did the black listening audience respond? This is the crucial question because it goes behind the fact of tuning in and strikes at the core of radio appeal, creating something special to share with the listener. There is a critical distinction between listening and enjoying. We have seen how black writer William Branch remembered sitting in front of the radio set with his family laughing at the antics of "Amos 'n' Andy," and how his childhood memories also include a vision of his father never laughing. Later, Branch had discovered why: Amos and Andy were supposedly "us."[8]

Being laughed at and derided produced mixed or negative feelings. To paraphrase an old blues lyric, blacks laughed to keep from crying. Or as 1950s black radio executive Leonard Evans explained, "The Negro may enjoy these shows ["Amos 'n' Andy" and a similar program about a black maid, "Beulah"], but he is embarrassed by them."[9]

The wide variance between Lester Weinrott's claim and the black response shows the irony of the black radio experience. Here was a medium whose appeal depended upon communication of imagery; but regarding whites and blacks the problem revolved around a failure of communication owing to the prevailing white image of blacks as people, audience, and consumers. This image blinded white radio executives to the viability of the black audience. It also made them deaf to the black protests that focused on the derogatory and stereotypical black image aired, in part because of the lack of balancing portrayals.

The result was that blacks had a very ambivalent radio experience, at least with the network broadcasting that dominated the radio before 1950. The medium itself had a strong appeal, and programs were aired that did appeal positively to blacks. Save for musical and isolated dance venues where art partially overcame negative stereotyping, however, such instances were few and far between. Continued protests by blacks and whites did bring some improvement after 1945, but generally blacks found broadcasting an unfriendly medium that mirrored the black situation in American society at that time. "All American radio takes its cue from the official government," explained black writer Carlton Moss. "We are automatically under a Jim Crow setup." [10]

The use of the term *Jim Crow* is very enlightening, as is Canada Lee's complaint that connects radio programs with minstrel shows. Both these examples not only reinforce the primacy of imagery as a barrier to communication but they also point out that the image problem was nothing new. A large number of blacks saw "Amos 'n' Andy" as the latest in a century-long series of entertainment and media presentations that projected a white image of blacks. It transferred the blackface minstrel comic to the airwaves.

To a great extent, the blackface minstrelsy image was a cause and a manifestation of a larger white mind set that saw blacks as inferior to whites. It arose at a time of racial questioning but persisted long past the day when the attitudes it espoused were relevant and the entertainment venue propagating this view was popular with the American masses.

JUMPING JIM CROW

A couple of young men, named Cain and Abel, respectively, did a brother act, though not necessarily a brotherly act, for the first-named gentleman one day in a fit of peevishness did smite Master Abel with such force that the breath did leave his body; Cain was punished, as he should have been; his complexion was changed from Caucasian to Ethiopian; that was the first black face turn. [11]

Grossly ludicrous, this biblical story epitomizes the blend of fact and fancy that characterized the blackface minstrelsy image. As told by minstrel performer Edward Leroy Rice, the tale of Cain and Abel was "an exaggerated or debased likeness, imitation or copy naturally or intentionally ludicrous." [12] In other words, it was a caricature like all the minstrel imagery. This fact, which defined the image and set the path of development it followed, was sometimes obscured by the needs and desires of minstrel audiences to learn about blacks during an era of expanding democracy and concern over slavery. Add to this situation claims of authenticity by performers as well as the influence of time, and we have uncovered the sources of the image problem blacks faced in entertainment, from the stage to radio to the movies and later to television.

Caricature humor has long been a staple of American comedy, just as comedy has been a dominant force in American entertainment. In the words of popular culture historian J. Fred MacDonald: "If one conclusion can be drawn from the history of popular entertainment it is that Americans like to laugh."[13] Newspaper comic strips by definition are formatted to amuse. They played a role in the popularization of certain newspapers at the turn of the twentieth century. The first movie superstar was comedian Charles Chaplin, who signed the first million dollar contract. The influence of "Amos 'n' Andy" on radio has been cited above. The comic antics of Lucille Ball and Milton Berle did as much to bring television into our lives as anything else.

In the integration of media into American lives, comedy has always been at the cutting edge of innovation and development. A good example is the evolution of the innovative newspaper comic strip to the radio serial and then to the television situation comedy, each of which represented significant breakthroughs.

Minstrelsy played a similar role in the development of American popular entertainment in the nineteenth century. It arose in response to the societal changes that both built and convulsed the United States between the 1820s and 1850s, particularly the mass movement known as Jacksonian democracy and the growing debate over slavery. The author of the most astute analysis of the connection between Jacksonian democracy and minstrelsy, Alex Saxton, links the two together almost from inception: "The rise of the first mass party in America and the dominance of the minstrel show as mass entertainment appear to have been interrelated and mutually reinforcing sequences."[14]

More to the point, minstrelsy served as the entertainment expression of this popular movement, a cutting-edge innovation that addressed the democratic tendencies of the developing mass society grappling with class and race questions. In addressing these issues, minstrelsy consistently reinforced "the politics of Jacksonian and neo-Jacksonian democracy"—including its class and racial contradictions.[15]

Reflecting the beliefs of its namesake, Andrew Jackson, Jacksonian democracy was selective rather than egalitarian in conferring democracy. Its mass connotation applied to whites occupying the middle rungs of society's ladder: the common man (and by default, the common woman). Minstrelsy reflected this bias with the very organization of the troupe onstage enhancing middling democratic tendencies. The semicircle in which the performers appeared was divided along symbolic class lines. The leader or interlocutor represented the aristocratic upper classes, serving as the butt of the symbolic middle-class end men's jokes.

The role played by the end men was double-edged, but always aimed at confirming the identity of the emerging white middle class. Regarding the relationship with the interlocutor, minstrel show chronicler Robert Toll explains: "From the beginning of minstrelsy, one of the functions of blackface had been to give the minstrel a position similar to the classic fool."[16] Patterned after writer Sir Walter Scott's character, Wat, in his popular novel *Ivanhoe*, the end men used their supposed mental inferiority to point out the folly of their higher bred, purportedly intellectual superiors. By lampooning the aristocracy, the minstrel show reinforced the masses' definition and application of democracy while exalting their status in society.

At the same time, blackface also imparted the character of the clown to the minstrel. There was no satirical connotation here. In this guise the minstrel reassured the masses that they were not at the bottom of the socioeconomic ladder. The lowest rungs were occupied by blacks who acted in real life much as the caricatures performed on stage. This portrayal meshed well with a major doctrine of Jacksonian democracy: white supremacy. "Although most northerners did not know what slaves were like," writes Toll, "they believed or wanted to believe that black slaves differed greatly from free, white Americans." During its early years, minstrelsy was largely a northern phenomenon centered around the increasingly urbanized New England and New York, where blacks remained largely unknown. The entertainment assured the "common white people's identity by emphasizing Negroes' 'peculiarities' and inferiority." [17]

Not surprisingly, caricature filled these needs by becoming the vehicle for 'educating' whites. But the needs of the audience played only a supporting role in determining that the blackface image revolve around caricature. Similarly, the purpose behind minstrelsy's creation and the black image it propagated was not to meet societal needs, though it capitalized upon them. First and foremost, minstrelsy was an entertainment vehicle designed to bolster the flagging careers of white performers.

In 1831 Thomas Dartmouth Rice was a 25-year-old entertainer on tour as a light comedian in Cincinnati. "He could tell a story, sing a song, and dance a hornpipe," recounted Robert P. Nevin in an 1867 *Atlantic Monthly* article. Rice also was experienced as a blackface Ethiopian delineator, but his specialty was Irish caricature. Though a versatile entertainer, as of 1831 he had not "attained to any noticeable degree of eminence in his profession." But, Nevin added, "he kept his wits upon the alert for everything that might be turned to professional and profitable use." [18]

Viewed from one perspective, Rice was a promising entrepreneur looking for an opportunity to innovate on change in order to move his career from a sphere of low to one of high productivity. He grasped this opportunity on a Cincinnati street watching a crippled black carriage driver, "his right shoulder deformed and drawn up high, his left leg gnarled with rheumatism, stiff and crooked at the knee, doing an odd-looking dance" and singing an equally odd-sounding song,

> Turn about an' wheel about an' do jis so,
> An ebery time I turn about I jump Jim Crow. [19]

Suddenly, Rice experienced a moment of artistic inspiration. The peculiarity of the performance certainly would appeal to audiences. The song-and-dance routine meshed well with his skills, and it provided a means of capitalizing on the increasing public interest in blacks in a uniquely American way. Or, as Nevin paraphrased Thomas Rice's thoughts, "As a national or 'race' illustration, behind the footlights, might not 'Jim Crow' and a black face tickle the fancy of pit and circle as well as the 'Sprig of Shillalah' and a red nose?"[20]

The centerpiece of Rice's new routine was the Jim Crow character he created, a classic caricature. Seeking authenticity in his performance, he borrowed the clothes of a black baggage handler for his costume. These consisted of "an old coat forlornly dilapidated, with a pair of shoes composed equally of patches and places for patches on his feet" and possibly "a coarse straw hat in a melancholy condition of rent and collapse." He blacked his skin and wore "a dense black wig of matted moss" to further enhance the ragged character of Jim Crow.[21]

As was true for all minstrel characters, reality provided inspiration rather than an example to copy exactly. Rice was less concerned with accurately portraying blacks on stage than capitalizing on the audience appeal of "peculiarities." The requirements of the routine certainly played a role here, too, as did his own perceptions of blacks. Because the peculiarity and uniqueness of the original performance attracted him and because he was skilled in caricature, Rice created Jim Crow in this image. He accentuated the peculiarities through distorted exaggerations in costuming and blacking up.

Similarly, the performance drew upon but apparently did not faithfully copy the original song and dance witnessed on the street. Adapted to the tune of an old Irish air and made more upbeat, the song's lyrics were revised to fit the stage act.

> O, Jim Crow's come to town, as you all must know,
> An' he wheel about, he turn about, he do jis so,
> An' ebery time he wheel about he jump Jim Crow.[22]

A number of other verses followed, most likely in the same vein. Reacting to the favorable audience reaction, Rice "ventured to improvise matter for his distiches from familiarly known local incidents." This enhanced audience identification, producing a "deafening" response from pit and circle.[23]

The original dance steps are lost but Rice's routine has been recorded and probably approximated, as the song did, what he saw and heard. It involved a wheel, turn, and jump in which Rice rolled his body lazily from side to side by shifting his weight from the heel of one foot to the toes of the other. Hans Nathan suggests that the jump came as Rice turned away from the audience. Using the words "jis so" as his cue, Nathan writes in *Dan Emmett and the Rise of Early Negro Minstrelsy*, Rice "jumped high up and and back into his initial position. While doing all this, he rolled his left hand in a half-seductive, half-waggishly admonishing manner."[24]

The "Jim Crow" routine touched a popular nerve producing "such a thunder of applause as . . . was never heard before within that old theatre.''[25] The song proved almost more popular than the blackface act. As for ''Jim Crow,'' this phrase became enshrined in the English language as a synonym for segregation.

Jim Crow was the starting point of the black image that minstrelsy created. Thomas Rice's character established the mold in which all other imagery followed from the stage to the radio microphone. Exaggerated distortions of blacks and black life presented in a caricature entertainment format became the rule. Blacks were depicted as ''foolish, stupid, and compulsively musical.'' They had wool for hair, fangs for teeth, bulging eyeballs, and flat noses. Their mouths were large with long, dangling lips. When ill they drank ink to remove any paleness. Their hair could not be cut, only filed. Best of all, you could grow them in the ground by planting their toes.[26]

By the advent of radio, these images had solidified, Fred MacDonald writes, into three major character types: coons, Toms, and mammies. The coon was the minstrel clown ''murdering the English language with malaprops, conniving to fleece a comrade out of money, bumblingly avoiding employment,'' and so on.[27] The inspiration for this character type was ''Zip Coon,'' a ''ludicrous black replica of the white dandy of Main Street or of New York's Broadway.''[28] This caricature antedated minstrelsy but was quickly integrated into the new entertainment form.

Modishly dressed and given to scholarly pretensions, Zip Coon had some basis in reality, as shown by this 1840s description of a real black dandy seen ''lounging down the street. He was a sable Count D'Orsay,'' explained Lady Emmeline Stuart Wortley. ''His toilet was the most elaborately recherche you can imagine. He seemed intensely and harmlessly happy in his coat and waistcoat, of the finest possible materials; and the careful adjustment of the wool and hat was not readily to be surpassed.''[29] For all his urbane pretensions, Zip Coon spoke in the Jim Crow dialect creating a peculiar contradiction well in tune with caricature. Wortley's description also substituted the word ''wool'' for hair, indicating that these caricature traits were applied by whites to blacks in real life.

A straight line of development can be drawn from Zip Coon to Andy Brown of ''Amos 'n' Andy'' and black actor Eddie Anderson's Rochester on the ''Jack Benny Program.'' The dress and some of the pretensions changed, but the character's traits remained much the same, with the lineage underscored by the name *coon*.

A simple, trusting fellow submissive to the will of others, the Tom was the coon's opposite. The models here were twofold. Jim Crow was one source. The evolution of Rice's character to the Tom represents an irony of the minstrelsy black image and a contradiction. Drawn from urban black examples, Jim Crow nonetheless came to represent minstrelsy's version of the southern plantation hand, later taking on many of the characteristics as well as the name of Harriet Beecher Stowe's classic Uncle Tom character. The amalgam of these two characters came early. Thomas Rice appeared as Uncle Tom jumping Jim Crow soon after publication of Stowe's *Uncle Tom's Cabin* in 1852.[30]

Originally, Zip Coon and Jim Crow represented opposite caricature extremes, physically indicating this fact by their placement as comic end men in the minstrel show. They represented onstage the dichotomy between urban America and the rural frontier. By the advent of radio, the two characters had developed to the point where the Tom acted as the foil for the coon's schemes, as Amos did for Andy.

The last character type was reserved for female actresses. The paragon of black womanhood, the mammy typically was fat, loving, and mother-wit smart. Frequently she possessed a quick temper and a shrill voice. Certainly, minstrelsy provided a role model for the mammy—always played by men—but the most popular female character had been the "yaller gal," whose beauty and skin color approximated those of white women.[31] The mammy had no such ambiguous racial connotations. On radio, the black domestic Beulah was the most blatant example. This female character drew the greatest opprobrium from black protesters, particularly since Beulah's creator and original portrayer was a white man named Marlin Hurt.

The minstrelsy imagery pervaded the entire entertainment world, painting a composite picture of blacks that was stilted and contradictory. Blacks were seen as either rascally and conniving or stupid and submissive. They either would not work for a living, preferring to "bamboozle" someone to get money, as Andy did, or they labored hard and long in faithful service to a family.

The one-dimensional blackface image was cut more out of cardboard and burnt cork than flesh. Its lack of depth had much to do with the fact of its being an entertainment image that by its very nature is superficial and seldom concerned with accuracy. 1950s television writer-producer Parke Levy explains that comedy works by exaggerating "a small hunk of life . . . for comic purposes. . . . People want a mirror held up to life, but at an angle so that it's humorous."[32]

Basically minstrels and others held up a mirror to blacks and black life at a skewed angle that produced a distorted, exaggerated image. The problem was not just the reflected imagery, however. Perhaps the biggest point of contention was origination. The minstrelsy image was a white creation. It was part of a larger white mind set and campaign dedicated to proving black inferiority that was translated into political and social terms by the strict color line that kept blacks separate but unequal. These white-inspired caricatures sent a strong message to blacks regarding their worth as human beings. The situation was made worse by performers who promoted their acts by using claims of authenticity, which duped ignorant whites.

Thomas Rice went to great pains to appear on stage as a black man. But burnt cork and a wig hardly reflected accurately black skin and hair color, no matter what the clothing was. Nor did Rice's act faithfully follow the original.

As had been true of the image so the same was true of the authenticity of the performance; Rice set the pattern that was followed. Again caricature is an apt description.

Other blackface performers built upon Rice's beginning, such as the equally famous Virginia Minstrels, who pioneered the familiar semicircle of performers that became standard in all shows. As shows became more grandiose, this semicircle evolved into the line of entertainers divided into end men and inter-locutor.

In 1843 veteran blackface delineators Frank Brower, Dan Emmett, Bill Whitlock, and Frank Pelham banded together as the Virginia Minstrels to increase their box office draw during a recession in the New York City entertainment scene. "Their choice of name fits the same opportunistic pattern," explains Robert Toll in *Blacking Up.* "Besides taking the name of a famous Southern state to enhance their claims of authenticity, they called themselves 'minstrels' instead of the more common 'delineators' because of the great success of the Tyrolese Minstrel Family which had recently toured America."[33] Thus even the name given this entertainment form lacked authentic black origins.

As for the performers' assertion of authenticity, it is claimed of Bill Whit-lock that "Every night during his journey south, when he was not playing, he would quietly steal off to some negro hut to hear the darkeys sing and see them dance, taking with him a jug of whiskey to make them all the merrier."[34]

Other minstrels also declared that close contact with blacks made their performances authentic. This line of proof became standard and was transferred to radio by Gosden and Correll. In their 1929 book *All about Amos 'n' Andy,* the two men claimed their popularity rested in part on their "true-to-life" portrayals of blacks. They wrote that frequent contact with blacks had given them "a thorough understanding of the colored race." Supporting this contention, Gosden explained that Amos and Andy were largely based on his black childhood friend Snowball.[35] While growing up in Richmond, Virginia, in the early 1900s, Gosden's household included Snowball and the black maid who raised him. His youth, therefore, did provide intimate contact with blacks that served him well in show business.

From the minstrel stage to radio, the assertion of authenticity was a potent promotional weapon. But even the minstrels could not truly believe their acts faithfully recreated black culture. As Toll wisely notes, "They were not ethnographers but professional entertainers. . . ."[36] Early observers of minstrelsy also recognized the fallacy of authenticity in minstrel performances. An 1845 critic called the acts "counterfeit because none but the negroes could give it in its original perfection."[37] Ten years later, Y. S. Nathanson, an early writer on black song, dated the decline of authentic black minstrelsy to the publication of "Ole Dan Tucker" in 1841. Afterwards all minstrel songs were white imitations that paled in comparison with black originals.[38]

The question of how authentic minstrel characters were is not the major issue. What matters is how the white mass audience responded to the claims of authenticity and to the performances themselves. Robert Toll asserts that before the publication of Harriet Beecher Stowe's *Uncle Tom's Cabin* in 1852, minstrelsy had "the greatest impact on the northern public's image of blacks." [39] Much of the public, the paying audience, often sat spellbound and convinced by the blackface performers.

Toll recounts the experience of minstrel Al G. Feld who, when he first saw minstrels, thought they were black. This belief apparently gained some credence to the point where jokes like this were used to emphasize that the entertainers were white.

> Why am I like a young widow?
> Because I do not stay long in black. [40]

Minstrel song sheets also included contrasting portraits of the performers. Group shots in formal wear without makeup were juxtaposed against portraits featuring burnt cork and costumes.

Perhaps the most striking example of authenticity creating misperceptions came after the Civil War when black performers began to appear on stage. Toll writes that "whites were astonished at the diversity of Negroes' skin color." [41] But even the appearance of black performers did little to alter the blackface image. The burnt cork figure remained standard. Blacks were as bound by the tradition as whites, frequently appearing in blackface, as singer Ethel Waters recounts in her autobiography. [42] These misconceptions concerning identity buttressed the performers' claim of authenticity even with the disclaimers. They also indicate why this appeal hit such a responsive chord among the white audience. Blacks were almost totally unknown to this population and the portrayals fit their preconceptions.

By definition and purpose the image may have been false, but the shows and the characters proved very entertaining and enduring. The blackface minstrelsy image remained monolithic in nature over decades, persisting as an entertainment characterization long after the minstrel show peaked and the form declined precipitously in popularity. The unchanging endurance of the imagery was the most vexing problem blacks faced. It proved so pervasive that almost no balancing portrayals were allowed to counter the distorted and ludicrous caricatures that prevailed.

Several factors contributed to the long-lived tenure of the blackface imagery. First, there was the strong influence that minstrelsy exerted on the development of American entertainment. A direct line of development can be drawn from the figures seated in a semicircle to vaudeville, radio, movies, and television as well as to developments in dance, song, and comedy. The minstrel newspaper, the New York *Clipper*, evolved into the show business Bible *Variety*.

The second factor was the role the minstrel show played as a springboard for aspiring performers. Singer and actor Al Jolson was probably the most famous entertainer to emerge from minstrelsy. Circus impressario P. T. Barnum appeared in blackface and the same may have been true of theatrical producer David Belasco as well as Broadway actor-composer George M. Cohan.[43] When these entertainers moved off the minstrel stage and into other areas of entertainment, they often brought something of minstrelsy to these new venues. Jolson, for example, appeared in blackface in what is considered to be the first sound movie, ''The Jazz Singer.''

Black performers also used minstrelsy as a career springboard. Famed black vaudevillian and ''Ziegfeld Follies'' star Bert Williams began his career with Lew Johnson's Minstrels. W. C. Handy has acknowledged the role minstrelsy played in his life. He entered the entertainment business as a cornet player with Mahara's Minstrels. Blues singers Ma Rainey and Bessie Smith performed with minstrel shows, too, as did black-appeal radio founder Jack L. Cooper.[44]

But the minstrel stage was much more than just a training ground for black talent. The shows virtually opened the world of popular entertainment to blacks, providing, Toll writes, ''their first large-scale entrance into American show business.''[45] W. C. Handy seconded Toll's contention, asserting: ''The composers, the singers, the musicians, the speakers—the minstrel show got them all.''[46] In addition to providing employment, minstrelsy supplied the natural opening wedge for blacks to enter and gain acceptance in vaudeville, film, and radio.

The opportunities opened, however, were circumscribed by blackface imagery, though wearing burnt cork was not a requirement for blacks. ''Emphasizing their authenticity as Negroes and claiming to be ex-slaves, black minstrels became the acknowledged minstrel experts at portraying plantation material,'' Robert Toll writes. ''But since they inherited the white-created stereotypes and could make only minor modifications in them, black minstrels in effect added credibility to these images by making it seem that Negroes actually behaved like minstrelsy's caricatures.''[47] Through performance, blacks certified the imagery, helping it endure and giving credence to white beliefs that blacks accepted and supported such characterizations.

Black protests against minstrelsy, interestingly enough, appear to have been class-motivated. Only the small black bourgeoisie registered complaints against minstrel shows and apparently shunned the performances. As was true of their white counterparts, the black masses—the common men and women—enthusiastically supported the fast-paced variety the minstrel shows offered. But the appearance of black performers on stage had an added appeal. It ''made clear . . . that it was possible for common blacks to become entertainers.''[48] Thanks to minstrelsy entertainment offered blacks an avenue of escape from a life of poverty and drudgery, much as religion and athletics did.

The last influence on the imagery's longevity was minstrelsy's emergence as an amateur venue for fund raising. The shows peaked as professional entertainment in the 1880s, but as late as 1925 veteran minstrel Willis N. Bugbee was publishing how-to stage minstrel show books through his company in Syracuse, New York. "There's money in a minstrel show," claimed one pamphlet, "so why not work up a good old time 'Burnt cork opry.' "[49]

The careers of Freeman Gosden and Charles Correll bring together these three factors, graphically illustrating minstrelsy's influence on show business. When Gosden entered show business, he perfected a blackface routine. He went to work for the Joseph Bren Company, which staged minstrel shows for churches and organizations throughout the United States. The company supplied professional management, costumes, and material for local talent. Gosden organized minstrel shows, reviews, and carnivals.

At this time Gosden met Charles Correll, a song-and-dance man who also worked for Bren. Born in Peoria, Illinois, Correll, like Gosden, included a blackface routine in his act. While rooming together, the two men decided to team up. In the mid-1920s, they began airing a blackface routine over Chicago station WEBH. Well-rounded performers, their singing prompted the Chicago *Tribune*-owned station WGN (World's Greatest Newspaper) to call them "a harmony team that is becoming most popular in the country."

Blackface humor remained their forte, however. In 1925, when *Tribune* executive Ben McGanna conceived the idea for a "talking comic strip," Gosden and Correll worked up an act about two black migrants to the city. Beginning on January 12, 1926, they appeared as "Sam 'n' Henry" on WGN but moved to WMAQ in 1928, where the show's name changed to "Amos 'n' Andy." That year NBC signed the comic duo to a $100,000-a-year contract.[50] One year later Gosden wrote his wistful remembrance of Snowball. The rest, as is so often said, is history.

Minstrelsy influenced Gosden and Correll's performance styles, the method by which they learned their craft, even their rationales for their success. The two men took the blackface clown off the minstrel stage and put him behind the radio microphone. Only the medium of presentation and the comic serial format distinguished their performances from "Daddy" Rice's in the age of Andrew Jackson.

To a certain extent, all black characterizations and all black appearances on radio between 1920 and 1940 were guided by the minstrel experience. It provided a gauge, a standard to follow. The few exceptions to this rule were significant, particularly the appearances of black singer and actor Paul Robeson.[51] They did little however to block the wider exposure and greater credence the minstrel image gained because of radio, which did provide many opportunities for black artists. In *Don't Touch That Dial,* Fred MacDonald writes that "The Afro-American was always part of popular radio," but this acceptance was "only in traditional terms of comedy and music."[52] The "traditional terms" MacDonald identifies date back to the venue where blacks first found opportunities as performers and where, as on the minstrel stage, whites could don burnt cork for black roles but blacks could not play white parts.

Black musicians alone seem to have escaped any negative aspects of performing, perhaps because the nature of their art freed them from caricature roles. Often black musicians had their own shows: Duke Ellington, Ethel Waters, Fats Waller, and the Mills Brothers, for example. Others found employment in the big bands that flourished during the 1930s, particularly after "swing" became popular.

The minstrelsy influence was also less prominent in drama. Here the color line apparently dictated opportunity: blacks typically played butlers, maids, and chauffeurs. Subservient roles underscoring their inferior status in society, the available dramatic roles were often just walk-ons, allowing for little emotional or intellectual range. Few whites could name the black actor playing a butler in a drama. The identification was with a voice-over role model, not a breathing human being.

In comedy, blacks took center stage. Black dramatic actors may have been plagued by lack of recognition but everyone knew Eddie "Rochester" Anderson, for example. Here the minstrelsy image was most apparent and hidebound; it provided an ironic and ambivalent opportunity for black entertainers.

Caricature humor as exemplified by the blackface minstrelsy image survived in radio in large part because of the show business maxim: if it works, do it again. Blackface appealed to audiences and so became engrained into performance. The fast pace of the minstrel show worked, so it became standard. As Robert Toll writes, minstrel audiences came to expect performers to tell certain jokes—the audience often supplying the punch line—and to sing certain songs—again with participation from those attending the show.[53] Similarly, on "Amos 'n' Andy," listeners expected Andy to exclaim, "I'se regusted" in certain situations just as they expected Andy to bamboozle Amos. The continued use of malapropisms in these catch phrases furthered the comic ploys.

The use of the proven jokes and characterizations lasted for so long—over a century—that the portrayals of blacks became bound by "rules unintelligently or slavishly followed to fettering conventionalities of usage, to beliefs held or professed out of mere acquiescence in tradition, etc."[54] In other words, the blackface image became an entertainment formula; it persisted in part because of the show business maxim of repeating what works and in part because the color line prevented blacks from balancing this image in other performances.

THE INFLUENCE OF THE COLOR LINE AND GEOGRAPHY

The combination of distorted imagery and racial separation kept blacks an unknown entity to the white masses. Even today neither race has a realistic image of the other, and this was more true 50 years ago. The racial situation in the United States between 1900 and 1930 featured institutionalized segregation sanctioned by law. This latest manifestation of a long-standing racial etiquette was based upon one central point: racial separation.[55] Economically, politically, and socially the color line kept blacks outside the American mainstream. In the early years of the twentieth century blacks had significant contact with whites as youths, domestics, in other work relationships, and less frequently as consumers.

Freeman Gosden's childhood illustrates a familiar interaction pattern of particular importance in the North. Census figures for black employment in Chicago during this period reinforce the dominance of the black domestic-white employer relationship. In 1900 the city's black workers numbered 17,986—13,065 men and 4,921 women. Of these, 12,379 were employed in domestic and personal fields. Eight of ten women and six of ten men were so classified by the census. Thirty years later after migration had swelled the black population of Chicago to 65,878, 13 of 20 women and one in three men still held personal or domestic jobs.[56]

In other labor fields, North and South, the color line kept most blacks on the bottom rungs of the employment ladder. They were residentially segregated into areas on the other side of the proverbial—and often very real—tracks and in large urban ghettos; or they were racially concentrated and isolated on southern farms.

The color line was not the only force keeping the races apart. Geography also played an important role. Until well after World War II, the rural South remained the home for the overwhelming majority of blacks. Looking at the above figures for Chicago and comparing them with contemporary national black population statistics the astonishingly low exposure of northern and western whites to blacks is underscored. There were 9 million American blacks in 1900. Fewer than 20,000 worked in the nation's second largest city, Chicago. Even after the Great Migration of World War I, 78.7 percent of the black population lived in the South.[57] The hundreds of thousands leaving the region tended to congregate in a handful of northern cities—New York, Chicago, Philadelphia, and Detroit. In these urban centers greater numbers did not translate into closer white contact because residential and other forms of segregation kept the races apart.

By the advent of commercial radio in the 1920s, the color line and geography combined to make blacks a largely unknown entity to whites. Most continued to learn about this minority group from entertainment and media venues.

IMAGERY AND COMMUNICATION

The image of blacks that minstrelsy created and propagated brought into being a sphere of communication between and among whites and blacks. The interconnected and interrelated dialogues, and in some cases monologues, that formed this interactive sphere revolved around three key elements: who, what, and how often. Whites opened the communication saying that blacks were inferior. This was the basic message of blackface minstrelsy and stands at the core of all communications between and among the races. Equally important was the unchanging content of this message and its repetition over time. How often, in this instance, acted as a primary component that strongly influenced the context as well as the content of the dialogues and monologues. For analytical purposes here, the basic communications formula is expanded to include this phrase.

By the advent of commercial radio in the 1920s, the cumulative effect of minstrelsy's long-standing, oft-repeated images had created a patterned cause-and-effect reaction in whites and blacks. Hardly any black portrayal was received solely on face value, as an individual example. Rather, reception was conditioned by deeply embedded impressions that triggered predictable responses that went beyond mere entertainment. Whites saw such imagery as reinforcing racial supremacist beliefs, and blacks responded with negative feelings of embarrassment and/or anger. Who sent the message further contributed to these patterned responses.

Whites in blackface, such as Gosden and Correll as Amos and Andy, clearly stereotyped blacks. But they also provided quality entertainment. White listeners enthusiastically supported the show more for its entertainment value than for its caricature of blacks. But there was another dimension to the white response. Whites saw Amos and Andy, or Beulah, or Rochester, as true-to-life imitations of blacks that fit comfortably within and confirmed their own racial conceptions.

Blacks were faithful listeners of "Amos 'n' Andy," too. Again, the undeniable comic genius was the appeal. The fact that blacks, even ersatz ones, were on the air contributed to the show's popularity. But the fact of white men playing blacks produced a mixed response. Not only the image of blacks aired, but the ability of whites to play black roles while blacks could not play whites aroused feelings of anger and embarrassment that led to protest. This unfair blackface turn symbolized the inequity of blacks in society. It also reduced black employment opportunities.

A contributing factor here was the monologue quality of the black protests before 1940. Though vociferous and continual, these protests largely fell on deaf ears. The popularity of "Amos 'n' Andy" among blacks plus the unwillingness of whites to recognize the existence and the viability of a separate black audience/consumer market obstructed communication.

After 1940, white and black critics achieved some success in airing more positive black images. But these were Pyrrhic victories, for minstrelsy-inspired caricatures were still debuting. "The Marlin Hurt and Beulah Show" premiered in 1945 after the character of the black maid had proved popular on the "Showboat" and "Fibber McGee and Molly" shows in the early 1940s. Hurt based his caricature on a black maid of his youth. He also appeared as her dumb boyfriend, Bill Jackson. Beulah raised the same protests that "Amos 'n' Andy" had raised and were still raising. The hiring of black actress Hattie McDaniel to play Beulah did not remove the character's blackface connection.

Black performers in minstrelsy-inspired parts sent different messages that elicited varying responses. Eddie Anderson achieved stardom and wide recognition as a master comedian through his role as Rochester Van Jones. He contributed much to the long-running success of the "Jack Benny Program," which produced high ratings for decades, on both radio and television. Anderson succeeded because he had crossover appeal to white audiences. His talent helped but so did the fact that his traditional character certified acceptance by blacks of the minstrelsy image and its authenticity. Anderson himself vehemently rejected charges of stereotyping but the passage of time and the traits of the Rochester character have negated his arguments.

Blacks responded in various ways to black performers in blackface. Middle-class blacks led the protests against such imagery, saying they were derogatory, offensive, and stereotypical. They were joined by some black performers, such as Canada Lee. These critics saw Rochester and Beulah, particularly when played by blacks, as working counter to race progress.

The mass of the black audience, composed largely of lower-class men and women, may have agreed in part with the protests, but for them Anderson and McDaniel symbolized something else as well. Just as black minstrels had, these radio stars beamed rays of hope and opportunity into black homes. Their success signaled the possibilities show business held: an ordinary person could escape the rigors and obstacles of racial segregation to gain kudos and acceptance in American society, not to mention wealth.

The question of opportunity was, of course, the focus of black protests against radio's treatment of the race. But the context differed from symbolizing hope. Here, opportunity meant expanding employment to all performance, production, and administrative levels—removing the job ceiling and the color line. It implied replacing blackface imagery with more positive likenesses. The goal was to use radio to promote race progress, not work against it.

This goal was never reached, or even approached. Gains made in the 1940s were negated by premieres of programs such as "The Marlin Hurt and Beulah Show." The question blacks faced but many never articulated was: is broadcasting the right medium through which to work for balance and appeal? The record answers no for reasons that extend beyond imagery into other areas of radio's commercial development.

NOTES

1. Lester Weinrott, "Chicago Radio: The Glory Days," *Chicago History,* vol. 3, no. 1 (Spring-Summer 1974), pp. 19–20.

2. MacDonald, *Don't Touch That Dial,* pp. 328, 358. See also Estelle Edmerson, "A Descriptive Study of the American Negro in the United States Professional Radio, 1922–1953" (unpublished M.A. thesis, UCLA, 1954), pp. 192–93. This study contains a wealth of information on blacks in broadcasting from the perspective of the performer.

3. MacDonald, *Don't Touch That Dial,* p. 328.

4. Mezz Mezzrow and Bernard Wolfe, *Really the Blues* (Garden City, N.Y.: Anchor Books, 1972, originally published 1946), p. 217.

5. MacDonald, *Don't Touch That Dial,* p. 341.

6. Ibid., p. 342.

7. Ibid., pp. 331, 345; John E. DiMeglio, "Black Pride and Protest: The 'Amos 'n' Andy' Crusade of 1931," *Journal of Popular Culture,* vol. 12, no. 2 (Fall 1979).

8. Cited in Erik Barnouw, *A Tower in Babel: A History of Broadcasting in the United States to 1933* (New York: Oxford University Press, 1966), p. 230.

9. Leonard Evans in "Away from the Blues," *Newsweek,* vol. 43, no. 3 (January 18, 1954), p. 51.

10. MacDonald, *Don't Touch That Dial,* p. 327.

11. Edward Leroy Rice, *Monarchs of Minstrelsy from Daddy Rice to Date* (New York: Kenny Publishing Company, 1911), p. 5.

12. *The Compact Edition of the Oxford English Dictionary,* vol. 1 (New York: Oxford University Press, 1976), p. 340.

13. MacDonald, *Don't Touch That Dial,* p. 91.

14. Alexander Saxton, "Blackface Minstrelsy and Jacksonian Democracy," Gary B. Nash, ed., *The Private Side of American History,* vol. 1: *To 1877* (New York: Harcourt Brace Jovanovich, 1979), p. 360.

15. Ibid., p. 378.

16. Robert Toll, *Blacking Up: The Minstrel Show in Nineteenth Century America* (New York: Oxford University Press, 1974), p. 161.

17. Ibid., pp. 34, 67.

18. Cited in Rice, *Monarchs of Minstrelsy,* p. 7.

19. Ibid.; Toll, *Blacking Up,* p. 28.

20. Rice, *Monarchs of Minstrelsy,* p. 7.

21. Ibid.

22. Hans Nathan, *Dan Emmett and the Rise of Early Negro Minstrelsy* (Norman: University of Oklahoma Press, 1962), p. 53.

23. Rice, *Monarchs of Minstrelsy,* p. 8.

24. Nathan, *Rise of Early Negro Minstrelsy,* p. 52.

25. Rice, *Monarchs of Minstrelsy,* p. 8.

26. Toll, *Blacking Up,* p. 67.

27. MacDonald, *Don't Touch That Dial,* p. 340.

28. Nathan, *Rise of Early Negro Minstrelsy,* p. 50.

29. Cited in ibid., p. 59.

30. Toll, *Blacking Up,* p. 92.

31. Ibid., p. 31.

32. Quoted in Rick Mitz, ed., *The Great TV Sitcom Book* (New York: Richard Marek Publishers, 1980), p. 3.

33. Toll, *Blacking Up,* p. 30. See also Nathan, *Rise of Early Negro Minstrelsy,* pp. 143–158.

34. Toll, *Blacking Up,* p. 46.

35. Correll and Gosden, *All about Amos 'n' Andy,* pp. 51–52.

36. Toll, *Blacking Up,* p. 40.

37. J. Kinnard, "Who Are Our National Poets?" in Bruce Jackson, ed., *The Negro and His Folklore in Nineteenth Century Periodicals* (Austin, Texas: American Folklore Society. 1967), p. 25.

38. Y. S. Nathanson, "Negro Minstrelsy: Ancient and Modern," in ibid., p. 42.

39. Toll, *Blacking Up,* p. 30.

40. Ibid., p. 40.

41. Ibid., p. 38.

42. Ethel Waters with Charles Samuels, *His Eye Is On the Sparrow* (Garden City, N.Y.: Doubleday, 1951), p. 139.

43. Rice, *Monarchs of Minstrelsy*, pp. 23, 280, 356, 363.

44. Ibid., p. 350; Stewart-Baxter, *Ma Rainey*, passim; Roi Ottley, "From Poverty to 90 Suits—Saga of a Negro," Chicago *Tribune* (January 10, 1954).

45. Toll, *Blacking Up*, p. 45.

46. Handy, *Father of the Blues*, p. 36.

47. Toll, *Blacking Up*, pp. 195–96.

48. Ibid., p. 228.

49. Mont Hurst, *The Tip-Top Minstrel Book* (Syracuse, N.Y.: Willis N. Bugbee Company, 1925), inside front cover.

50. Correll and Gosden, *All About Amos 'n' Andy*, pp. 21–22, 51–52; Weinrott, "Chicago Radio: The Glory Days," p. 19.

51. See MacDonald, *Don't Touch That Dial*, pp. 346–50.

52. Ibid., pp. 328, 340–46.

53. Toll, *Blacking Up*, p. 11–13.

54. *The Compact Edition of the Oxford English Dictionary*, vol 1, p. 1061.

55. Many works exist on the subject of racial segregation in the United States. Regarding racial etiquette, see Bertram Doyle, *The Etiquette of Race Relations in the South* (Chicago: University of Chicago Press, 1937). Also of interest are Ray Stannard Baker, *Following the Color Line* (New York: Harper & Row, 1964, originally published 1908); John Dollard, *Caste and Class in a Southern Town* (Garden City, N.Y.: Doubleday & Company, Inc., 1949, originally published 1937).

56. U.S. Bureau of the Census, *U.S. Twelfth Census, 1900, Special Reports: Occupations* (Washington, D.C.: U.S. Government Printing Office, 1902), pp. 516–23.

57. Ibid. In 1930, 37.4 percent of the northern black population lived in these four cities. U.S. Bureau of the Census, *Negroes in the United States, 1920–1932* (Washington, D.C.: U.S. Government Printing Office, 1935), pp. 5, 50, 290.

2

FINE-TUNING
THE DIAL OF
OPPORTUNITY

The white preconceptions that determined what black images were aired influenced the white image of the black audience/consumer market. Here, too, imagery hindered communication, obstructing opportunity. John Asher, CBS Los Angeles research director in 1950, illuminated the problem. "Once the sponsors realize the Negroes' purchasing power is great, programs will be designed to appeal to Negroes."[1]

Asher's comments were made at a time when enough stations were producing black-appeal programming to constitute a boom. An obvious failure of communication was occurring that deafened one side of the dial to black viability while promoting it on another. Asher indicates that the question was not whether blacks could support specifically designed shows. It was making white sponsors "realize" that they could and would and were, a fact that underscores the influence of imagery on racially ignorant whites.

The task of educating whites continued to be a priority for black-appeal promoters and remained one as late as 1987. The general manager of Chicago black-appeal station WJPC, Charles Mootry, claimed in 1979, "We make sales calls all the time . . . and most of these calls are to young white women who buy time for the major corporations. . . . They know little about black people and even less about black radio."[2] This ignorance combined with negative perceptions inhibited the ability to fully capitalize on available opportunity, even in the face of seemingly overwhelming evidence. "A black station can have the highest listenership in a city, yet not be able to attract maximum advertising rates—the lifeblood of radio," a 1987 New York *Daily News* article reported, "because too many of its listeners are presumed to be people without money."[3]

These quotes stimulate questions about blacks and radio both regarding and beyond the question of imagery. The contradiction between John Asher's statement and the fact of the black-appeal boom raises the issue of whether the development of commercial radio, broadcasting in particular, adversely affected blacks. Did the white image of the black consumer as "inferior" have any basis in fact? Were the blacks (and whites) who looked to broadcasting for change and appeal fine-tuning to the wrong channel on the dial of opportunity?

THE RISE OF BROADCASTING

What is commercial radio? Is it a medium of enlightenment, entertainment, and information? Its name indicates its focus. Commercial radio may enlighten, entertain, and inform, but its primary function is to sell. The programming aired lures listeners to hear the commercial message of sponsors whose purchases of airtime pay for the programming.

The relationship between the ads and the shows is symbiotic; each feeds upon the other. Sponsors vie for time on the most popular—not necessarily the best—shows because their sales pitch will be heard by the most people. Since commercial radio's inception in 1920 the advertising mechanism has been its core. In fact, writes Daniel J. Czitrom in *Media and the American Mind,* "Radio broadcasting began as a marketing tool, a service designed by large electrical manufacturers to sell privately owned receivers." As market exploitation proceeded, broadcasters "added a totally new dimension to modern communication by bringing the outside world into the individual home." Part of the outside world entering American homes was advertising. By the close of the 1920s, Czitrom adds, "advertising had established itself as the basis for American broadcasting."[4]

Until the advent of television after World War II, the dominant marketing/ programming strategy was broadcasting. It evolved naturally from radio's earliest days, influenced by technology and the growing commercial emphasis of the medium. Initially radio transmissions were aired in the hope that someone, anyone, would hear them. You could be sure the transmission went out but there was no way to know if it was received. Later the context was experimentation in long distance transmissions to test how far signals could travel. This was followed by a consolidation of the industry for military purposes during World War I.

The wartime collaboration continued after the conflict ended, leading to the institution of broadcasting. On October 17, 1919, the Radio Corporation of America was formed by American Marconi, General Electric, American Telephone and Telegraph, and Western Electric, later joined by Westinghouse and United Fruit. This erstwhile monopoly attempted to divide up the radio industry among large corporations.[5] It did dominate the airwaves for a while, but it never controlled them.

A major question asked about radio's maturation was: should the medium act as an adjunct of the telephone providing one-to-one communication, or should it be developed for mass use? In 1920 in Pittsburgh the answer came, setting radio on the path it follows today. Here as throughout radio's history, entrepreneurship played the pivotal role in defining and advancing the commercial medium's development, not so much by creating something new as by innovating on changes evident already in how radio was used. Often, the innovation moved the focus of the medium from the area of low productivity to a higher one.

Westinghouse engineer Frank Conrad was meeting a growing audience need for programming by airing "ham" concerts from his garage. Conrad was not the first or the only ham operator and his broadcasts initially attracted little attention. But they did stimulate two entrepreneurial schemes that established radio as a mass commercial medium based on advertising.

Pittsburgh's Joseph Horne Department Store used Conrad's shows to promote sales of receivers. An ad in the Pittsburgh *Sun* summarizes their strategy and indicates the role of entrepreneurship. The copy said that Conrad's concerts were picked up by a receiver in the store. "Amateur Wireless Sets, made by the maker of the set which is in operation in our store, are on sale here $10.00 and up."[6]

The entrepreneurial innovation, probably repeated nationwide by other retailers though without the ramifications of Horne's advertising, consisted of making the vital connection between sets and programming. More specifically, this connection was used to lure customers to the store where they could hear the wonders of radio and overcome any skepticism. Horne moved to a higher level of productivity by directing the sales message at the public emphasizing the ability to receive programming. There was no appeal to radio "hams," amateur aficionados, who needed no persuasion.

The mass appeal of the Horne Department Store was important more for its influence than as a marketing ploy. Aware of Conrad's transmissions, Westinghouse Vice President Harry P. Davis paid the broadcasts little attention until the Horne ad caught his eye. Suddenly, Davis's conception of the role of radio changed. His entrepreneurship involved adapting Horne's mass strategy to the commercial development of the medium. "The efforts that were then being made to develop radio-telephony as a confidential means of communication were wrong," he exclaimed, "and instead its field was really one of wide publicity." Davis considered radio as "the only means of instantaneous collective communication ever devised."[7]

Davis moved radio from an adjunct to the telephone to a mass medium developing the first regularly broadcasting station, KDKA, in Pittsburgh. Debuting on November 2, 1920, it covered the presidential election won by Warren Harding. The heavily promoted premiere broadcast emphasized, broadcasting chronicler Erik Barnouw explains, "the activity as something for everyone, a social delight for home and country club. References to the equipment were fairly casual, suggesting ease of operation rather than the need for mysterious knowledge and ritual."[8] The election broadcast caused a national radio mania. In 1922 almost 100,000 receivers were sold. This figure reached 500,000 the following year with sales revenues totaling $136 million.[9]

KDKA's success and the promotional campaign that put it in the public eye moved radio into the highest possible sphere of productivity, the national American consumer marketplace. Its first priority mirrored that of the Horne Department Store, though on a larger scale: place a radio set in every American home. "Early broadcasting . . . was a merchandising offshoot," explains Daniel Czitrom, with the programing acting as the advertising vehicle. Czitrom's statistics on station ownership further demonstrate this point. "Of the 570 stations licensed in 1922, radio manufacturers owned 231; newspapers owned 70; . . . and department stores owned 30."[10]

The concept of using the air waves to advertise goods and services also debuted in 1922. On January 12, AT & T entered the broadcasting business by again using an entrepreneurial scheme that had a novel twist. Its interest lay not in selling sets but in opening its transmission studios to the public on a fee basis. "Anyone who had a message for the world or wished to entertain was to come in and pay their money as they would upon coming into a telephone booth, address the world, and go out," explained AT & T executive Lloyd Espenchied.[11]

Toll broadcasting, as it was called, evolved because of AT & T's unique market position regarding radio-telephony. As part of the agreement that created RCA the phone company received exclusive rights to telephony.[12] By carefully choosing its language to explain and promote the new service, AT & T removed any likelihood of complaints, or to a certain extent competition, from Westinghouse, General Electric, or RCA. However, there were mass ramifications readily evident. Part of the plan was to open up AT & T's long lines to link up the 38 AT & T radio telephone stations.

Initially the phone company produced no programming and acted merely as the means of transmission. The experiment began at station WEAF, New York City. Not surprisingly, the first broadcast to the world was an advertisement. A ten-minute "message" promoting the sale of apartments in Jackson Heights, New York, was aired by the Queensboro Corporation. Apparently there was some positive response because the company aired five more "messages."[13]

AT & T switched the marketing stress from sets to airtime, basically transferring its traditional role of communications facilitator from the telephone to radio. It also opened up a new market. The consumer was no longer the marketing target, at least from AT & T's perspective. Businesses serving the public became the customers of the phone company, again a move away from competition and into a higher productivity area.

As the concept developed, AT & T changed its policy on nonproduction of programming. It may have "wanted no more responsibility over content than it had in the case of phone calls," explains Erik Barnouw. "But sale of time to address the public was hardly feasible unless people were listening."[14] The phone company improved its service by upgrading its production facilities, the technical aspects of broadcasting, and the programming aired. Having made the vital connection between ads and programming, AT & T realized a net profit of $150,000 in 1925.[15]

Five years after radio began developing mass dimensions, the ground was laid for its emergence as a household item and an advertising vehicle. Two higher productivity markets that complemented each other had been identified and targeted for different products that radio could provide. The public was sold sets to receive programming, and businesses were sold airtime and along with it opportunity to reach the largest number of people possible instantaneously with the same sales message. In both cases entrepreneurship spearheaded the evolution of the medium.

By 1927, radio sets had developed into pieces of furniture. The Sears, Roebuck catalog not only touted that store's own station, WLS, but offered sets for sale ranging from small, desk-top models to a genuine walnut console with all the accessories selling for $115. The more expensive consoles were designed as sound systems whose appearance would grace any living room. And they could be bought for $14 down and $14 per month. The catalog ads emphasized: "No radio knowledge is necessary"; "the range you want, the tonal quality you appreciate and the dependability you expect." Another key feature was ease of installation.[16]

Sears's introduction to the catalog's radio section illustrated the ideas behind the advertising approach to selling sets. The first paragraph deals with ease of installation and use, concluding, "Thousands of people annually buy radio sets from us, install them themselves and tell us of results that are truly marvelous." The next paragraph focuses on placing a set in every home. It deserves full coverage. Underneath the headline—"A Home Necessity"—the copy reads:

Radio has become an almost indispensible part of homelife. It brings to the fireside, from points far and near, the world's most inspiring music, the voices of great singers and the words of our country's most notable men and women. It brings the news of the day; many things of interest to the housewife; entertainment and education to the young and comfort to the old. It keeps the family together; no roaming around seeking entertainment.

The copy ends with this statement: "Radio is the most marvelous gift of the present age and no family should be without its untold advantages."[17]

The advertising strategy is easily discerned. First, people were assured that radios were not too technical for them to use. Second, the need to own one was emphasized; then came the clear keeping-up-with-the-Joneses message that without a set they would be missing something their neighbors enjoyed. Finally, radio as a triumph of human ingenuity was highlighted. In between there were appeals to keep the family together safe and sound in the home. The purpose, like that of all advertising, was to improve sales. But hype and hyperbole aside, radio did bring the world into the home and it did provide almost free entertainment and news. As a result, owning a set actually was the best advertising; and this point was stressed by the Sears catalog.

But to keep people listening there had to be worthwhile programming aired. On September 9, 1926, in Delaware, RCA moved to strengthen its marketing and programming efforts by forming the National Broadcasting Company. The driving force behind the first national radio network was a man whose life was inextricably entwined with radio's development, David Sarnoff.[18]

The son of Russian Jewish immigrants, Sarnoff came to the United States at the age of nine, in 1900. Rapidly adapting to his new surroundings, he worked first for the Postal Telegraph and then for American Marconi. While manning a wireless station in 1912, Sarnoff picked up the faint distress signals from an ocean liner: "S.S. Titanic ran into iceberg. Sinking fast." From his station, Sarnoff passed messages of the rescue efforts to the press, acting as the link between these events and the world. His heroic tour of duty made him well-known to the public.

Sarnoff's business acumen brought him recognition within the radio industry, and he quickly climbed American Marconi's corporate ladder. Not only was he familiar with the technical aspects of radio and its ability to capture the public's attention—demonstrated by the Titanic incident—but he recognized the medium's commercial potential. His entrepreneurship extended into both the consumer potential of radio and the organization of the radio industry itself. In 1916 Sarnoff presaged Harry P. Davis's idea in a memo proposing "a plan of development which would make radio 'a household utility' in the same sense as the piano or phonograph." The key, he explained, was designing and marketing an easy-to-use receiver, or as Sarnoff called it, a "radio music box."[19] His idea was to maximize the potential of radio in regards to the American consumer. Sarnoff's reasoning was much in tune with that behind the advertising strategy Sears used to market sets more than a decade later.

Following the formation of RCA, Sarnoff implemented his idea with similarly prescient results. He predicted first-year sales at $7.5 million, rising to $22.5 million the second year and $45 million the third. In 1922, when RCA began marketing sets, sales surpassed his figures, totaling $11 million. The second year totals equaled Sarnoff's estimate, and the third year produced sales of $50 million. "These estimates," writes Erik Barnouw, "were to win Sarnoff legendary repute as a prophet."[20] His growing stature and farsightedness led to the agreement to form NBC and the widespread acceptance of toll broadcasting.

Since NBC's parent company, RCA, was the largest distributor of radio sets, the network's creation was the culmination of the efforts at consolidation begun under government direction during World War I. Where RCA consolidated set production and marketing, NBC performed the same function for programming and advertising. Recognizing that radio's mass potential reached from coast to coast, Sarnoff capitalized on that fact through a unified approach that allowed listeners from Maine to California to receive the same programming. In this respect, entrepreneurship aimed at getting the most out of the least, that is, reaching the entire population with a single broadcast. On another level, the network's formation tapped into a different market, one of big name performers who could use radio to further their careers. By appearing on the air, these performers drew larger numbers of listeners, thus increasing sale of sets and enhancing advertising potential. The result was that radio changed from a local or regionally oriented medium to a national one.

A full-page announcement introducing NBC underscored this switch in emphasis to the nation. The company's commitment was to placing a set in every home with programming acting as the sales pitch. "The market for receiving sets in the future will be determined largely by the quantity and quality of the programs broadcast." The network would "provide machinery which will insure a national distribution of national programs, and a higher distribution of programs of the highest quality." [21] Although programming would lure the consumer, NBC's success was much in doubt: radio was hardly a household item. In 1926, the NBC ad reported that five million of the 26 million American homes had a radio set. A national network, however, could amass resources beyond those of local outlets, thereby providing programming that would entice people to buy sets. They could hear top stars perform, get up-to-the-minute news, and so on.

The formation of NBC heralded the age of network broadcasting. The developing philosophy of broadcasting meshed well with the network concept. The word *broadcasting* itself means sowing seeds over the entire field rather than placing them individually in drills or rows. [22] Regarding its applicability to radio the NBC ad contains both a definition and a summary of the broadcasting philosophy that it put into practice. "We say quantity because they [the shows] must be diversified enough so that some of them will appeal to all possible listeners." [23] The formation of the network allowed universal programming to be beamed from a central location to stations throughout the nation, blanketing the country with NBC shows and the accompanying commercials. One show could attract millions of people as "Amos 'n' Andy" did. This strategy not only optimized the entertainment and other functions of the medium but it also enhanced the marketing of sets and the spreading of the advertiser's message.

By 1940, the primary goal of placing sets in American homes was largely realized. Out of 35 million households, 28.5 million owned at least one set. In other words, four of five families owned a set compared to the one in five thirteen years earlier. Those listening in 1940 heard commercials costing advertisers $216 million, while radio revenues totaled $147 million for eight networks and 765 individual stations (not all of which were network affiliated). In turn, stations spent $114 million on programming, operations, and so on, and employed over 25,000 people. Total income stood at $33 million.[24] The promise heralded by Harry Davis in Pittsburgh and prophesized even earlier by David Sarnoff had come true. Radio was a national mass medium of culture, information, and service financed by advertising.

The programming strategy of providing something for everyone did produce substantial results. By the 1930s, the recruitment of top performers, writers, directors, and producers had ushered in the golden age of radio. By the end of the 1930s, radio had furthered the careers of Jack Benny, Bob Hope, Bing Crosby, Gosden and Correll, the Mills Brothers, Fats Waller, Orson Welles, and a host of others whose names were to become household words. Comedy, drama, mystery, science fiction, music, soap operas, adventure, sports, and news were available with just a twist of the dial.

Yet the goal of providing programming of universal appeal fell short. Several groups felt left out. They did not experience the intimate, individual communication that Marshall McLuhan saw as the essence of the medium's appeal.[25] The attempt to please everyone was doomed to failure because the American populace was not welded into one big, homogeneous audience. Capturing the mass audience meant that programming was designed for the lowest common demographic denominator—white, English-speaking Americans. For example, neither foreign-language speakers nor blacks were served by broadcasters. Under the philosophy of broadcasting should these groups—and could they—have been appealed to with specifically designed programming? The criterion of appeal was the phrase from the debut NBC ad: "some of them will appeal to all possible listeners."

FOREIGN-LANGUAGE PROGRAMMING
AND BROADCASTING

Foreign-language speakers overwhelming were immigrants who looked to radio to provide news and culture from their homelands. They wanted programming in their native languages. The premise of broadcasting omitted such programming on a regular basis because foreign-language shows certainly did not provide something for everyone. The potential listening audience was too small, but more important, too specialized to merit attention by broadcasters. Outside of the fact that not every immigrant desired such shows, a contributing hindrance was that most were clustered in big cities in the North and on the West Coast. Geographically, they did not constitute a mass audience.[26]

The need for programming was also fueled by the image of immigrants aired by radio broadcasting. Here, too, the root of the problem goes back to minstrelsy. After the Civil War, the competition of black minstrels hampered white blackface routines, while the flood of immigration from Europe and to a much lesser extent Asia provided new performance models.

Using what Robert Toll calls, "the technique of the caricaturing cartoonist," a popular feature in newspapers of the post–Civil War years, minstrels played upon exotic and peculiar ethnic traits. "Asians had odd-sounding languages, bizarre diets, and wore pigtails," he writes. "Germans spoke 'Dutch,' drank lager beer, and ate sauerkraut and sausage; and Irishmen had brogues, drank whisky, partied, and fought."[27] The portrayals of these newcomers fulfilled the same needs as blackface. They "made America's human heterogeneity and complexity seem comprehensible and psychologically manageable to members of the audience."[28] The use of caricatures also embedded ethnic stereotypes in the American consciousness and, of course, in popular entertainment. As with blacks, these were exercises in education through inferiority.

By the advent of radio, ethnic humor had become institutionalized into comedy and drama. "Life with Luigi" satirized the Italian experience just as wickedly as "Amos 'n' Andy" did the black. "Frank Watanabe and Honorable Archie" told of a white American and his Japanese houseboy, and Clifton Finnegan and Clancy the policeman of "Duffy's Tavern" played on Irish stereotypes. "Abie's Irish Rose" followed the misadventures of a Jewish man and his Irish wife, again relying on stereotypes for laughs.[29]

Supporting characters in ethnic caricature roles were a staple of many shows. Bert Gordon played "The Mad Russian" on Eddie Cantor's weekly program. He was joined by Harry Einstein as the Greek Parkyakarkas. The "Judy Canova Show" featured Mel Blanc as Pablo, a Mexican caricature.[30] There are many other examples but these suffice. Like blacks, members of virtually all ethnic groups could find something entertaining but offensive on radio.

BLACK-APPEAL PROGRAMMING AND BROADCASTING

In one respect, blacks and foreign-language speakers faced a similar situation. Both were minorities who were not being served by broadcasting but desired relevant programming. However, the reasons behind these desires differed greatly. For blacks, the crucial factor of appeal revolved, not surprisingly, around imagery and the airing of racially designed shows. There is a cause and effect to this formula of appeal. Negative imagery, in large part, created a need for more positive programming. How and why this need arose is less germane here than the question of whether or not blacks merited special consideration within broadcasting.

At best, blacks were neglected or taken for granted as a viable segment of the one big audience. At worst, they were ignored or disdained. To achieve redress, as John Asher counseled above, blacks had to show they had the numbers—population, set ownership, listening levels, and consumer power—to sway skeptical white executives. Most important, they had to demonstrate this viability within the constructs of broadcasting, a critical requirement.

In 1930, the midway point in radio broadcasting's golden age, the U.S. population stood at 123,077,000. Of these, 12,518,000 were blacks, meaning that roughly nine out of ten Americans were not black. Though 10 percent of the total population represented a large segment, demographically blacks did not exhibit national settlement patterns. They were clustered in one region and in a handful of northern cities. Over 10 million blacks called the South home; 2.4 million lived in the North, primarily in New York, Chicago, Philadelphia, and Detroit, and only 128,000 lived in the West.[31]

Even more illuminating—and detrimental to blacks—is a comparison of the size of the foreign-language and the black communities. In 1930 Chicago's population was 3.3 million. The foreign-born numbered 866,861. Figures for blacks were 233,903.[32]

Using population totals and settlement patterns as criteria, blacks hardly constituted a separate big audience. But the crux of radio ratings is listener levels. Here, too, black numbers were puny. The 1930 census painted a woeful picture of black support for radio as determined by ownership of sets, particularly in comparison with white figures. One in two urban, about 20 percent rural farm, and one in three rural nonfarm white, native-born Americans owned a radio. Foreign-born white totals were 46.2, 32, and 35.1 percent respectively. Of blacks, 14.4 percent urban, 0.3 percent rural farm, and 3 percent rural nonfarm had a set.[33]

Local figures from cities with 100,000 or more inhabitants further illuminate the black ownership problem.[34] The scale of black ownership extended from coast-to-coast, but the level of possession was mixed. The two largest black communities, in New York and Chicago, registered competitive figures of 40.1 and 42.6 percent ownership respectively.

Nationwide, scattered communities also reported possession ratios in the 30–40 percent range. Two hundred thirty out of 750 black families in Paterson, New Jersey, owned a radio. In Massachusetts, one in three or more black homes in Boston, Cambridge, Fall River, and Lynn had a set. Of the 200 black families in Salt Lake City, Utah, 64 owned radios. In California, ownership rates in Long Beach, Los Angeles, San Diego, and San Francisco ranged from 31.2 to 46 percent. But Los Angeles, with the largest black population, had only 11,164 families. Of these, 5,136 had radios. Still these statistics indicate scattered but widespread black support for radio outside the South.

The South, containing three out of four of the nation's black families, recorded the lowest ownership rates, causing the low national figures. A total of 23,450 black families lived in Atlanta. Only 740, or 3.2 percent, had a radio set. New Orleans had the largest black population but a very low 3.3 percent (1,154) of its 34,461 black families owned a radio. A paltry 1,087 of the 29,057 black homes in Memphis had a set. The South registered low ownership rates generally. In the above three cities, total set ownership stood at 26, 21, and 24.5 percent respectively, with the black statistics surely bringing the numbers down.

Finally, there were a number of black-appeal failures that confirm the above dismal statistics. In *Don't Touch that Dial,* Fred MacDonald lists a number of black-appeal shows, all dramas and all short-lived. In 1933, "Deacon Brown and His Peacemakers" aired in San Francisco for a short time. WJZ in New

York City offered an ensemble show of black life in the early 1930s, and another New York outlet, WMCA, produced "A Harlem Family" in 1935.[35] The failure of black-appeal programs reflected poorly on black consumer status, since sponsor support to a certain extent determined a show's tenure on the air. Studies on black economic status, particularly during the depressed 1930s, compounded the problem with their depictions of abject black poverty.

In the South, rural blacks outnumbered urban dwellers by an almost two-to-one ratio. A total of 881,683 blacks were farm operators—most likely with family dependents—but only 182,019 owned the land they tilled. Almost 700,000 were employed as tenants, with the majority working as sharecroppers, "dependent upon the plantation operator for credit, both for current crop expenses and for subsistence." This short-term credit per family amounted to $161 in 1934, rising to $252 in 1937. Blacks averaged $331 and $385 in gross cash income for these two years.[36]

"The low income for large families provides only a meagre subsistence," concluded a 1934 WPA study of cotton plantations. "About one-third of the net income is in the form of products raised for home consumption—a few chickens and eggs, home killed pork, syrup, corn meal, cowpeas, and sweet potatoes." The second third, amounting to about $13 a month, was spent during the cultivation months "for food, mostly flour, lard, and salt pork—and also for kerosene, medicine, and such clothing purchases as cannot be postponed till fall." After the harvest, when accounts were settled, the final third was spent on incidentals and clothing of the poorest quality.[37]

The rural black consumer living on a southern plantation had minimal consumer initiative. His or her purchases revolved around essentials for existence, barely meeting survival requirements. In addition, the typical practice of employers was to require all blacks to patronize plantation-run commissaries. The owners stocked the stores solely according to price, obviously seeking to keep cash flow down, as they also lived on credit.[38]

The conclusion we can draw here is that the mass of southern blacks possessed neither the money nor the opportunity to exercise their consumer initiative. Their situation was more feudal than capitalistic and continued to be so until the late 1930s, 1940s, and 1950s, when wage labor replaced tenancy in the southern countryside.

Urban blacks had enjoyed considerable progress in the 1920s, but the depression probably hit them hardest of all. "Almost 70 percent of the Negro families in Chicago in 1935–1936 had less than $1,000 a year ($83 a month) to spend," according to St. Clair Drake and Horace Cayton in *Black Metropolis*. "Their situation was just the reverse of the white population's—only a little over 30 per cent of the white families received incomes of less than $1,000 a year."[39] Whereas almost one in two black families was on relief, only one in ten white families were welfare recipients. Still, in 1934, black consumer purchasing power in Chicago stood at $84 million.[40]

Given black population, set ownership, or consumer status, broadcasters were right to be wary of black-appeal shows. By all traditional measures blacks did not qualify as a potent radio market. However, the black situation was not traditional or typical. It was special, because of racism. Black protests implied if they did not state this fact. Much of what occurred behind the color line remained hidden from whites, obscuring the potential the black community held for radio if appealed to correctly, even in depressed times.

"The last inch of space was filled, yet people continued to wedge themselves along the walls of the store. Uncle Willie had turned the radio up to the last notch so that youngsters on the porch wouldn't miss a word. Women sat on kitchen chairs, dining room chairs, stools and upturned boxes. Small children and babies perched on every lap available and men leaned on the shelves or on each other."

This was the scene in a small, black-owned grocery store in Stamps, Arkansas, in the 1930s. As recounted by Maya Angelou in her autobiography, it shows the tumult that accompanied the fights of Joe Louis, the black heavyweight boxing champion of the world. Most likely, this scenario was repeated in every black community throughout the United States, for Louis was the preeminent symbol of black pride and progress. "If Joe Louis lost we were back in slavery and beyond help," writes Angelou. "It would be true, the accusations that we were lower types of human beings. Only a little higher than apes."[41]

More to the point, the mob scene around the radio in the small Stamps grocery demonstrated that blacks could be willing and fervent radio listeners. Lack of set ownership proved no obstacle to tuning in programs. Most important, since all ages and both sexes were present for the broadcasts of Louis's fights, advertisers were reaching all segments of the black population at once. Broadcasters were missing the fact that blacks constituted a potent source of revenue to sponsors if approached correctly. Undoubtedly, other programs did not draw the crowds Joe Louis did, but then they did not have the strong appeal of the black boxer.

The final obstacle blacks faced in broadcasting directly related to the philosophy of the one big audience as influenced by segregation. Broadcasters obviously produced shows for audience segments, designing programming for families, women, men, and children. And the varying formats ranging from comedy to drama attracted certain viewers, too. Race, however, was not a criterion so much as a secondary assumption. The only black shows to last on broadcast stations were those with crossover appeal to whites, like musical programs featuring the Mills Brothers, Ethel Waters, and Duke Ellington.[42] White-appeal was the primary consideration as evinced by the crossover factor. Blacks would tune in these shows and support them. However, as was true in society, they were considered a secondary audience whose support was not pivotal to the show's success.

The major thrust behind black-appeal was to balance comedies in the blackface vein and black caricature portrayals. Here, the blackface image complicated matters, causing many broadcasters to believe that they were appealing to blacks with shows like "Amos 'n' Andy."

Thus a number of forces combined to hamper black access to broadcasting's airwaves. But there is no doubt that even under the most favorable conditions, black programming would have played a minor role in broadcasting. The prevailing philosophy of universal appeal dictated that a prime criterion would be white crossover appeal. Blacks attempting to change broadcasting's racial image were blocked by an institutional barrier buttressed by weak socioeconomic statistics, a strong philosophical commitment, and an even more pervasive negative racial situation. In addition, business was booming in the 1930s, so broadcasters could afford to ignore small markets, especially ones they profoundly misjudged.

Even today, in 1988, broadcasting—be it radio, television, or film—permits little deviation from the images and opinions approved by the majority. If blacks fare better in these media, and that is highly debatable, it is because the white majority has either changed its racial perceptions or accepted the need to cater to blacks.

In other words, blacks looking to broadcasting for change and appeal were in the wrong market niche. They had to look outside broadcasting, to get in a game where the odds were more in their favor. They needed a venue where their clustering and numbers would seem impressive, not puny. They had to enter the world of narrowcasting.

NOTES

1. Cited in MacDonald, *Don't Touch That Dial,* p. 357.
2. Cited in Muslimah Muhammed, "Chicago Black-Oriented Radio," *Dollars & $ense* (April/May, 1979), p. 32.
3. New York *Daily News,* (1987).
4. Daniel J. Czitrom, *Media and the American Mind: From Morse to McLuhan* (Chapel Hill: University of North Carolina Press, 1982), pp. 60–61.
5. Barnouw, *A Tower in Babel,* passim. On the creation of RCA, see ibid., pp. 57–61.
6. Ibid., p. 68.
7. Cited in Czitrom, *Media and the American Mind,* p. 71.
8. Barnouw, *A Tower in Babel,* p. 70.
9. Czitrom, *Media and the American Mind,* p. 72.
10. Ibid.
11. Barnouw, *A Tower in Babel,* p. 106.
12. Ibid., pp. 106–7.
13. Ibid., pp. 110–11. Apparently this novel concept took time to gain acceptance. Over a month went by before AT & T found its first toll broadcasting customer.
14. Ibid., p. 109.
15. Ibid.
16. Alan Mirken, ed., *1927 Edition of the Sears, Roebuck Catalog* (New York: Crown Publishers, Inc., 1970), p. 708.

17. Ibid., p. 707.

18. Sarnoff's biography comes from Barnouw, *A Tower in Babel*, pp. 75–78.

19. Ibid., p. 78.

20. Ibid., p. 79.

21. The NBC ad is reproduced in ibid. on the page before p. 88.

22. *The Compact Edition of the Oxford English Dictionary*, vol. 1, p. 280.

23. Barnouw, *A Tower in Babel*, p. 88.

24. U.S. Bureau of the Census, *The Statistical History of the United States: From Colonial Times to the Present* (New York: Basic Books, Inc., 1976), pp. 796–797.

25. Marshall McLuhan, *Understanding Media* (New York: McGraw-Hill, 1964), p. 299.

26. Ross M. Robertson and Gary M. Walton, *History of the American Economy*, 4th ed. (New York: Harcourt Brace Jovanovich, Inc., 1979), p. 329; St. Clair Drake and Horace Cayton, *Black Metropolis*, rev. ed., vol. 1 (New York: Harper & Row, 1962), pp. 7–12.

27. Toll, *Blacking Up*, p. 18.

28. Ibid.

29. MacDonald, *Don't Touch That Dial*, pp. 98–99.

30. Ibid.

31. U.S. Bureau of the Census, *Negroes in the United States, 1920–1932* (Washington, D.C.: U.S. Government Printing Office, 1935), pp. 5, 50, 290.

32. Drake and Cayton, *Black Metropolis*, vol. 1, p. 8.

33. MacDonald, *Don't Touch That Dial*, p. 333.

34. These low national figures hid the relatively high set ownership rates in cities such as Chicago, where 42 percent of the black families owned a radio in 1930.

35. MacDonald, *Don't Touch That Dial*, pp. 330, 332.

36. U.S. Bureau of the Census, *Census of Agriculture: 1930*, The Negro Farmer'' (Washington, D.C.: U.S. Government Printing Office, 1932) p. 18; William C. Holley, Ellen Winston, and T. J. Woofter, Jr., *The Plantation South, 1934–1937*, Works Project Administration, Division of Research, Research Monograph 22 (Washington, D.C.: U.S. Government Printing Office, 1940), pp. 26, 43.

37. T. J. Woofter, Jr., *Landlord and Tenant on the Cotton Plantation*, Works Project Administration, Division of Social Research, Research Monograph 5 (Washington, D.C.: U.S. Government Printing Office, 1936) pp. 27–28.

38. Ibid., p. 28.

39. Drake and Cayton, *Black Metropolis*, vol. 2, pp. 513–14.

40. Ibid., p. 437.

41. Maya Angelou, *I Know Why the Caged Bird Sings* (New York: Bantam Books, 1971) pp. 111, 113.

42. MacDonald, *Don't Touch That Dial*, p. 330.

PART II

BEHIND THE BOOM: PATTERNS OF BLACK-APPEAL DEVELOPMENT

INTRODUCTION

Whereas broadcasting means spreading the seeds over the whole field, narrow-casting implies placing the seeds in rows or drills. One casts a wide net as far as possible, blanketing an area. The other is tightly focused, dividing an area into neat segments. As applied to media, the term *narrowcasting* was coined when cable television began offering viewers options beyond network broad-casting. The tightly formatted movie, health, news, and sports channels tar-geted specific audience wants. Radio had been doing the same thing for de-cades. It was just never called narrowcasting.

The targeted audience concept provides alternatives to listeners and viewers seeking a certain type of programming. Blacks sought the kind of radio shows that appealed to them but that network broadcasting seldom supplied. Earlier successes, particularly in race records, indicated that black-appeal radio would work. But there is no direct evidence of any link between black-appeal pioneers and race records except on a tenuous, or personal, level. Jack L. Cooper, the father of black-appeal radio, was a close friend of black record company pro-ducer Mayo Williams and Cooper did innovate the disc jockey format. But his motivation apparently was the absence of appeal in radio rather than its pres-ence in recording.

Actually the race record experience was just the tip of the black-appeal ice-berg. Just as minstrelsy opened doors of opportunity for black entertainers, it gave birth to a racially separate black entertainment industry catering solely to blacks. Following the Civil War, in black cities and sections throughout the United States, entertainment centers grew up. There were Beale Street in Memphis, Tennessee; Storyville in New Orleans, Louisiana; and south State Street in Chicago, among others. In small southern towns in the rural countryside, juke joints combining gambling and music proliferated. Outside city limits the aptly named roadhouses and frequent barbecues provided entertainment.

To meet the growing demand, a black circuit developed, stretching from Atlanta to Kansas City, from New Orleans to Chicago to New York and covering many points in between. On it traveled minstrel shows, medicine shows, vaudeville troupes, theater companies, and individual performers, all appealing to the black audience. There was even a Theatre Owners Booking Agency to coordinate scheduling, and naturally each locale generated its own entertainers.[1] The TOBA was owned by whites, as were most of the theaters; the lucrative nature of black entertainment was not hidden totally from whites. Rather its viability was self-evident to those in the business.

Equally important, the black circuit provided many of the black entertainers who later achieved fame. W.C. Handy enjoyed a good, rewarding career as a bandleader playing largely to black audiences in the Memphis area. His decision to accept employment with a black band over a white one, in fact, led him directly to the blues and entrepreneurship. Perry Bradford and the singer who broke open the race record market, Mamie Smith, both worked on the black circuit. So did Eddie "Rochester" Anderson and Jack L. Cooper.[2]

Regarding black-appeal radio, Cooper is the starting point of any analysis. He sired the concept and proved that it would work. Jack L. also developed, among many other things, the entertainment-religion-service format that became standard in black radio. By 1941, Jack L. Cooper had a national reputation, and his influence in other ventures was national in scope. Because he worked in Chicago, that city became the black-appeal capital before World War II and remained so after the war. His success was directly due to his previous entertainment experience.

In the context of the black-appeal entertainment continuum, radio was a natural and typical incursion into the media, a logical result of its development. And like all other such undertakings, it was an entrepreneurial activity seeking to switch to a higher level of productivity and requiring biracial cooperation between blacks and whites.

Cooper provided a model to follow. But the concept and practice of narrowcasting dictated that local conditions determine each black-appeal venture. While extreme individuality is evident in specific black-appeal development, all were shaped by the same general forces—including the influence of Cooper. Thus a combination of uniqueness and generality characterizes the explosion of black-appeal radio after 1945. The boom was evident nationwide but obviously programming could only surface where blacks were in residence. So we can narrow the options down generally to large metropolises in the South, North, and West, and mid-size and small southern towns.

What were the patterns of black-appeal development and what factors determined the path that it followed? What lay behind the boom that resulted in six hundred stations airing black-appeal by 1955? Who programmed black, why, when, and where? What went out over the air and into black homes? What was the content of programming?

NOTES

1. This agency was founded in 1909 by a white man named A. Barasso. Over 40 theatres from Jacksonville to Chicago to Dallas to Detroit booked acts through the TOBA. Paul Oliver, *Story of the Blues,* pp. 69–71.

2. See Chapter 3 for a profile of Cooper.

3
GETTIN' 'EM TOLD

With remarkable similarity the story has been told over the years. Jack L. Cooper relished the tale of how he entered radio through the front door, and after his death in 1970, his widow, Gertrude continued to fuel the legend. This story epitomizes the difficulties blacks faced within the microcosm of society known as radio, and it portrays the character of the man who created black-appeal programming.

Seated in her comfortable Morgan Park home on Chicago's far South Side, with his pictures prominently displayed on the walls, Gertrude Cooper once again tells how her late husband got into radio. "He worked for the *Defender* here [Chicago]. They sent him to Washington to open an office."[1] It was early 1925 and the nation's mania for radio continued, with Cooper joining in the fun. He brought a set with him to the nation's capital and, earplug in place, tuned in the shows being aired. One day he happened upon a musical variety program hosted by a German bandleader. A black singing group was featured. The station was WCAP, broadcasting from the Wardman Hotel. While listening, Cooper reflected that although he had heard blacks sing on the air, he had yet to hear one talk. To him, this was like "taxation without representation and so I made up my mind to do something about it."[2]

Gertrude Cooper continues the story. "He wanted to talk to the fellow about some way of getting into radio, some form of it, because he did a lot of comedy." Earlier in the interview, she had mentioned her late husband's commitment "to help the race grow and prosper," surely a consideration here. "There was no way of getting in [to the hotel]. At that time the racial bias was strong."

The color line even barred blacks from using the front door except under unusual circumstances.

Cooper subverted the color line with ease.

So he put on a cap backwards and had an envelope, went to the front desk, and said he had to deliver a message to this fellow [the German bandleader]. They said, "You can't do it. You have to take a back elevator. Or we'll send it." He said, "No. I have to deliver it in person." So they allowed him to do this. Then when he talked to the man, he told him his real purpose. And his purpose was to do dialect if necessary, but some form of comedy—he would write the script—back and forth with this orchestra leader. So the man agreed. And this was his advent into radio. I think he got five dollars a performance three times a week. That's how it all began.[3]

Cooper proved a popular performer and he did achieve his goal of being a black man talking on the air. But the act called for the use of many accents, including black dialect. As a result, the symbolism of his actions went unnoticed. Years later, the *Defender* reported, "Nobody knew what color he was (outside the station) and nobody cared."[4] For all intents and purposes it appeared that blacks still did not talk on the air.

Cooper's WCAP experience raises some interesting points about radio and blacks. Unlike film, the stage, and later television, the medium itself was colorblind. Employment in roles free of minstrelsy's stigma was possible because the limitations of sound potentially offered a shield of racial anonymity to performers. Similarly, by expanding the bounds of ethnic humor to all groups, versatile comedians such as Cooper could use traditional opportunities to get jobs in which they could lessen racial bias, achieving a dubious level of equality. Blacks, like everyone else, would be caricatured, but there would be no singling out of one group as the primary target.

However, the cost was high, as Cooper's experience shows: submerging racial identity, sacrificing any black-appeal focus that implied progress, and removing the race pride factor—a powerful motivation. Whether blacks would have shared more fully in the radio boom under such conditions is a question that defies answering. What we can conclude is that Jack L. Cooper demonstrated that radio could and did remove the onus of minstrelsy. But full realization of this potential was blocked by the fact that both blacks and whites were still responding to the blackface image.

Frustrated by his tenure at WCAP, Cooper returned to Chicago in 1926, determined to make blacks share in the radio boom. He may have found part-time work helping produce a religious program on station WWAE, a small local outlet. Even if there was a black perspective to the show it was an isolated, short-term venture. Cooper's major task was persuading local stations to buy the idea of a black program. For fourteen months he knocked on station doors but none opened. Then he met Joseph Silverstein, a kindred spirit. Silverstein's vision of beaming shows to all ethnic groups included blacks as long as the programming had value. After several meetings, the two men struck a deal.

On Sunday, November 3, 1929, at 5:00 p.m., WSBC premiered "The All-Negro Hour," starring Jack L. Cooper and his gang. Though advance publicity was sparse for the 60-minute variety show, the *Defender* reported that it was received enthusiastically in the black community.[5] At this point, the hero flush with success, the story usually ends. Cooper's radio career, however, had just begun. It would continue well into the 1950s, with the concept he created becoming accepted as an integral part of the radio industry. Much of black radio today is directly traceable to the ideas and practices of Jack L. Cooper, a man fated by temperament and experience to change radio forever.

JACK L. COOPER: THE MAN

Cooper's life serves as a primer for those determined to escape the life of manual labor that the color line dictated for so many blacks. His varied career followed two traditional paths traveled by others similarly purposed: athletics and entertainment. But there was a distinct difference. Cooper also combined a penchant for business, for entrepreneurial initiative, a path often overlooked by scholars examining black modes of progress. Entrepreneurship played a vital role in racial advancement and the furthering of black-appeal radio. Jack L. Cooper's life exemplifies this pattern of progress.

The grandson of a white French-Canadian named Kupincheaux and a black Virginia woman, the son of a gambler who died before the child was one year old, Jack L. Cooper was born on September 18, 1888, the last of ten children. He left school after the fifth grade to work as a race track yard boy. "The family was named Black," Gertrude Cooper explains. "At the age of ten he went to Cincinnati with them. That was where he finished growing up."[6] In fact, working for Black entailed traveling the race track circuit through the Midwest and mid-South. Life on the road gave Cooper a broader vision of the world than most youths his age had. During the off-season, Cooper lived in Cincinnati, working first as a newsboy and later as a bellboy and porter. But his real passion was boxing. He fought 160 amateur bouts and won several championships, including the Cincinnati newsboy title in 1901 and later the Ohio Negro welterweight crown.[7]

Briefly Cooper played second base for a semi-pro baseball team but soon entered show business in traditional fashion. A 1954 interview with black writer Roi Ottley revealed his beginnings as a singer, buck-and-wing dancer, and even as an end man in a minstrel show.[8] In entertainment he found the opportunity athletics did not provide. In addition to singing and dancing, Jack L. performed as a comedian and actor, soon branching out into writing and producing. By the early 1920s he had his own troupe traveling the black theater circuit. In fact all his experience was in the black world. Cooper apparently never sought to cross over to white venues, except for the short stint on WCAP.

Cooper's vaudeville/theater background provided good training for his future radio career. Not only did he hone his performance skills and come into close contact with the wants of the black audience, he also received training in the business of entertainment. A playbill and some newspaper clippings from his files show what sort of entertainment Cooper favored and how the audience responded. These documents also reveal much about the man.

Jack L.'s troupe was called the Cooper and Lamar Music Company. Madam Lamar was the stage name of Estelle Mansfield Cooper, Jack's first wife.[9] She served as musical directress and composed most of the songs. A 1923 tour brought the company to the Belmont Theatre in an unnamed city. Written by Cooper and starring him in the title role, "Unlucky Joe" was the featured act. "Picturizing life today," it was a morality play billed as "a Stupendous drama brimful of Thrills, Pathos, Melody, and Mirth." This musical comedy and dramatic tearjerker all in one provided something for everyone. Its message is evident from the synopsis. "Vow to make good" is the title of Act 1, Scene 1. "A chance to make good" summarizes Act 2. Scene 3 in the third and final act demonstrated that "Might is right."[10] Uplift and progress were the company's underlying concepts, as this plea from the playbill demonstrates: "The shows presented by this company is a study in the art of clean shows. . . . Come out and help us pave the way for clean, moral refined shows."[11]

The Belmont engagement offered full entertainment. After "Unlucky Joe" on Monday and Tuesday, the audience could enjoy "The Vaudeville Question" and a comic afterpiece, "Whose Baby Is That," the following two days. Friday and Saturday customers laughed at "A Wife for a Hundred Dollars," which was billed as "a comedy traveling at the rate of 65 laughs a minute."[12]

Such broad-based yet respectful entertainment was well received by black audiences. A review of their Tyler, Texas, engagement reads: "The Cooper and Lamar Musical Company with their two weeks engagement at the Rapeed Theatre are carrying a crowded house and management says it is the best company that ever played at this place."[13]

The varied career of Jack L. Cooper allows for little chronology. Though he left athletics for entertainment, he still remained active in sports, at least sporadically. His files contain documentation of his managing a boxer called "Six Cylinder" and a short tenure as a boxing promoter in Palm Beach, Florida. Cooper also managed theaters in that city and in Texarkana, Arkansas. Between approximately 1910 and 1924, he worked as a journalist, writing for a number of black newspapers: the *Freeman, Ledger,* and *Recorder* in Indianapolis, Indiana (on the last two he was theatrical editor); and two Memphis, Tennessee, papers, *Bluff City News* and *Western World Reporter.*[14]

In 1924 Cooper left the stage but not the theater. On June 10 he was hired as assistant theatrical editor by the Chicago *Defender.* He also wrote a regular column, "Coop's Chatter," spreading the gospel of hard work and progress. "Were we to spend half the time between the pages of good books that we spend between the curbstone and the building," he wrote on November 24, 1924, "there would be less crime, more business, and better understanding." [15]

Cooper's message, as evidenced by his life and work, was simple and forthright. Black progress depended upon black self-help with special emphasis on and recognition of the importance of the individual. In the 1954 Ottley interview, Cooper reflected on his life and motivation. His poverty-stricken childhood acted as the catalyst for his personal philosophy and his determination to succeed. It probably contributed to his goal-oriented, practical, and entrepreneurial bent. "Sow no valued seeds among the weeds, for therefrom can come no harvest," he told Ottley. Other quotes provide further insight into his character. "To grow old with nothing is disaster," he said, revealing the accumulation of wealth as one of his major goals. But money was not his only motivation. "The more I accomplish the more I become the servant of those who are not so fortunate." He wanted "to pave a better road, an easier path for Negroes who came along behind." [16]

Radio provided Cooper with the means to acquire wealth and to help the race progress. His concept for a black show extended far beyond just airing something of appeal. Cooper's idea was to gain as much black control and participation as possible, and Joseph Silverstein proved a willing ally. Silverstein owned the World Battery Company, which manufactured, among other things, the "WORLD Storage 'B' Battery" for radios. A 1926 direct mail ad claims 10 million sets were powered by this battery. [17] Seeking to maximize his advantage and to pursue a dream, Silverstein founded WSBC in 1925, building studios on the seventh floor of the New Southern Hotel at 13th and Michigan on Chicago's near South Side. Located at 1210 kilocycles on the AM dial, WSBC (Storage Battery Company) was a part-time station sharing the frequency with WEDC and WCRW. Its signal strength of 250 watts was too low to reach all of the Chicago metropolitan area. [18]

Advertising his battery company by providing programming for listeners was only part of Silverstein's goal. His vision was to use the radio for beaming shows to each and every ethnic group living in Chicago—which meant airing foreign-language shows. By 1930, the census reported that such groups comprised a population of 842,057, a very significant market of one in four Chicagoans. [19] Even today the station operates under the banner "News and Music of all Nations."

Cooper's idea of airing shows for blacks fit in with Silverstein's format and vision. In part, Silverstein may have recognized that Cooper's idea would enhance his station's share in the increasingly competitive ethnic radio market. Certainly, the notion was entrepreneurial in that Jack proposed moving the station into new audience territory of potentially higher productivity. This is particularly true given Cooper's objective and the show's comprehensive format. The connection between black programming and ethnic stations was also a primary pattern of black-appeal development in large northern urban centers with significant immigrant and black populations, such as Chicago, New York, Philadelphia, Los Angeles, and Detroit.[20]

"THE ALL-NEGRO HOUR"

In pioneering the black-appeal concept, Jack L. Cooper had one goal in mind. He wanted it to be a 100 percent black effort. When "The All Negro Hour" debuted, a white announcer "put the carrier on the air," meaning that he introduced the show, and took "off the carrier," meaning that he closed the show. In both instances this involved naming the station and providing transitions to the ethnic program following it.[21] Unhappy with this arrangement, Cooper had the white announcer replaced with a black one: himself. Success provided greater latitude. Cooper was issued a card designating him "official announcer of the 'all Negro' programs" as well as commercial announcer of all advertising accounts whose messages were aired during the black segments.[22]

Building a new studio solely for the production and airing of black shows was the next step. As had happened with the program itself, Cooper spent nine months knocking on doors seeking funding, but the black community's resources were sorely strained by the depression. A story in *The Bronzeman,* a short-lived local black newspaper, reports on how the money was found. Cooper "took his idea to Messrs. R. A. Cole and Fred Lewing, President and Secretary, respectively, of the Metropolitan Funeral System Association, who took hold of the idea and built a studio, equipped it, and contracted with WSBC for time on the air."[23] The new studio included seating for the audience who came to watch live what others only heard over the radio. As *The Bronzeman* story notes, "Each Sunday, regardless of weather conditions, the usual big crowd of admiring spectators is on hand to enjoy the program."[24]

For several reasons Cooper never succeeded in making "The All-Negro Hour" an all-black effort. Although he did attain management status, the first black to do so, WSBC remained a white-run and -owned radio station. In addition, the engineers handling the technical end of airing the show were white men, one of whom was named Edward Jaecker.[25] As will be shown later, the advertising came largely from white-owned businesses in the black community. In other words, the institutional, technical, and financial support was largely in white hands, but what went out over the air was black-controlled—that is, by Jack L. Cooper. Since the show was popular and made money, he was given free rein.

The reasons behind the show's success are varied, complex,and interrelated. In part, it was a direct result of a larger black self-help movement popular in the 1920s. Having helped win the "war for democracy"—World War I—and having experienced significant gains socially, politically, and economically through migration and the wartime prosperity, the new black urban enclaves looked to the future with hope, confidence, and determination. W. E. B. DuBois put it best, writing in *Crisis:* "Make way for democracy! We saved it in France and by the Great Jehovah, we will save it in the United States, or know the reason why." [26]

During the 1920s, blacks in northern cities such as Chicago made tremendous strides toward democracy. Black migrants in particular enjoyed more freedom, more opportunity, and more excitement. Coming to Chicago was like a dream come true. They could vote and they did. Their swelling numbers provided the base for a political machine that elected black state and federal representatives. School attendance for children was regular and consistent, not determined by the needs of agriculture. Blacks moved freely around the city on public transportation and in commercial centers. Black culture boomed as a renaissance of music, literature, and art characterized the age. [27]

Most important, jobs paying unheard of salaries were plentiful for much of the 1920s. [28] As migration transformed small, established enclaves into large, growing communities, so prosperity imparted economic power and initiative to black consumers. In 1928 prominent black Chicago banker Jesse Binga reported that blacks had $4 million on deposit in banks, paid taxes on $4 billion worth of property, and had contributed $2 million to charity. [29]

Blacks recognized that, in the spite of all these gains, white racism backed by the color line was thwarting their efforts to fully realize democracy. Ambivalence characterized black city life, as evidenced by the rise of the inner city ghetto. Historian Allan Spear sees the physical ghetto resulting from white hostility to black population growth. Violence and housing covenants restricted expansion into white areas. These conditions caused severe overcrowding, straining the physical and service resources of the black community.

The black response to white racism was, Spear explains, "the institutional ghetto." [30] Seeking to beat whites at their own game and drawing inspiration from the experiences of other ethnic groups, black leaders espoused the doctrine of self-help, aiming to build an independent black metropolis within Chicago. The keystone of this effort was the building of an economic foundation, but inexperience and insufficient time doomed it to failure.

The black consumer's buying criteria were quality goods and services at the lowest price, not racial pride as most black leaders had hoped. [31] White businesses continued to capture the black trade, since black-owned operations typically had neither the experience, the resources, nor the expertise to compete. Nor were black ventures afforded the luxury of time to develop. The economic depression hit blacks long before 1929, sweeping away the black metropolis dream. Sounding the death knell was the failure of the Binga Bank, a very visible symbol of success. Ironically, the racial self-help concept survived and thrived in the radio shows of Jack L. Cooper, whose "All-Negro Hour" premiered at a most unpropitious time: five days after the stock market crashed.

Cooper was certainly a supporter of the black metropolis idea. A self-educated and self-made man, he espoused the cause in his newspaper column for the *Defender,* urging blacks to learn to help themselves. His insistence on a

100 percent black effort and the very name of the radio show, "All-Negro Hour," underscore his commitment to race pride, to working within the black community to achieve progress.

However race had little to do with Cooper's success on the air. Race would have been evident in some fashion no matter what the black-appeal undertaking. "The All-Negro Hour" prevailed because its founder knew his audience and based the format and content of the show on tried-and-true entertainment formulas. With sixty minutes each week on a station whose signal paled in comparison with the network outlets and working with meager capital, Cooper provided quality along with pride.

At the same time that Cooper was building an audience, he had to convince advertisers, local merchants in the black community, to try a new means of reaching customers with a sales message: radio. Success rested on proven expertise, long years of experience learning the market, and business acumen— the attributes that many advocates of the black metropolis had lacked.

The show starred Cooper as host and featured a gang of regular performers. Representing virtually every age group and both sexes, the cast included Lucretia Knight, the prima donna of the group; ukelele player and novelty singer "Big Boy" Edwards; Lennie Stratton, the "Boo Doope Doop" girl; crooner David Mozee; Buddy Burton, recording star; a female singer named Ezra Shelton; pianist Claude "Clink" Rhodes and his five-year old daughter, June; the silver-haired sweetheart, Mrs. Hattie Andrews; and preacher D. E. Milton of "A Little Prayer for Me" fame. Supplementing Coop's gang were guest stars such as blues singer Lovie Austin, "Showboat" actress Rose Summerville, and the Original Cotton Pickers singing group, among others.[32]

Featuring an encyclopedic, fast-paced entertainment format that stressed music and comedy, "The All-Negro Hour" was like a vaudeville revue on the air. Actually it was in the vanguard of radio programming circa 1929. Cooper's program rivaled "The Rudy Vallee Show" as "the first variety series to revolve about a single celebrity and employ famous guests as a supplement."[33] Vallee's program also debuted in Autumn 1929.

An accomplished innovator, Cooper also capitalized quickly on popular developments in radio. Within months of "Amos 'n Andy" 's skyrocket to popularity, Cooper had developed his own comic strip serial about two black migrants. "Luke and Timber" premiered on February 27, 1930. Certainly, Cooper knew about "Sam 'n' Henry," the local precursor of "Amos 'n' Andy," and this knowledge aided him. He wrote the serial and appeared as Luke, while Brunswick recording star Arnold Wiley played Timber. The theme song "I Ain't Never Done Nothin' " indicates the thrust of the serial.

By August 1930, two more serials were introduced. "Mush and Clorinda, the Alabama Sunflowers" followed the misadventures of a husband and wife. "Horseradish and Fertilizer" told the story of two lovers. This last was written by Cooper, who played Horseradish. Mamie Porter played Fertilizer. This serial lasted for over 12 years on the air.[34]

Cooper's files contain several scripts for these serials as well as other musical and comedy bits. They allow a typical show to be traced from beginning to end. "The All-Negro Hour" opened with the "Two Black Diamonds of Radio," Jack L. Cooper and "Clink" Rhodes singing:

How-dee do, Friends how are you,
We're here to cheer, two black diamonds,
to stop your pining,
Before we're thru, you'll be smiling too. . . .

This opening theme was followed by several musical numbers, such as "I'll Never Do That Again," "Without A Song," "The Old Paper Dollar," and "River Stay Away."[35]

In all probability, a serial followed the music. "Well here are Mush and Clorinda in person. Last week we found things still buzzing about the case of the lost heirloom. Madam Mystery, the lady who lost the heirloom, as you recall, has a hunch that Mush took the heirloom from her home when he visited there for a lesson in how to make love."

The scene opens in the Slick Shave barbershop and pressing club. Mush is there with Zacaria, Miss Sadie Green, and his lawyer, Mr. D. Westbrook Richards. We hear Miss Green as she says:

Sad: You said the case will be called tomorrow Richards?

Law: Well that depends wholly on howsomeever my client here acts bout my emolument de retainer.

Mus: Is de jedge gon put dat again me too, Mr. lawyer?

Law: Well not exactly the judge, but I will.

Mus: But I don't see how come you got to go holdin anythin lak dat gainst me when I gotts to pay you ter handle dis thing.

Miss Green explains that the lawyer means his fee, to which Mush replies, "Well, how come he don say dat, stid o talkin bout molement de tainer and stuff." The episode continues with the lawyer pressing for payment. Finally Mush calls Clorinda, who comes to the barbershop to handle matters. She rejects the lawyer's demand for $20, telling Richards to take $2.50 or leave it. The lawyer accepts and Clorinda takes Mush home so he can beat some rugs.[36]

Here a commercial was probably aired, so this is a good place to stop the show and analyze the above serial excerpt. In many ways it appears well in tune with the blackface humor prevalent at the time. Mush seems a good-hearted Tom, who is always getting into trouble. The lawyer parodies the legal profession, using big words and pressing for payment. But Richards can also be viewed as a coon speaking in malapropisms and always trying to get something for nothing. Clorinda is obviously the boss, seeing through Richards's ploy for more money. She could be considered a mammy with mother wit.

None of these negative blackface images, however, were attributed to Cooper's serials. The performers were black. The scripts were written, produced, and directed by a black man. The audience was black. All of these points take the serial out of the blackface realm. They were self-parody using universal comic formulas such as malapropisms and caricature humor. And as noted before, the big determining factor in blackface was who was saying what to whom, and how often. Basically, Cooper acted in classic entrepreneurial fashion, switching from blackface to black-appeal humor in order to achieve a higher return. Beyond the absence of any white perspective here, there is the further distinction that the program presented wide-ranging entertainment. There was balance in the images presented and not all the humor had this tinge of caricature.

For example, the following excerpt from a comedy segment called "Giggles and Grins" has no racial aspects. Featuring Cooper and his second wife, Billie, this exchange was aired August 30, 1931.

B. What is wrong with your brother, he looks tired and worn these days?

J. Well the poor sap isn't getting any sleep.

B. Why what seems to be wrong[?]

J. His wife accuses him of snoring in his sleep, he declares he doesn't and now he is laying awake nights to catch himself in the act.[37]

The show probably closed with a musical number or two and undoubtedly a sermon by D. E. Milton. To take it off the air, the "Two Black Diamonds" sang the theme song:

> We're two "Black Diamonds" direct from Dixie,
> Where the corn and cotton bask in the sun,
> We hate to leave you, we hoped we've pleased you,
> And you've really enjoyed our fun,
> We aim to chase your blues, and kill old gloom,
> and fill you with glee,
> When we appear on station Double You See Bee See.
> The Two Black Diamonds, direct from Dixie,
> From the place called Cotton town.[38]

Cooper compressed into one show and one hour what networks devoted many programs and hours to. "The All-Negro Hour" was, in many ways, an amalgam of proven vaudeville and radio formulas. But it was also distinctively black-appeal, as evidenced by the inclusion of preacher D. E. Milton in the cast. Recorded sermons were popular among blacks, often becoming top-selling hits.

Cooper's mix of entertainment and religion found a ready, supportive audience. The show stayed on the air during the worst years of the depression. One facet of its appeal was the novelty of radio programming for blacks. Another was the opportunity the new studio provided for blacks to watch the program live. Gertrude Cooper recalls that as a teenager she and a friend went down to the show. "It was new to the public and just like the kids flocked to television they flocked to radio at that time," she explains. "So this was one thing where you could peek behind the curtains and look." [39]

GETTIN' 'EM TOLD

After six years on WSBC, "The All-Negro Hour" ended its run in 1935. But Cooper's career in radio had yet to begin in earnest. Throughout this period he produced new programming and expanded his time on WSBC. Though records are sketchy it is possible from surviving advertising contracts to trace this expansion beginning in 1933. "The All-Negro Hour" aired from 5:00 to 6:00 p.m. on Sundays.

In the early and middle 1930s there was steady growth in WSBC's black-appeal schedule, but always at off times—weeknight late evenings and weekends. By 1935, Cooper controlled approximately nine and a half of the station's 56 hours of weekly airtime. On Sundays his shows were aired from 6:00 to 8:30 a.m., and from 5:00 to 6:00, 7:00 to 7:45, and 9:15 to 10:00 p.m. On Tuesdays through Fridays he occupied the 11 p.m. to midnight slot, and he was on the air Saturday afternoon from 1:30 to 2:00. There was some shifting of time slots, some gains and losses, but generally Cooper's schedule was stable. Prime time, however, remained an elusive goal.

The programming followed in expanded fashion the popular entertainment-religion formula. The Saturday afternoon "Colored Children's Hour" was a short-lived effort. But the main trend was away from live performance to recorded music on the late weeknight shows. Live entertainment posed three substantial problems: recruiting talent, keeping them employed, and paying the artists. "We'd take anybody we could find and put them on the air," Cooper recalled during a 1963 *Defender* interview. [40]

A dispute over money precipitated the switch to records. Gertrude Cooper explains: "What happened in his case was there was this woman piano player. This was an important item at the time. Hammond hadn't done anything either at that time [with the organ], so piano was it. And on a Saturday night, which was very important to him in his production, she wanted more money." Cooper couldn't pay more money so the performer left. That night, his wife continues,

He got a barrel and set some little record player on it and held a mike to it. And that's the way he carried on the show for that night. And that was his start into the record business. And, of course, after that the station got equipment. Then there was a fella now named Al Jarvis in California and according to my husband Jack there was a little dispute about which of the two was first . . . in the whole country to play a record.[41]

The dispute was not over who played the first record, because recorded music had been a programming mainstay before live entertainment replaced it. The question was who was the first disc jockey, the first to intersperse the playing of records with the now familiar disc jockey patter that links the music with the talk of the person behind the microphone. If Cooper's dates are correct—and 1931 has appeared in print many times—then he predated Jarvis by a year.[42]

Playing records solved the live-performance problems. It was cheaper, more reliable, and, Gertrude Cooper says, provided "much more variety." Producing recorded music programming was also much less time-consuming than producing a variety show, leaving Cooper more time to develop programming and advertising strategies. As a result the vaudeville-of-the-air format was abandoned and the serials declined too. Only the fifteen-minute "Horseradish and Fertilizer" stayed on the air throughout the 1930s. Its run ended in 1942.[43]

Religious offerings served as Cooper's financial base during the lean years. Live gospel and spiritual concerts were aired but the major thrust was Sunday live remote broadcasts from various churches. The fact that the Unity Independent Spiritual Church and others were sponsors shows how important these remotes were. Another illustration of this is Gertrude's account of her first meeting with Jack, which occurred several years after she went down to the radio station to see "The All-Negro Hour."

Gertrude's father was Bishop William Roberts of the Church of God in Christ located at 40th and State Street. He had moved his family from Memphis to Chicago in 1917 when Gertrude was seven. An accomplished pianist and organist, Gertrude started playing in her father's church when she was 13. Several years later Cooper signed a contract with Bishop Roberts to air church services. "Our church was broadcasting with him," Mrs. Cooper explains. "He served as broadcaster and engineer. I think we were the third church in Chicago to come on. Shortly after they were there, he and his wife (he was married and they had a break-up). And then I discovered he played drums. We had a band. And one time there was nobody at the drums so he took over the drums and we became acquainted." Gertrude was 28 and Jack 50 when they married on June 25, 1938.[44]

For all this activity and growth, the failure to break into prime time—weekday mornings and afternoons—kept Cooper at the fringes of radio success. He struggled to make a profit, recognizing that his career was at a standstill. Soon after they married he asked his wife, "What can we do to increase sales and stuff?" Gertrude recalls her reply. "And I said, 'I don't know about other people but I do things from habit. If there was some consecutive programs then people would establish the habit of listening.' "[45] Becoming habit-forming is an essential part of audience building, but it requires regular, reasonable air times.

The breakthrough came in 1938 when WSBC's afternoon drive hours from 2:00 to 3:30 p.m. opened up and so did time on other stations. The key was buying up the WSBC afternoon hours. Cooper formatted three disc jockey shows in this slot: "Rug Cutter's Special" from 2:00 to 2:30, "Gloom Chasers" between 2:30 and 3:00, and "Jump, Jive, and Jam" in the last half hour. At last, there was consecutive programming at reasonable times. Programs could become habit-forming and they did. Bob Roberts, Gertrude's brother, went to work for Cooper in 1938. He says Cooper reached into half the black homes in Chicago, a statement that provides strong commentary on the number of blacks owning radios.[46]

It was also in 1938 that Cooper expanded beyond his WSBC base of operations with the opening up of time on WHFC. During the late 1930s and 1940s Cooper exponentially increased his schedule. The zenith was reached in 1947 when shows produced by Jack L. Cooper Presentations comprised 40 hours of air time weekly on four or more stations. According to an undated *Defender* article in his files, Cooper had 154 programs on the air at one time. On WSBC, Cooper controlled 19 1/2 hours out of 56 total hours on the air.[47]

This rapid expansion of air time necessitated more program development in a number of categories. As with "The All-Negro Hour," only more so, Cooper was still providing something for everyone via narrowcasting. A closer examination reveals this comprehensiveness. Those unable to attend religious services could tune in a variety of narrowcasts from a number of churches, including: the Church of Englewood, South Park Baptist Church, Beth Eden Baptist Church, the First Church of Divine Science, the Evangelist Temple, Saint Paul Church, Wesley Memorial Church, the Thankful Baptist Church, and the aforementioned Unity Independent Spiritual Church and the Church of God in Christ. "Bible Time" and "Know Your Bible" provided religious education. Spiritual and gospel music fans had a choice of shows, among them "Spiritual Music" and "Song of Zion," hosted by Gertrude's brother Isaiah Roberts.[48]

As noted, popular programming centered on recorded music formats and spanned the tastes of listeners. The thrust of "Songs by Request" is obvious. Besides "Rug Cutter's Special," Gloom Chasers," and "Jump, Jive, and Jam," there was "Stomp Time," "Evening Heat Wave," and "Music for Anybody." An unusual offering was "Polite Music," which featured spiritual, gospel, and popular music. Gertrude Cooper played live organ music on WHFC's "Organ Interlude" and also hosted "Tips and Tunes with Trudy" on WBEE.[49]

In addition, there were quiz shows, programs analyzing handwriting, and the very popular serials that continued into the 1940s. Cooper even forayed into the dramatic realm. Featuring Mannie Mauldin, Jr., and Lucky Cordell, both of whom became popular radio personalities, "The Nitemare" was a mystery-drama aired at 10:00 p.m. on Saturdays on WHFC in the later 1940s. Cooper financed the program initially by appealing to racial pride. " 'Nitemare' proved to the radio audience that such dramas can be written and presented by Negro talent. This will lead to other opportunities which will give us a chance to display our talent," he said in a *Defender* interview.[50] Cooper was at least a decade late with his idea. The program attracted neither listeners nor sponsors, who looked to the new medium of television for such shows.

Perhaps the most influential and important aspect of Cooper's programming was in the realm of public service. The black-appeal effort in this area and the energy behind it was as important as entertainment in gaining the allegiance of the black audience. Again Cooper was the pioneer. The first example of public service programming was aired on December 9, 1938, when he launched the "Search for Missing Persons" show at his father-in-law's Church of God in Christ. Aimed at reuniting people who had lost contact with friends and relatives through migration and over time, the program was produced in cooperation with the Chicago Police Department. It began as a 15-minute show and soon was expanded to include the original spot and an additional 45 minutes on Friday evening. Aired over WSBC, it had allegedly reunited 20,000 people by 1950. A mother and son who had been separated for 35 years were among those brought together.[51]

Developed largely in the 1940s, the public service area was comprehensive in its approach. On Saturdays at 11:00 p.m., "veteran social worker" John M. Ragland offered advice on "Our Community Marches On." "May We Help You" featured Gertrude Cooper's brother Isaiah counseling callers. Those seeking employment found out about jobs by tuning in "Situations Wanted" on WHFC Monday, Wednesday, and Friday at 10:00 a.m. "Social Security For You and Your Family" explained the workings of this program to WSBC listeners. In addition, there was a program on "Your Legal Rights."[52]

Local news of interest to blacks was covered as well. Cooper remodeled a van into a mobile unit to relay "on-the-spot news events directly to four radio stations in the Chicago and suburban area," according to *Ebony* magazine.[53] At 11:45 p.m. news flashes from the black newspaper, the Pittsburgh *Courier,* were aired. Often famous personalities who had come to town were interviewed on the air by Cooper, as, for example, boxer Joe Louis. Gertrude Cooper remembers that her husband could only get one word out of him.[54]

Special events in the black community received special coverage. The annual Bud Billiken parade is perhaps the major black event in Chicago. Cooper aired the twenty-first annual edition of the parade over WHFC and he reported on the first Exposition of Black Business.[55] Cooper did play-by-play sportcasts of black baseball games as well. The greatest innovation and triumph was a news discussion show called "Listen Chicago" aired Sunday from 4:00 to 4:30 p.m. Listeners heard a panel of experts discuss topics of interest first on WAAF and later on WHFC. Newsworthy and educational, the show was an exercise in both freedom of the press and freedom of speech. As Cooper, subbing for regular moderator Virgil Williams, said on March 27, 1949, "Before proceeding with our program for today, we wish it known that we reserve the right to differ with you on what you say, but will champion with equal vigor, your right to say it.'' Bob Roberts called "Listen Chicago" "one of our best programs." It provided blacks with their first opportunity to use the medium of radio as a public forum and ran about seven years on the air, from 1946 to 1952.[56]

To a certain extent, "Listen Chicago" was the apotheosis of Cooper's career, his shining and last achievement. It capped the programming initiatives of the previous two decades that expanded the bounds of his radio commitment to entertaining, informing, and serving the black community. The show was probably the last of the "firsts" that spanned his career. He had pioneered the very concept of black-appeal programming and made it work by building a mass following. He had been the first black radio station executive in the United States, the first black news and sportscaster, perhaps the first disc jockey, and the first to use radio as a service medium.

GETTIN' 'EM SOLD

But developing programming of appeal was only half of Jack Cooper's formula of success. The other was building an advertising base among local retailers serving blacks and local churches. These two facets worked in tandem, reinforcing each other. The greater his audience following, the better his prospects were of selling advertising time. The more time he sold, the more capital he received to expand black-appeal's air time and to produce more shows. The linchpin of this synergistic relationship was an institutional oddity of narrowcasting in Chicago.

"A time broker was what Jack L. Cooper was," explains Bob Roberts. "He would broker the time by buying it from the station and reselling it. For instance, you buy an hour's time for x number of dollars and sell it in five minute segments, one minute segments, or even 30 minute segments."[57] By buying a large block of time and subdividing it for resale at a higher rate to sponsors, Cooper assumed responsibility for all aspects of his programming. The station had no risk. It neither financed the show nor sold the advertising. It just provided the facilities necessary for narrowcasting programs to the public.

The concept of buying and reselling air time allowed Cooper to expand his schedule on WSBC and to diversify to other stations. This, in turn, allowed the growing local advertising market to be nurtured. Later the same would be true for national accounts.

In many respects, time brokering resembled the original AT & T idea of opening up its studios to anyone able to pay the tariff for air time. It also acted as a marvelous vehicle for innovative programming to unknown audiences, such as blacks. To sum up, narrowcasting provided black-appeal radio in Chicago with opportunity while time brokerage provided the means to commercially exploit this opportunity.

Ironically, "The All-Negro Hour" was not produced under the broker concept. Apparently, Cooper received a small salary plus commission for selling advertising from WSBC. Sometime in the 1930s he switched to the more risky but potentially more lucrative brokerage arrangement.[58]

Cooper's initial problem was opening wider the doors of opportunity through audience building and advertising successes. Race was a minor hindrance compared to that of time. Jack L. worked in an environment where airtime was limited owing to the part-time status of WSBC and the station's need to provide comprehensive ethnic programming. For nine years he labored on the fringes of late nights and weekends. This "spotty" schedule, as Gertrude Cooper described it, was hardly an inducement for potential sponsors. But it was balanced by the fact that only Jack L. Cooper was programming black-appeal in the Chicago area. Without any competition, he built a stable, growing base of sponsors that kept him on the air even if they didn't make him wealthy.

Cooper's records contain enough advertising contracts to reconstruct a profile of his sponsors in the 1930s. With the exception of the ubiquitous churches, the common thread among these advertisers was retailing. All delivered goods or services to the black public. Shoe and clothing stores, beauty shops, groceries, auto repair shops, restaurants, a doctor, a coal company, a funeral home, and even a bus depot all bought time on Cooper productions. Another similarity was location. All but two were located in the area around Indiana and 43rd Street on Chicago's South Side.[59]

Some of the businesses forged long-term relationships with Jack L. Cooper. Bill's Bootery at 302 East 43rd Street began advertising in April, 1933, if not earlier, and continued to buy time until the mid-1940s. Bob's Radio Store at 540 East 47th Street advertised with Jack from at least 1934 to 1937.[60] As will be shown later, after Cooper hit prime time in 1938, both national and some prominent local sponsors also entered into long-term advertising relationships. Obviously, even in less than perfect circumstances, Jack could and did get 'em told.

The major advertising drawback was Cooper's inability to attract black sponsors. Throughout his long radio career spanning parts or all of four decades, white businesses overwhelmingly bought ad time. At best, Gertrude Cooper claimed, one in five sponsors was black. She frequently heard her husband complain about this situation,[61] which worked counter to his quest to make black-appeal radio an all-black effort.

A review of the black business situation in the 1930s indicates that perhaps Jack L. was fortunate to have as many black sponsors as he did. Both economics and attitude—the same problems that had plagued the black metropolis—proved formidable obstacles to overcome.

The onset of the depression erased much of the business progress of the prosperous 1920s. But phoenixlike, the black community experienced an even larger resurgence of black-owned businesses. Of 5,400 businesses in the black area in 1937, almost half—2,464—were black. Over half again of these had been founded after 1927, "as many people with some savings saw in the opening of a small store one means of insuring themselves against starvation." [62]

But rising numbers did not translate into greater strength or a larger market share. St. Clair Drake and Horace Cayton write that "Most of these [new businesses] were small retail stores and service enterprises on the side streets, or in the older, less desirable communities." Bad location was not the only drawback. Contributing negative factors included lack of experience and a dearth of capital. Most important though was the absence of motivation. Many people opened their own business more out of necessity than choice. "If work was plentiful, these small places would not exist," claimed one successful black shop owner. Drake and Cayton second this assertion.

White stores continued to capture the black trade, garnering over 90 cents of every black consumer dollar expended. Black stores received less than a dime. In the grocery sector, the second most popular black business, only 5 percent of the $11 million dollars spent by blacks in 1937 went into black-owned cash registers.

The only areas where blacks could compete were in undertaking, beauty parlors, and barber shops, where there was no white competition. Not surprisingly, beauty parlors ranked first and barber shops third as popular black businesses. [63]

From the above statistics and from surviving contracts, we can more accurately recreate the potential black market for radio advertising at that time. Of the 5,400 businesses, fewer than half represented the potential market. However, as it is doubtful that Cooper could have marketed to the newer, marginal retail outlets, the total number is reduced to 1,296. Instead of speculatively subtracting the noncompetitive operations, we can further reduce this number by drawing upon Cooper's contracts to see who did buy time. The fact, however, that he sold time to a grocer does not mean that a black owned the store, for the level of black patronage then was dismally low.

Comparing the list of contracts to the list of the ten most popular black businesses (accounting for two-thirds of the total), Cooper's potential market comprised approximately 569 out of 2,464 total black businesses, or a little under one in five. This ratio is somewhat deceptive because of the large number of beauty parlors in operation—287 of the 2,464—not all of which would take ads. [64] In addition, the potential market for black sponsors was buttressed by churches, which probably served as the most numerous black ad takers.

A similar reduction in the black sponsor figures would result if the attitude of the shop owners was included in the tally. Here again economics enters into the discussion, because price is the determining factor in selling ad time. How many blacks owners could afford to buy time? How many would experience enough return to merit the purchase? Given their inexperience and motivation, how many would even listen to Cooper's sales pitch?

The last question is easily answered. Few of the newer black shop owners would find air advertising appealing since they were often biding their time until the job situation improved. Or they were stocking the shelves of their groceries to prepare for the worst possible scenario. "We were at the height of the Depression," explained one erstwhile black grocer. "I had just a small amount of money and could not find a job so I decided to open a grocery. If worse came to worst, I would at least have something to eat."[65]

The advertising costs also presented a barrier, though Cooper provided many options for both buying and paying for time. In addition, his rates remained stable throughout the 1930s and usually included copywriting and announcing, eliminating a major concern of inexperienced sponsors. Time signal and spot announcements cost $4.50 and $2.50 each respectively. The most popular vehicle was the 100-word ad running from $2 to $5 depending upon the time slot and the length of the contract.[66] Blocks of time—15, 30, and 60 minutes— were also available.

Both to maintain his capital pool and enhance the effectiveness of the advertising campaign, Jack preferred long-term contracts. William Friedman of Bill's Bootery bought six, 100-word announcements to be aired on the colored children's program between April 1, 1933 and May 6, 1933. The total cost was $15 with one-third due upon signing the contract and the remainder payable in $2.50 weekly installments before the "current broadcast." In March, 1937, Robert Chambers of Bob's Radio Store purchased the Tuesday evening 11:30 to midnight slot for 26 weeks. He paid a total of $910 on terms similar to the above.[67]

Most black shop owners could not have afforded air time purchases like that of Chambers. But if there was a sale promotion through radio, advertising was possible. Thus, sporadic rather than regular advertising would be the norm for the majority of black businesses if Cooper could overcome prevalent negative attitudes.

The attempt to recruit black sponsors so as to make black-appeal radio a 100 percent black effort was part of the original black metropolis idea. As the larger crusade met resistance from black consumers, we can infer that Cooper encountered similar responses from black business owners. Blacks would not patronize black businesses to help them grow and strike a blow for race pride. "The Negro should not be expected to trade with another Negro because he is a black man," explained one woman. "People of any race should have some respect for their people, but any people naturally want to get things where they can get the best bargains."[68] That meant shopping at white stores. Complicating matters was the popular black image of the black merchant. "Negroes rate their businessmen as the scum of the earth," complained one angry black owner.[69] The weekly antics of Amos and Andy may have contributed to this image.

The mix of image and economic reality made blacks wary of air advertising. In some cases the cost was too high. In others, the merchant probably realized the return would be too low. Finally, given the motivation for opening a business and the inexperience of the operator, few would have recognized that a well-constructed ad campaign could improve their image and help overcome such variables as a bad location.

Even the black preachers' forceful and continual advocacy of buying black fell on deaf ears. "Tomorrow I want all of you to go to these stores. Have your shoes repaired at a Negro shop, buy your groceries from a Negro grocer . . . patronize your own, for that is the only way we as a race will ever get anywhere," exhorted a black preacher in the 1930s.[70] Such appeals did bring black consumers to black-owned shops, though usually only for token purchases. Still a major key to retailing success is getting people inside the store. Once the customer is in the store, through solicitous, respectful service and the sale of goods at competitive prices, a relationship between owner and customer can be built—and some black owners succeeded in doing so.

One new shop owner thought business was "lazy work." He quickly learned the work was "exceedingly hard, and that the hardest thing is trying to please the public and encourage them to buy."[71] This man probably would have recognized the value of air advertising.

From the above discussion, it is evident that a whole range of interrelated forces affected Jack L. Cooper's marketing of air time to black businesses. The total market statistics were illusory, masking severe deficiencies in the black business sector. Jack probably achieved as much success as possible given the economic realities and the prevailing attitudes of black consumers and retailers in the 1930s. The return of prosperity in the 1940s and 1950s witnessed no upturn in the racial sponsor ratio, indicating that attitude was the primary obstacle.

Race was a secondary consideration for Cooper, particularly in his advertising efforts. Like all other businessmen he was out to make a profit and that meant exploiting the market open to him—white-owned outlets catering to blacks. In 1937 he opened the Jack L. Cooper Advertising Company in what was a logical culmination of events. The company's motto illustrates its thrust: "When we get 'em told, you got 'em sold."[72]

Since Cooper was the acknowledged expert in the field, it made sense for him to enhance his market position by founding an ad agency. It basically professionalized and organized services Cooper already provided to present a more businesslike image to sponsors and radio stations. Equally important, the agency provided self-advertising for his shows, since Cooper usually, though not exclusively, sold time on programs produced under his aegis.

Also the company was a persuasive selling force. Small businesses leery of buying time because of their inability to design air advertising found Cooper's operation filling a deeply felt void. Like a one-stop shopping center, the agency handled everything a sponsor needed, from placing an ad to writing one that would attract black consumers. Cooper played on this image and touted his record of success in brochures, coverage of his activities in the Chicago *Defender,* and possibly other avenues not evident from his files or interviews with wife Gertrude and brother-in-law Bob Roberts. The result was that when Cooper's career began booming in 1938 he was well positioned for success.

The purchase of WSBC's weekday afternoon slot was the pivotal point in Cooper's career. "That's when we began to make some money," recalled Gertrude Cooper. Having finally broken into prime time, her husband expanded his advertising market locally and nationally. "We had some good sponsors. Large accounts," said Gertrude. "Atlas Prager Beer, at that time was one. Tip Top Bread was one." By 1949, Cooper's advertising clients included the American Giants black baseball team, Thomas J. Webb Coffee, Parker House Sausage, Lipton's Tea, and a large number of local businesses. Many of these, like Tip Top Bread and Atlas Prager Beer, enjoyed long, fruitful relationships with Cooper.[73]

In securing accounts, Jack L. proved very innovative. He recruited the Chattanooga Medicine Company, a white-owned Tennessee firm that sold hair products to blacks, by drawing upon a childhood tie. "Because as a little boy he had delivered papers to the owner and he sent this in communication he got the account. I think it was through the J. Walter Thompson Agency," Gertrude Cooper recalls.[74]

Cooper's most potent selling weapon, however, was his following in the black community. A late 1940s advertising brochure for Jack L. Cooper Radio Presentations, the companion company for radio show productions, promoted the results of a survey conducted by "one of Chicago's largest clothing and furniture retailers with over 60,000 active accounts—95% Negro." Two hundred customers selected at random were asked about their listening and buying habits. Asked if they listened to Cooper's shows (then on four stations), "74 or 37% said 'Most of them,' 120 or 60% said 'Some of them.' " Only six respondents did not tune in any Cooper programming.

The poll's results assured sponsors that not only did people listen but they also bought the products advertised. One hundred twenty-two said they purchased most advertised products. Forty-nine bought sponsor goods and services some of the time. Only 29 did not patronize Cooper's advertisers.[75] Though not definitive in its results or totally scientific in its polling, this survey did indicate Cooper's strength in the black community and the willingness of black consumers to support those serving them.

At the peak of his career in the late 1940s Cooper was a truly commanding figure. In 1951 he was voted the top radio man in Chicago. Soon afterward, failing eyesight and age forced him to cut back his schedule.[76] Although he died in 1970, his legacy lives on. The eulogies spoken by black radio personalities after his death demonstrate his profound influence.

"How can you begin to assess or evaluate this man's many contributions within and outside the communications media?" asked Daddy O'Daylie, whose own radio career centered on making jazz accessible to listeners. "He opened many doors for many of today's black disc jockeys and gave them opportunities." Former employee Lucky Cordell echoed O'Daylie's sentiments. "Certainly in his life span, he helped countless numbers of people . . . interested in radio broadcasting. So many of today's black radio personalities at some time or other worked with or for Mr. Cooper and I believe that he has made an indelible mark.'' Vince Saunders of WBEE called Cooper the ''forerunner of black announcers across the country.''[77]

A major fact of Cooper's career is that, although he was a pivotal figure, he was never alone on the air. ''The All-Negro Hour'' and other live venues provided entertainers with great career opportunities. His expansion on the airwaves opened up an entirely new field of employment for blacks. Gertrude Cooper became almost as ubiquitous an air personality as her husband. ''I helped with the announcing. If anybody came up to do a little song I played for them,'' she said. ''Her voice soon became as familiar to listeners'' as Jack's, according to the *Defender*.[78]

In the 1950s when WBEE hired Gertrude to host ''Tips and Tunes with Trudy'' the station praised her work. ''Negro radio programs in Chicago have long been in search of a radio personality with an elusive combination of talent, pose [poise], natural sagacity, appeal, experience, 'presence of mike,' and community influence. In Trudy Cooper WBEE Radio has such a person.''[79] She was on the air over 25 years. Her brothers also worked in the Cooper organization. Bob was chief of staff and his duties ranged from announcing to selling to writing. Isaiah focused on religious programming.

Other blacks found employment with Jack L. Cooper Presentations. One newspaper ad shows his staff totaling 16. Of the five people listed as announcers, two were women and another woman worked as a commentator.[80] In the days before affirmative action, Cooper practiced equal employment opportunity.

But perhaps Cooper's greatest contribution was his influence on black-appeal development nationwide. He became the example to follow. ''Since June 1 of this year,'' reported the *Defender* in 1946, ''radio and advertising men all over the country have focused their attention on Cooper's successful experiment in beaming a variety of programs during 36 hours of air time per week.'' The test involved a series of shows sponsored by the National Credit Clothing Company and ''represented the first time an advertiser attempted to deal directly to colored audiences—and to the tune of $50,000 per year.'' While the *Defender* inaccurately described this as the first radio advertising directed at blacks, the industry's scrutiny probably was a first.

In checking Cooper's progress the *Defender* explained that radio executives were thinking of introducing similar programming ''in New York, Detroit, Pittsburg [sic], Los Angeles and other metropolitan centers with large Negro populations.''[81] The boom was on, not only in Chicago but across the United States.

NOTES

1. Interview, Gertrude Cooper, Chicago, Ill., June, 1982.
2. "Meet Jack L. Cooper," Chicago *Defender,* March 5, 1949.
3. Interview, Gertrude Cooper.
4. Bob Hunter, "74 and Blind, Jack L. Cooper, First Negro Deejay, Still Airs Radio Show," Chicago *Defender* Magazine, May 14, 1963.
5. Chicago *Defender,* December 3, 1929.
6. Interview, Gertrude Cooper.
7. Undated newspaper clipping, Jack L. Cooper Files, Chicago Historical Society (hereafter referred to as JLC Files). The Cooper Files contain a large scrapbook of newspaper clippings and other memorabilia. These and other materials constitute the written data used to support information collected in interviews.
8. Ottley, "From Poverty to 90 Suits."
9. Interview, Gertrude Cooper.
10. Playbill, Belmont Theatre, January 8–9, 1923. JLC Files.
11. Ibid.
12. Ibid.
13. Undated newspaper clipping, JLC Files.
14. Undated newspaper clippings, JLC Files; interview, Gertrude Cooper.
15. Chicago *Defender,* November 24, 1924.
16. Ottley, "From Poverty to 90 Suits."
17. This ad was obtained from WSBC station manager Roy Bellavia.
18. Roy J. Bellavia, *A Capsule History of Past and Present Radio Stations in the Chicagoland Area* (unpublished pamphlet, Chicago 1978), p. 5.
19. Drake and Cayton, *Black Metropolis,* vol. 1, p. 11.
20. See Chapter 4.
21. Wilbur Wright, "Chicago's All Colored Radio Hour," *The Bronzeman* (1934?), JLC Files.
22. Ibid.
23. Ibid.
24. Ibid.
25. Interview, Edward Jaecker, Chicago, Ill., June, 1978.
26. W. E. B. DuBois, editorial, *Crisis,* May, 1919.
27. See Huggins, *Harlem Renaissance.*
28. Florette Henri, *Black Migration: Movement North, 1900–1920* (Garden City, N.Y.: Anchor Press, 1976).
29. Drake and Cayton, *Black Metropolis,* vol. 1, pp. 78–83.
30. Allan Spear, *Black Chicago: The Making of a Negro Ghetto, 1890–1920* (Chicago: University of Chicago Press, 1967), p. 91.
31. See Drake and Cayton, *Black Metropolis,* vol. 2, pp. 430–69 for a discussion on the problems faced by black-owned businesses.
32. Undated Chicago *Defender* article, JLC Files.
33. MacDonald, *Don't Touch That Dial,* p. 28.
34. Chicago *Bee,* August 17, 1930, JLC Files; interview, Gertrude Cooper.
35. "All-Negro Hour" radio script, JLC Files.
36. "Mush and Clorinda" radio script, JLC Files.
37. "All-Negro Hour" radio script, JLC Files.
38. "All-Negro Hour" radio script, JLC Files.

39. Interview, Gertrude Cooper.

40. Hunter, "74 and Blind, Jack L. Cooper, First Negro Deejay, Still Airs Radio Show."

41. Interview, Gertrude Cooper.

42. Arnold Passman, *The Deejays* (New York: Macmillan, 1971), p. 48. Based on interviews he conducted in Chicago in 1984; Passman told me he believes Cooper predates Jarvis.

43. Chicago *Bee*, August 17, 1930, JLC Files; interview Gertrude Cooper.

44. Ibid.

45. Ibid.

46. Interview, Bob Roberts, Chicago, Ill., July, 1982.

47. WSBC Program Schedule, JLC Files.

48. Advertising contracts; undated Chicago *Defender* article, JLC Files.

49. Ibid.

50. Undated Chicago *Defender* article, JLC Files.

51. Undated Chicago *Defender* article, JLC Files.

52. Undated Chicago *Defender* advertisement, JLC Files.

53. "Disc Jockeys," *Ebony,* vol II (May, 1957), p. 24.

54. Interview, Gertrude Cooper.

55. Undated Chicago *Defender* articles, JLC Files.

56. "Listen Chicago" radio script, March 7, 1949; interview, Bob Roberts.

57. Interview, Bob Roberts.

58. Interview, Gertrude Cooper.

59. Advertising contracts, JLC Files.

60. Interview, Gertrude Cooper.

61. Ibid.

62. Drake and Cayton, *Black Metropolis,* vol. 2, p. 436.

63. Ibid., pp. 438–55.

64. Ibid., pp. 450–51.

65. Ibid., p. 454.

66. Advertising contract, JLC Files.

67. Ibid.

68. Drake and Cayton, *Black Metropolis,* vol. 2, p. 445.

69. Ibid., p. 444.

70. Ibid., p. 431

71. Ibid., p. 454.

72. Advertising contract, JLC Files.

73. Interview, Gertrude Cooper; Jack L. Cooper Radio Presentations promotional brochure, JLC Files.

74. Interview, Gertrude Cooper.

75. Jack L. Cooper Radio Presentations promotional brochure, JLC Files.

76. Interview, Gertrude Cooper.

77. "Jack L. Cooper, 1st DJ, Is Dead," Chicago *Defender,* January 12, 1970.

78. Undated Chicago *Defender* article, JLC Files.

79. Ibid.

80. Undated Chicago *Defender* advertisement, JLC Files.

81. "Jack L. Cooper Opens Door of Radio to Negroes," Chicago *Defender,* c. 1946, JLC Files.

4

FROM ONE VOICE TO MANY

Between 1940 and 1954, the transformation of both Afro-America and the radio industry allowed Jack L. Cooper to realize his dreams of hearing many black voices on the air. Changes precipitated by World War II produced the black-appeal boom after peace returned in 1945. The black community became more urban than rural, more demanding of progress, and more receiving of the prosperity that spread throughout the United States. Even those blacks who remained employed on the farm experienced substantial gains as wage labor and mechanization plowed under the tenancy-operated plantations. So long neglected and scorned as an audience and consumer market, blacks now found radio stations and advertisers catering respectfully and solicitously to their needs.

There was good reason for the new treatment radio accorded blacks. Between 1940 and 1953, the black population grew and progressed at a faster rate than the white. The number of blacks rose to over 15 million, an increase of 15.8 percent compared to 14.4 percent among whites.[1] Black migration reached record proportions as blacks were pushed by mechanization and pulled by the promise of better-paying jobs to cities throughout the country. Between 1940 and 1944 alone, the number of blacks living in Chicago increased by 60,000. By 1953, six in ten blacks lived in urban areas.[2]

Just as important was the 129 percent climb in black urban home ownership that translated into one in three black families owning their own residence. The increase for whites was 84 percent. This statistic had particular meaning to radio executives and advertisers. "The home owner, as any adman knows, is one of the prime targets for the advertiser," counseled the industry trade journal *Sponsor*. "He is in effect 'a purchasing agent,' both for his family consumption needs and for the maintenance and improvement of his home."[3]

Behind the rise in black home ownership were some strong trends in black earnings. Though white income levels remained higher than those of blacks, the gap was closing. Black median income rose 192 percent between 1940 and 1953 whereas whites experienced a 146 percent growth rate. Nine out of ten blacks were gainfully employed in 1953.

Perhaps most revealing to whites were black radio-set ownership rates. In 1953, 98 percent of all Americans owned a radio. Nine in ten blacks did. In the North and the Pacific West, there were sets in 90 to 98 percent of black homes. In the South, the figures were approximately 75 to 85 percent, but urban radio ownership jumped into the 90 percentile range.[4] The question of whether blacks owned enough radios to merit attention had been answered with a resounding yes.

The strong signal all these numbers sent to the radio industry was that "The country's Negro population is gradually acquiring better disposable incomes, and is spending it more and more in urban areas." This conclusion *Sponsor* supported by "8 key facts to remember about the Negro market," from which the above statistics were taken.[5] It achieved maximum impact because this industry trade journal narrowcast the news of black progress to those best able to capitalize on these gains. The message to station owners was brief and clear—opportunity.

Bert Ferguson, the co-owner of WDIA, Memphis, Tennessee, touted black-appeal as "the sales opportunity of the decade." He described the black listening audience as "plump and juicy, the succulent plum of a $15,000,000,000 Negro market."[6] *Sponsor* supported Ferguson, claiming that "The average Negro household . . . is a better-than-average consumer of nearly all of the products regularly advertised on radio."[7]

Black improvement was part of the general prosperity spreading across the United States after fifteen years of depression and war. True, the economy wavered temporarily at times, dipping into stalls and short recessions, and inflation was a problem, but "The tonic of prosperity affected almost every segment of the economy," as Arthur S. Link and William B. Catton write in the *American Epoch*. That major indicator of economic well-being, the gross national product, rose from about $310 billion in 1946 to $487.7 billion in 1960. Most important for radio, the disposable income of Americans jumped 50 percent between 1940 and 1960. Construction, manufacturing, service industries, technology, all boomed.[8]

There was also a boom in race relations, beginning with the successful 1941 black protest against job segregation in war plants. It was followed by the 1948 integration of the armed forces and President Truman's campaign visit to Harlem to court black voters that presidential election year. The peak was reached in 1954 when the Supreme Court struck down legalized segregation in the case of Brown v. Board of Education.[9] As depression and war had transformed the socioeconomic black community, so had it similarly affected black consciousness, as will be shown in detail in Chapter 7. But some discussion of the subject is needed here.

The winning of the war against the Fascist threat, particularly from Germany, was seen by all as a victory over the past. Blacks saw it as a triumph over racism. "There was no need to discuss racial prejudice," wrote black writer Maya Angelou, a teenager in 1945. "Hadn't we all, black and white, just snatched the remaining Jews from the hell of concentration camps? Race prejudice was dead. A mistake made by a young country. Something to be forgiven as an unpleasant act committed by an intoxicated friend."

Reality was much different. The war had not removed the color line, nor had it changed white racial attitudes. Black perceptions had been altered, however. "They were free or at least nearer to freedom than ever before and they would not go back," explained Angelou.[10] The altered black consciousness created a new concept of what it meant to be black and new cultural expressions to express this emerging self-concept, among many other things.

While the black community was being transformed, radio underwent its own revolution. Television had almost been ready for commercial development in the late 1920s but first the depression and then the war delayed its entry into the market. After the war, RCA introduced a new, more efficient video receiver that enhanced its appeal and ignited an explosion in the marketplace.

In 1946, 6,000 American homes had television sets. Three years later, 3.5 million sets were in use and by 1952 almost 28 million had been sold.[11] Radio had taken 20 years to fulfill its goal of a set in every home. Television became a part of everyday life in half that time, no doubt in part because radio had prepared Americans for future advances such as putting visuals to the familiar sounds.

As more and more performers switched to the new medium, fears arose. Would television relegate radio to the same scrap heap to which the automobile had banished the horse-drawn carriage? "Pessimists said radio was finished; it would never survive," writes Robert St. John in the *Encyclopedia of Radio and Television*. But, he continues, "Radio was not dying. It just needed a new and different diet."[12]

Television usurped radio's broadcasting crown, ending the network hegemony. The stars moved to the TV studio so they could be seen as well as heard. The audience switched, too, turning to the new marvel in their living rooms for entertainment and news. Conceptually, the networks faced a revolution in programming and marketing that many affiliates were ill-equipped to face. Many outlets possessed no studio facilities or sales staffs. They had merely thrown a switch and caused Jack Benny or "Gunsmoke" to reach into people's homes. This arrangement kept costs low while allowing the airing of the shows people wanted. It also inhibited responses to changing conditions. Time and preparation were necessary for the former kingpins of radio to regroup and carve out their audience shares anew.

The decline of network broadcasting opened up new opportunities for independent stations—a blessing, since the number of outlets on the air increased dramatically after 1945. Competition was intense but the one big audience was no longer the target. Instead, the population was segmented and targeted by stations as narrowcasting became the dominant strategy for survival and black-appeal became the darling of the industry.

FROM ONE VOICE TO MANY IN CHICAGO

Jack Cooper's boom started earlier, in 1938, when he finally obtained prime time shows and began multistation programming. He continually expanded his schedule throughout the forties, helping to fuel the rise of Chicago black-appeal by increasing program development and providing employment for other blacks. The socioeconomic forces at work nationally helped Cooper.[13]

The midwestern metropolis became the acknowledged capital of black radio. A 1947 *Ebony* of "sepia spielers" profiled 16 black radio personalities. Five were from the Chicago area and represented five different stations, although at least two, Cooper and newcomer Al Benson, had shows on more than one outlet.[14]

But the impact of migration to Chicago changed the audience. Cooper, the urban New Negro, found himself growing out of touch with some listeners. He refused to play records of the new electric blues style so popular with black newcomers to Chicago. He was 57 in 1945 and represented an older generation than most of the migrants. And he did not speak their language; there was no hint of a southern accent in his speech patterns. He was middle class and most of the migrants came from working-class origins. These differences, combined with his health problems, particularly his failing eyesight, and his advancing age opened the door for a successor. Al Benson became the king of black-appeal in Chicago, far surpassing Cooper in air time and eventually in earnings.

Not surprisingly, there was some animosity between Cooper and his heir apparent. Even in 1982 when I interviewed Gertrude Cooper it was obvious hard feelings existed. They were two very different and yet very similar men. Perhaps the major career difference was that Cooper had labored so long and hard at the fringes of success while Benson had reaped the rewards of Jack's toil virtually overnight. Al owed his rise to timing. He came on the air as the boom began and so was in the proverbial right place at the right time. He also had the right stuff.

Like Cooper, Al Benson was an entrepreneur with no previous radio experience. He was born in Mississippi in 1910. Before attending Jackson Normal College in Jackson, Mississippi, he worked in music shows traveling the black circuit. As was true with Jack L., Arthur B. Leaner (his real name) had a varied career working as "cook for the Pennsylvania Railroad, an interviewer for the Works Progress Administration [after he moved to Chicago during the depression], and a Cook County probation officer."[15] He, too, had extensive and intensive contact with the black audience, contact that was furthered by his job as a pastor for a nondenominational storefront church at 40th and State Street.

Unlike that of Cooper, Benson's experience was with the black masses. Professionally he worked with the lower classes seeking employment from the federal government in the thirties, trying to make it on the streets after jail, and seeking spiritual guidance. He was no New Negro appealing to urban blacks and the small middle class as Jack L. had. Instead, "Ole Mushmouth," as he was called, spoke the dialect of the migrant on the air and was a strong supporter of the new Chicago blues sounds percolating up from the South Side clubs. His entrepreneurship did not involve challenging Cooper's hold on established residents but in moving to a higher level of productivity by becoming the radio voice of the former farm worker turned city dweller.

Benson's work as a pastor brought him to radio. In August 1945, the Reverend Arthur B. Leaner launched his narrowcasting career with a fifteen-minute remote from his church on station WGES. "Within two months," writes Norman Spaulding, a former disc jockey and author of a study on black radio in Chicago, "he had 'sold' his time and expanded his program to one hour each Sunday." [16]

Apparently Benson moved to the radio studio, because Gertrude Cooper recalled, "My first awareness that he existed was that I would see him—we were there until midnight on Sundays—and we were on the air from eleven to twelve because the station was." WSBC shared facilities with WGES. "And I would see him and he would be lookin' through the windows watching the performance. . . . He would wait until the program was through and then take his little singing group" into the studio. [17]

Here the story becomes vague; apparently Leaner switched his name to Al Benson and his format to popular music because WGES allowed no commercials on religious programs. From there, according to Spaulding, Benson "proceeded to build a legend and a fortune." [18]

By 1948 the former pastor was on the air a purported ten hours a day over three stations—WGES (his base), WAAF, and WJJD. "His schedule became so heavy between selling his time and broadcasting that he was eventually forced to broadcast from his home and later—around 1949—to hire young protégés who became salesmen and on-the-air personalities under his auspices." Spaulding estimated that Benson earned $2 million between 1945 and 1965. [19]

The similarities between Al Benson's career and that of Jack Cooper are striking. Each came to radio in mid-life. Cooper was 41 when "The All-Negro Hour" premiered. Benson was 35 when he started. Each had diverse backgrounds that included entertainment and that kept them attuned to black audience needs. Finally each was an astute businessman with an appealing on-the-air personality. To paraphrase Cooper's motto, both could get 'em told and get 'em sold. Cooper's sales ability already has been demonstrated.

Former WGES owner Elizabeth Hinzman called Benson "the greatest salesman that I have ever known.'' Al's brother, record dealer Ernie Leaner, said that Benson ''was so strong and popular that he could pick and choose his own sponsors.'' Spaulding writes that some South Side merchants would buy an hour of time just to get on his shows. By 1949, national accounts began signing up: Coca Cola, Schlitz Beer, Italian Swiss Colony Wine, and Continental Bakers, to name a few.[20]

Two factors contributed greatly to Benson's rise to the top of what was to become a crowded black-appeal market. The first was that he did not work at WGES under a time-brokering arrangement. This practice had allowed Cooper the opportunity to build black-appeal radio into a viable concept. After the war, as more and more stations entered the black-appeal fold (between Benson and Cooper alone we can name nine outlets), competition intensified. ''There were over 75 Black personalities [in Chicago] during the period of 1945 to 1960, who worked at various stations in the city,'' Spaulding reports. ''Many of them lasted only a few weeks because of the 'brokeraging arrangement.' ''[21]

Basically time brokering still opened doors of opportunity to blacks. It also allowed the marketplace to swiftly weed out those ''unable to cut the mustard,'' as WGES disc jockey Richard Stams put it.[22] The point was that sales superseded all other skills. ''It is important to realize that the first group of Black radio personalities were not hired as 'performers or stars,' '' Spaulding writes, ''but rather as salesmen, who if they had a style that appealed to the public became known and developed audiences for their shows.''[23] Many found the demand for weekly payments on the time they purchased too onerous a burden and soon left the air.

At WGES, the black disc jockeys were responsible for sales of ad time but not under the brokerage concept. ''Benson was not charged for his time by the station, but rather acted as a salesman and received a commission for the accounts he sold.''[24] There was pressure to sell but there was no out-of-pocket expense. As a result, Benson had the opportunity to build up his audience and his sponsor base without striving to make those weekly payments. He, Stams, Sam Evans, and others proved very durable personalities for WGES.

The dual nature of black disc jockey employment in Chicago may have been unique. The common practice was for air personalities to pitch sponsor products and services on the air while a separate sales staff sold air time. By combining both tasks in one job, Chicago outlets reduced manpower expenses while providing greater returns for success. But there is no denying that the personal costs were higher, too, particularly regarding time and stress.

Another aspect of WGES operations worked in Benson's favor. It was a twenty-four-hour station with a 5,000-watt signal that far surpassed Cooper's base, WSBC with 250 watts. Though he did expand to other stations, Benson was heard by all Chicago area blacks from WGES. Like WSBC, this outlet had engaged in ethnic programming, but by the 1950s black-appeal had taken over the bulk of its airtime including prime time.

Unlike Jack L., who expanded into advertising, Benson moved into the burgeoning music and record industries. He founded Parrot Records and was a prominent concert producer for black music acts.[25] This was a natural progression because of the role radio came to play in the music industry as a maker or breaker of discs and performers. Radio airplay was the prime method for promoting new songs. Without it few records achieved success. Benson played the pivotal role in introducing blues records by artists such as Muddy Waters on new independent labels, Chess, for instance, to Chicago audiences. As noted above, Cooper had considered such music too raw for airplay.

Throughout the 1950s, Al Benson ruled black-appeal radio, but his dominance was continually challenged by other personalities on and off WGES. For example, station mates Sam Evans and Richard Stams proved extremely popular; Stams claimed that he was breathing down Benson's neck. On WOPA, another ethnic station that beamed black shows, Big Bill Hill and popular nightclub owner McKie Fitzhugh carved out substantial audience shares. Daddy O'Daylie championed jazz on the air and Lucky Cordell, a Cooper protégé, also achieved success, as did many others.

In 1962 WGES was sold, and Benson moved to WHFC. This latter station was then sold to the Chess brothers, who ran the record company of the same name. They were major purveyors of the Chicago blues sound and hoped to use their radio acquisition to sell more discs. They renamed the station WVON (Voice of the Negro), indicating its focus. WVON became the Chicago black station of the 1960s, but blues continued its decline in popularity among blacks, a trend analyzed in Chapter 8. As for Al Benson, his radio career ended. Spaulding claims that Benson was "paid over $25,000 a year *not* to broadcast over WVON or any other station within 300 miles of Chicago." He retired in 1964 and moved to Three Oaks, Michigan, where he died on September 8, 1980.[26]

The Chicago black radio experience after World War II followed the trail Cooper had blazed and was somewhat typical of that of other large, polyglot cities. It was both unique and exemplary in its pattern of development. The biggest question here involves time brokerage. The scanty information available indicates neither the use of this concept outside of Chicago nor its lack of use. In fact, though evidence exists that the FCC outlawed the practice of brokering time, when I spoke with WSBC manager Roy Bellavia in 1982, he seemed unaware of any law outlawing it.[27] Another factor mitigating against the use of time brokerage was the traditional division between on-the-air selling of sponsor products and the sale of airtime to these advertisers. We can surmise that time brokering was only applicable to large cities with the necessary resources needed to make it viable: a goodly number of stations; enough entrepreneurs willing to take the risk; and, naturally, a large black population concentrated in a relatively small area.

What made Chicago unique—and at the same time representative—was the person of Jack L. Cooper. As early as 1940 *Variety* touted him as having "a rep that extends through all the Negro communities in the nation."[28] The 1946 test (discussed in Chapter 3) followed closely by representatives from other stations is proof of Cooper's influence coast-to-coast. So are some program features adopted by other stations. WDIA in Memphis, Tennessee, for instance, aired a missing persons show and a news forum remarkably similar to "Listen Chicago." In addition, Cooper employees gained work both in and outside Chicago, helping spread his influence. Sam Evans of WGES first worked on a Cooper show. Richard Stams claims to have cobroadcasted black baseball games with him. Mannie Mauldin worked first for Cooper and then moved to Milwaukee, where he enjoyed a long radio career.

The influence of Chicago was furthered by the fact that it was, as *Ebony* reported in 1947, "the mecca for colored wax workers" or disc jockeys.[29] Cooper played a part in the midwestern city's achieving status as the capital of black radio. But the strong ethnic radio industry and the fact that the city contained the largest single black community in the United States also played a role.

Conditions similar to those in Chicago existed in other urban centers such as New York, Los Angeles, San Francisco—any city with a large ethnically diverse population, a radio industry serving these groups, and a growing black population. In these areas black-appeal followed the Chicago example, with ethnic radio as the starting point for programming. The large New York City independent WLIB aired ethnic shows with black offerings. In Los Angeles, Spanish-language programming vied with black-appeal for time. KSAN, San Francisco, was an ethnic outlet with a black component. The northern California metropolis had large Chinese and Italian populations to serve.

The other similarity in the pattern of development was part-time multistation programming. By 1954, six stations in the Los Angeles area were airing black shows. Two stations in New York City and two in neighboring Newark, New Jersey, served the resident black population. Philadelphia had three stations beaming black-appeal shows and the San Francisco Bay area had two. None was 100 percent black. Interestingly, except for Philadelphia, the other metropolitan areas listed all had had stations airing black-appeal programming before the post–World War II boom.[30]

Sometimes it was an individual who launched the concept, as Cooper did in Chicago. Joe Adams pioneered black-appeal in Los Angeles on KOWL, Santa Monica, during World War II. He later became Ray Charles's manager, introducing another pattern of general development, the growing relationship between radio, records, and music. Radio historian Larry Lichty told me that some Los Angeles stations were tied to record stores.[31] Even though the scanty written data provides no corroboration for his claim, it does seem likely that this was true, because of the strong role Los Angeles played in rhythm and blues music.

To sum up, large metropolises throughout the United States, often in ethnic venues, gave rise to significant black-appeal radio components. They followed a pattern of development similar to that of Chicago, the acknowledged leader.

The emergence often was led by a single pioneer and usually involved or evolved into some tie-in with the music and recording industries. During the boom, programming was aired on a number of stations, typically as part of an overall schedule.

But the black-appeal boom was not restricted to large cities. Nor was the Chicago pattern relevant to all cases, though Cooper's influence may have been present.

THE BOOM IN BLACK-APPEAL RADIO

Perhaps the most potent symbol of the black-appeal radio boom was the creation of the National Negro Network in 1954. Its first show, a soap opera called "Ruby Valentine" starring Juanita Hall, was carried by 45 stations in 21 states from Alabama to California and from New York to Texas. The sponsors were Pet Milk and Philip Morris cigarettes. Other black stars appearing on its programs included Ethel Waters, Hilda Simms, and Cab Calloway. The NNN owned no stations; it distributed its shows and commercials to affiliates, providing advertisers with almost national exposure. But whereas the time was right for black-appeal radio, the day had passed for golden age programming as produced by the NNN. It quickly disappeared, but the very appearance of a black-appeal network indicates that the concept had come of age.[32]

By 1952 the radio industry was well aware of the explosive growth of black-appeal. "Negro-appeal radio programming has been in a boom period for the past five years," reported the industry trade journal *Sponsor*. Actually the boom spanned the period from 1946 to 1955, when the number of stations airing black shows jumped dramatically from 24 to 600.[33]

Geographically, the trend to black-appeal was evident nationwide but was most apparent in the South, reflecting population patterns. A 1954 *Sponsor* survey disclosed that there were 269 stations in the South, 102 in the Northeast, and 27 in the West. Obviously black-appeal would only appear where an audience was in residence to support it. Yet towns and cities as disparate as Fresno, California, Flagstaff, Arizona, Tampa, Florida, Newman, Georgia, and New York City had outlets airing black shows. This fact underscores the widespread dispersion of the black population.

The state with the most stations appealing to blacks was Texas, with 47. Reflecting the heavy influx of blacks during and after the war, California reported 19. But one California outlet, KWBR, Oakland, had been appealing to blacks since 1934.[34]

The *Sponsor* survey from which these statistics are taken was representative and indicative rather than comprehensive and definitive. It shows that wherever blacks lived in significant numbers, radio was appealing to them. Another obvious but difficult-to-prove aspect of the boom was the entry and exit of outlets to black programming. Not all who experimented with black shows remained committed to the concept. There was a continual expansion and retraction of airtime depending upon that sole determinant, sale of advertising.

The sales imperative mostly worked to black-appeal's advantage. The *Sponsor* annual surveys contain many stories of blacks passing tests overwhelmingly. In Memphis, Tennessee, a 1949 campaign by the General Home Service Corporation brought station WDIA a faithful sponsor. For 13 weeks, a 15-minute spot on a disc jockey show was used to sell clothes washers. The result was that "a total of 546 washers had been sold—more than any other dealer had disposed of and almost as many as all the GE dealers in Memphis together had sold." A satisfied General Home Service Corporation increased its advertising to "10 to 12 quarter hours weekly."[35]

Even tract homes were sold on the air. In 1954 in Compton, California, a city in the Los Angeles area, Holly Manor Estates used one-minute spots on KOWL exclusively to sell 33 new homes. Each cost $11,500, and a down payment of $1,500 was required. "The results were spectacular," the station reported. "Every home was sold within three weeks representing a gross sale of $379,500." Advertising costs were under $400. In addition, tract developers said that if the down payment had been modified, "they could have sold out the first week." Sixty percent of the buyers "said they heard about the homes through the 'Joe Adams Show,' " on which the ads had been placed.[36]

Each year *Sponsor* included such success stories in their black radio annual. There were 15 in 1954 alone and they involved everything from bleach to snuff. Radio stations and advertisers quickly learned how lucrative the black consumer market was and how potent an ad medium radio could be.

Who was likely to program shows for blacks? "This boom has been confined to independent stations for the most part," *Sponsor* said, "and it is continuing in this direction."[37] This statement accurately reflects the black-appeal situation. Narrowcasting was the strategy of independent stations often possessing weak signals and a small capital base that made them noncompetitive with network affiliates engaged in broadcasting. Jack L. Cooper's experience in Chicago supports this contention, as do the other stations studied in the following chapters.

Of 130 stations surveyed by *Sponsor* in 1954 only 20 reported affiliations with the big three networks, CBS, NBC, and ABC. Twenty-one mentioned a Mutual Broadcasting System connection. The remaining 89 stations either responded to the questionnaire as independent or noted an affiliation with NNN, which was quite different from the other networks.[38]

Independent narrowcasting is what made the national dimensions of the boom possible. The local emphasis of the outlets meant that even in isolated areas where the black population was relatively small but significant locally, black shows would be aired. This was particularly true in the West. Flagstaff, Arizona, for instance had a population of 7,663 in 1950. The black community numbered 667. Station KGPH aired seven hours of black-appeal shows in 1954.

Fresno, California, outlet KGST scheduled ten hours of shows for the 11,492 blacks living there.[39]

In the South and the North, where the population concentration was high, stations used their weak signals as their strength. They promoted their ability to zero in on the black community. WWRL claimed it had a "larger audience in the 1,045,371 New York Negro Market than any other stations—network or independent." Touting itself as the first black-owned station, Atlanta's WERD said its "listening audience is made up predominately of the 290,000 Negroes in the WERD coverage area." WDAS, Philadelphia included a "map for time buyers" showing the 450,000 black population in the city's "basic 7 wards."[40]

Independence was not the only trait of the black-appeal station. The overwhelming majority were new ventures. Only 19 of 135 stations in the *Sponsor* survey were on the air prior to 1940. Sixteen opened for business during the war, meaning that 100 were postwar babies.[41]

The post–World War II character of black-appeal and its rapid growth was graphically shown by the December 1947 *Ebony* profile of the top 16 "sepia spielers," or black disc jockeys. Though inaccurate on some details, such as Cooper's tenure on the air, the general trend identified was that this was a new field of employment. The on-the-air experience ranged from 26 years for Jack L. Cooper (really 21) to nothing for Philadelphia disc jockey Sam Price, who was too new to the microphone to merit a number. Only two besides Cooper were veterans. Bass Harris of Seattle had 15 years experience and Eddie Honesty of WJOB, Hammond, Indiana, had 14.[42]

Honesty deserves further scrutiny because he may actually have predated Cooper on the air. Norman Spaulding dates Honesty's debut behind the microphone to 1925. Ironically, WJOB was originally WWAE, where Cooper got his start in Chicago radio. But the pivotal question is how long Honesty and the station were involved in black-appeal programming. Spaulding claims that Honesty was the first black to regularly air a show in Chicago. But he also notes that these programs were not black-appeal. Honesty, a native of Memphis, Tennessee, and son of a college professor, "had a language style that sounded white" and "his musical selections and comments were beamed to a white audience." Both Richard Stams and black record dealer Ernie Leaner confirm that Honesty did not enter black-appeal until the 1940s.[43] He may have been a pioneer black in radio, but he was not a black-appeal pioneer, a significant distinction.

Of the others profiled in *Ebony,* three had logged eight years of airtime, two had been working five and four years respectively, and the rest—ten—had two or fewer years radio experience. The newness of the concept and the tremendous growth are demonstrated by the air time controlled by the 16 men. Most significant is the fact that two newcomers, Harold Jackson of Washington, D.C., and Al Benson of Chicago controlled 20 hours of airtime each though the two had only been on radio for two years.[44]

Since most stations opened for business during the boom, not surprisingly many integrated black shows into their schedules virtually upon going on the air. Eighty-four had a black-appeal component within one year of operation. Often this decision was one of necessity. "Many of them came on the air in the first post-war rush of new radio outlets, found that the going was pretty tough when they tried to use a 'shotgun' programming approach, and then switched in whole or in part to Negro programming."[45] Again the advantage of narrowcasting is demonstrated. Significantly, though, 25 stations were on the air five or more years before adding black shows.

A major aspect of the boom was that stations did not turn their entire schedule over to racially designed programs. Part-time black-appeal was the norm. In 1954, 21 of 398 stations were 100 percent black-appeal outlets. The rest reserved from as little as a half hour to as much as 100 or more hours for black shows. The overwhelming majority, 226, allotted between one and ten hours to blacks.[46]

The question of what comprised programming for blacks is covered in depth in Chapter 7 and will only be summarized here. Stations devoting limited time to black-appeal opted for a popular disc jockey and religious music format that allowed use of records. This combination was the staple for other outlets with a larger black component. News, home economics, and possibly a variety venue rounded out the schedule. Often public service programs comprised a significant share of air time as was true with Jack Cooper in Chicago and on WDIA in Memphis, Tennessee.

To sum up, the black-appeal phenomenon was an independent narrowcasting strategy adopted nationwide predominantly by new stations who either opened their doors with such a component or added one within a year. The trend was to devote some but not all airtime to the concept; thus black-appeal stations were rare. The plan was to change relative weaknesses in signal strength and capital into strengths through targeted programming/marketing to the black population in the coverage area.

The development of black-appeal reflected the independent nature of the phenomenon. Local conditions made each experience unique. However geography and size determined that certain general patterns of development be followed. The Chicago example was unique because of Jack L. Cooper. This city was the first to air shows for blacks achieving a special prominence and exerting an influence on other experiments in large urban areas. But typically in the metropolis black-appeal arose within an ethnic radio venue and featured part-time multistation programming to a growing, disparate black audience swelled by migration from the rural South. In addition, there is a strong possibility that time brokerage provided an incentive to development.

None of these conditions was present in small southern towns where the population was bisected by the color line. Here the impetus behind black-appeal was the agricultural revolution, which created a new black consumer class while depopulating the countryside. The black numbers were smaller but those remaining had finally gained some buying power. Classic market exploitation created the need for black-appeal. Nowhere was this more true than in Helena, Arkansas, which gave birth to an extremely significant and influential black-appeal radio component.

In small cities North, South, and West, black-appeal arose in response to two factors. First was the network stranglehold on the white audience that virtually forced independent stations to program black. Second was the explosion of stations after World War II. New outlets experimenting with other formats failed and then turned to black-appeal. These two factors often worked together, survival being the key word. In both small and large cities, public service programming also became of vital importance in capturing a black following. The experience of Memphis, Tennessee, exemplifies all these trends and more. WDIA became the most powerful and influential black-appeal station of the 1950s.

Local, regional, and national forces then came together to produce the black-appeal radio boom after 1945. Jack L. Cooper's vision was at last a reality. Radio had become the only mass electronic medium to truly appeal to blacks and it remains so to this day.

NOTES

1. "1. The Negro Market: $15 Billion Annually," *Sponsor,* vol. 7, no. 17 (August 24, 1953), p. 66. Sources for this information were the Census Bureau, Joint Radio Network Committee, and the magazine's survey of black-appeal stations.

2. Ibid.; Drake and Cayton, *Black Metropolis,* vol. 1, p. 8.

3. "The Negro Market: $15,000,000,000 to Spend," *Sponsor,* vol. 6, no. 15 (July 28, 1952), p. 75.

4. "1. The Negro Market: $15 Billion Annually," p. 66.

5. "The Negro Market: $15,000,000,000 to Spend," p. 72.

6. "Mr. Sponsor Asks . . . ," *Sponsor,* vol. 6, no. 15 (July 28, 1952), p. 42.

7. "1. The Negro Market: $15 Billion Annually," p. 30.

8. Arthur S. Link and William B. Catton, *American Epoch: A History of the United States,* vol. 3: *1946–1973,* 4th ed. (New York: Alfred A. Knopf, 1974), pp. 10–11.

9. On Brown v. Board of Education and the black legal struggle for civil rights, see Richard Kluger, *Simple Justice: The History of Brown v. Board of Education and Black America's Struggle for Equality* (New York: Alfred A. Knopf, 1976).

10. Maya Angelou, *Gather Together in My Name* (New York: Bantam Books, 1974), p. 2.

11. Cited in Judy Fireman, ed., *TV Book: The Ultimate Television Book* (New York: Workman Publishing Company, Inc., 1977), p. 7.

12. Robert St. John, *Encyclopedia of Radio and Television Broadcasting* (Milwaukee: Cathedral Publishing Company, 1967), p. 75.

13. See Chapter 3.

14. "Disc Jockeys," *Ebony,* vol. II (May 1947), p. 44.

15. Chicago *Tribune,* September 8, 1980.

16. Norman Spaulding, "History of Black-Oriented Radio in Chicago" (unpublished M.A. thesis, University of Illinois at Chicago, 1974), p. 36.

17. Interview, Gertrude Cooper.

18. Spaulding, "Black-Oriented Radio in Chicago."

19. Ibid.

20. Ibid., p. 37–39.

21. Ibid., p. 31.

22. Interview, Richard Stams, Chicago, Ill., August 1978.

23. Spaulding, "Black-Oriented Radio in Chicago," p. 31.

24. Ibid., p. 42.

25. See Mike Rowe, *Chicago Breakdown* (New York: Drake Publishers, Inc., 1969) for details of Benson's outside careers in music and recording.

26. Chicago *Tribune*, September 8, 1980.

27. Interview, Roy J. Bellavia, Chicago, Ill., May 1982.

28. Dan Goldberg, "Chicago's Negro Station," *Variety* (January 3, 1940), p. 121.

29. "Disc Jockeys," p. 44.

30. *Sponsor*, vol. 8, no. 19 (September 20, 1954), pp. 139–142, 145.

31. Conversation, Professor Larry Lichty, Chairperson, Northwestern University Radio/TV/Film Department, Evanston, Ill., February 1987.

32. "NNN: Negro's Radio Network," *Sponsor*, vol. 8, no. 19 (September 20, 1954), p. 54.

33. "Negro Radio: 200-Plus Special Stations—More Coming," *Ibid.*, vol. 6, no. 5 (July 28, 1952), p. 32; "3. Negro Radio: Over 600 Stations Strong Today," *ibid.*, vol. 9, no. 19 (September 19, 1955), p. 112.

34. Ibid. (September 20, 1954), pp. 139–42, 145.

35. "Negro Results: Rich Yield for All Types of Clients," *ibid.*, vol. 6, no. 15 (July 28, 1952), pp. 38–39.

36. "Negro Radio Results," ibid., vol. 8, no. 3 (September 20, 1954), pp. 53, 153.

37. "Negro Radio: 200-Plus Special Stations—More Coming," p. 32.

38. *Sponsor* (September 20, 1954) pp. 139–42.

39. U.S. Bureau of the Census, *U.S. Census of the Population: 1950*, vol. 2: *Characteristics of the Population:* Pt. 3: *Arizona;* pt. 5: *California* (Washington, D.C.: U.S. Government Printing Office, 1952) pp. 3–36, 5–96.

40. Advertisements, *Sponsor* (September 20, 1954), pp. 143, 157; *ibid.*, vol. 7, no. 17 (August 24, 1953), p. 96.

41. Ibid. (September 20, 1954), pp. 130–42.

42. "Disc Jockeys," p. 44.

43. Spaulding, "Black-Oriented Radio in Chicago," p. 29. Spaulding interviewed Stams and Leaner.

44. "Disc Jockeys," p. 44.

45. "Negro Radio: 200-Plus Special Stations—More Coming," p. 32.

46. *Sponsor* (September 20, 1954), pp. 139–42.

Figure 1. A labor dispute made Cooper the first disc jockey.

Figure 2. Jack L. Cooper found boxer Joe Louis a difficult interview.

Figure 3. Gertrude Cooper joined her husband on the air soon after their marriage in 1938.

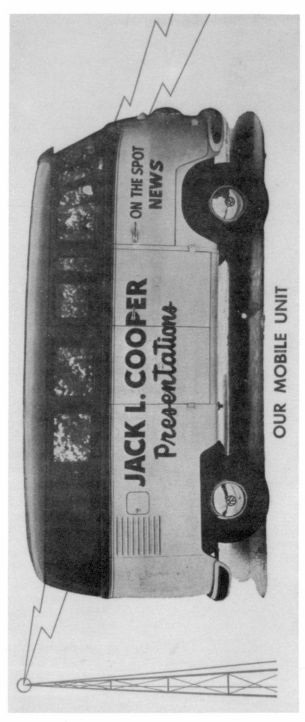

Figure 4.

5   "PASS THE BISCUITS, 'CAUSE IT'S KING BISCUIT TIME"

Black-appeal radio's development depended upon the presence of certain factors, the most important being a viable listening audience/consumer market. People had to tune in shows, and they had to support sponsors at the cash register. As shown in chapter 2, farm tenancy effectively blocked the rise of a black consumer class in the rural South, where the majority of blacks lived until after World War II.[1] It did so by helping to obstruct any change in agricultural production, particularly in cotton culture areas such as the lush Arkansas-Mississippi delta, the alluvial flood plain, or bottom lands, of the Mississippi River running from approximately Memphis, Tennessee, at the north down to Louisiana in the south. The delta was described by Clarksdale, Mississippi, *Press Register* editor Joseph F. Ellis, Jr. as "fairly typical of the general Deep South, only more so. The delta has historically been an area of big farming operations. . . . And it's historically been a cotton-producing area, a hand labor crop area ever since it was first developed."[2]

Delta farm operations were more traditional than scientific. One writer characterizes the system thus: "It . . . involved intense, and over a period of time, wasteful specialization in the production of a single staple commodity for which it was believed vitally necessary to maintain an abundant supply of low-cost labor." Maintenance implied "control over the labor force and hence over the distribution of return."[3]

Tenancy supplied the necessary control over farm operations. Because of the furnishing provision, it immediately placed the tenant in debt to the planter, and the tenant's earnings were not received until the crop was marketed. The result was too often, as an 1890s black song lyric says, "all for the white man, none for the nigger." Tenancy also isolated the black population in areas of large plantations with the delay of payment insuring an ample work force until after the crop was sold.

While cultivation of other crops became more scientific, cotton culture "tended to preserve conditions which were increasingly out of step with the remainder of American industrial and agricultural development." Southern planters adhered to this intensive hand labor system largely because mechanization of cotton culture proved illusory.[4]

The invention of the cotton gin in the 1790s remained the only technological innovation for 100 years. As of 1880, writes James Street in *The New Revolution in the Cotton Economy*, "Of the various types of mechanical cultivators which were devised, none succeeded in actually supplanting the primitive hand hoe as a necessary tool."[5] The same was true of the other hand labor intensive activity, harvest. Even in the late 1940s, cotton was still hand-picked by gangs of workers dragging long bags behind them.

Similarly, reliance upon king cotton as the sole cash crop hindered change and economic progress. Part of the problem rested with the merchants and bankers who offered financing for crops. They showed a marked "preference for cotton as security for the loans they granted."[6] The result was a pernicious cycle of boom and bust that largely kept tenants in debt and planters on the edge of solvency. In describing the plight of black tenants, W. E. B. DuBois aptly summarized the situation faced by all concerned: "A good season with good prices regularly freed a number from debt . . . a season poor either in weather or in prices resulted in ruin to many."[7]

The feudalistic plantation system had an impact on all aspects of life and commerce in areas like the delta. For example, the furnishing of tenants with foodstuffs was the sole prerogative of the planter or merchant who owned the commissary. Their only concern was "in buying as cheap a merchandise as they could," according to wholesale grocer Max Moore.

In the 1930s, Moore ran the Interstate Grocer Company in Helena, Arkansas. The company was started in 1913 by his father and uncle. "The biggest operation we had was from the farm angle," he explained. "Back in those days [when] we needed corn meal we'd buy about eight or ten mills for quotation. The mill that had the cheapest price got the business. It didn't make a difference what kind of meal it was or anything else. It was jus' price," he said. "Everybody want price. We sold by price." These conditions created an extremely competitive market that turned the delta into a "dumpin' place for cheap flour and meal." Profit margins were so low, Moore complained, that "we didn't make anything out of it. Retailer didn't make anything out of it."[8]

As long as plantations predominated, little change was forthcoming for anybody, from the tenant to the planter to the wholesale grocer. But this system that proved so hide-bound and restrictive also was extremely brittle. In the 1930s, the devastating effects of the depression combined with the entry of government programs and money began a process of change transforming southern, and delta, farming operations. Under federal government pressure, crop diversification became the norm, along with a more scientific and less wasteful method of cultivation.[9] Mechanization finally came to the delta, though it would be the 1950s before an economical cotton-picker would reduce harvest manpower needs.[10]

Eventually, four full-time workers using machinery produced the crop instead of 200 families working by hand. Planters began calling themselves farmers. They subdivided the larger, unwieldy plantations into more manageable 2,000-acre farms. Having been dictated to for so long by outmoded nineteenth-century beliefs, southern landowners finally entered the twentieth century. And this entry had ripple effects on all aspects of life in the South, including the rise of black-appeal radio.

In transforming southern plantations into modern agribusinesses and precapitalist tenants into a potent consumer class, the agricultural revolution also instigated a mass migration that almost depopulated the region. The growing number of urban blacks and the return of prosperity after 1945 were key factors in the black-appeal boom, as shown in Chapter 4.[11]

In areas like the delta, black-appeal radio arose in classic, textbook entrepreneurial fashion. Either observing or experiencing the effects of the agricultural transformation, entrepreneurs innovated on the changes to exploit the new black consumer class. Here the emphasis was on responding to socioeconomic changes at a very basic level and nowhere was this more true than in Helena, Arkansas.

KING BISCUIT TIME

Phillips County, in which Helena is situated; was and is a typical delta area. Two-thirds of the county's population were black in 1940. Of the 5,744 farmers counted by the census, 4,690 were tenants. Eighty percent of the farmers were black and 86 percent of these were tenants. Over half of the 495 white farmers also worked as tenants. In 1939, cotton accounted for more than three-fourths of the total value of crops harvested.[12]

Max Moore began noticing changes in Phillips County in the late 1930s. "The farmers begin to get rid of their tenants and begin to hire what they call day labor. And the mechanical machinery came into vogue; the tractors and combines and them to take the place of the old mule-drawn machinery." Day labor implied paying wages instead of furnishing tenants on credit. This meant, Moore explains, that those working the fields "had a little chance at buying a better grade of food, particularly flour and meal."[13]

Moore decided to introduce a new flour on the market, something "the retailer could make a profit out of and we could, too." Instead of continuing the multimill purchasing system, Moore consolidated his operations by making an exclusive deal with Buhler Mills of Buhler, Kansas, to provide him with a high quality flour. The result was King Biscuit Flour, "fine, dainty, and light."[14]

The next step was advertising the product. Moore continues, "And that was when we thought about radio."[15]

Moore's plans coincided perfectly with those of Sam W. Anderson, an educator turned radio station owner. In 1940 Anderson looked forward to the end of both the school year and his tenure as superintendent of schools in Dyess, Arkansas. Though his $3,600 annual salary made Anderson one of the state's higher paid educators, he sought a more lucrative career. During a previous term as superintendent for the Nettleton, Arkansas, school district his friendship with radio station owner Jay Beard made Anderson aware of radio's potential. Owning and operating a radio station seemed an interesting and promising enterprise.[16]

Forming the Helena Broadcasting Company with partners John Thomas Franklin and J. Q. Floyd, Anderson received a station license. KFFA would operate at 1360 kilocycles on the AM dial and have 250 watts of power. On November 19, 1941, the first program was aired.[17]

Like other successes in radio, Anderson's rested on building an audience and an advertising base. And like other entrepreneurs in a new business, he was open to new ideas and innovations. "I was lookin' for any kind of customer I could get back in those days," he said during a 1976 interview.[18]

When Max Moore contacted him, Anderson agreed to look for a suitable program to promote the new flour. Since King Biscuit was being marketed largely to blacks, the program and the advertising had to appeal to this audience.

The station and the sponsor were ready. All KFFA needed to launch its black-appeal venture was the programming. This ingredient was supplied by a six-foot-four-inch black man named Rice Miller. In 1941 Miller was in his late thirties or early forties. Born in Glendora, Mississippi, he had spent most of his life playing the small bars and juke joints that dotted the delta countryside. Calling himself Sonny Boy Williamson, he was a local favorite, but the all-important career breakthrough—making records—had eluded him. The opening of KFFA apparently gave him an idea. If records could not further his career maybe the radio could.[19]

Soon after KFFA opened its doors Williamson went to see Sam Anderson. "I was sittin' in the office one day and Sonny Boy walked in and said he wanted to play on my radio station. I said, 'Well, what do you play Sonny?' He said,'I play mouth harp and sing.' So I went back in the studio and had him play me a couple of numbers and I thought he had the potential of maybe a saleable program."

Anderson called Max Moore suggesting he sponsor a program featuring Williamson. After recruiting guitarist Robert Jr. Lockwood to accompany him, Williamson played for Moore. Interstate Grocer's owner decided that "it was just about what we needed." A deal was made for the two musicians to perform fifteen minutes daily, Monday through Friday, beginning at 12:15 p.m. They would receive no salary, but Williamson could advertise over the radio where he was playing that week. Apparently, that was why he wanted to go on the air. Like Moore, Williamson had a product to sell.[20]

The common thread running through these three men's ideas was entrepreneurship. Each had a different innovation on the changes transpiring in the delta but all sought to move to a higher level of productivity. Moore did so not only through marketing a quality flour but in relying upon radio to advertise the product. Anderson opened up the airwaves to blacks neglected by radio in the past. Williamson perceived radio as his star vehicle, since the normal path, records, was blocked. All three gambled on the potential of the emerging black listening audience/consumer market. None were disappointed.

In part they succeeded because all three tried something new in the delta. Moore's flour was new. Anderson's station was new, and Williamson's idea was new. Actually Williamson was following a pattern set early in radio's history when performers began to realize what kind of exposure the medium provided.[21] However he was the first to propose such an arrangement in Helena, and certainly one of the first blues singers to recognize the value of radio exposure as an alternative to records. Most important, the audience was entering a new era of work because of the changing face of southern agriculture.

Audience response to "King Biscuit Time" was overwhelming. "It began just blooming over night," Moore recalled. "It just exceed our expectations more than we ever thought."[22]

Blacks living in the range of KFFA's signal, which reached as far as Little Rock, Arkansas, found the program habit-forming. Jesse "Hot Rod" Carter, a black disc jockey at KFFA from the early 1950s through the 1970s, recalled his introduction to Williamson's program. "It was right around noon and I heard the King Biscuit Boys playing and we stopped." Carter had tuned in the show by accident. "And we thought we knew their voices but we didn't. Sounded familiar, downhome fellas playin' blues an' everything. And so I got into the habit of listenin' to KFFA."[23]

Blues singer B. B. King remembers that when he was a teenager working the cotton fields "King Biscuit Time" was a noontime event. He and his fellow workers would anxiously await the noon hour "when they would be rushin' out of the field to try and get to the house where we could catch Sonny Boy comin' on."[24]

Another bluesman whose career was profoundly affected by the show was James Cotton. After his appearance at the 1976 Monterey Jazz Festival Cotton told us: "I know the sound of harmonica and I heard peoples play the blues right across the field farmin'. I heard blues as a kid but I never heard it put together like I heard it when I heard it on 'King Biscuit Time.' And I used to listen to that show every chance I get."[25] Cotton did more than listen. When he was ten he ran away from his Tunica, Mississippi, home and traveled the 20 or so miles south and west to Helena to play with Williamson. Quite literally, Cotton learned to play harmonica on Williamson's knee.

Not all listeners were attracted to the show by the music. The pride of having a black man on the air and the progress it signified was the main attraction for many. "We never heard blacks on the radio 'cause Sonny Boy was the first," said J. C. Danley, a millworker living in West Helena, a suburb of Helena. "He came in representin' the King Biscuit Flour. Well, then, that was our first. So, then, I was inclined to listen to him." Danley had little interest in, or, for that matter, liking for the blues. But hearing Williamson perform on the air was "something new . . . something we had never been able to witness." As a result, "when Sonny Boy Williamson came on, we would turn that on because he were black. And that's the only reason we would turn it on." [26]

Blacks turned on "King Biscuit Time" and they kept listening. Sonny Boy Williamson's name became a household word in the area. Williamson, and Lockwood, became overnight successes. Their meteoric rise was demonstrated by an incident that occurred soon after they went on the air. Max Moore recalled that a rumor swept through Helena that the two musicians had been killed in an automobile accident while returning from an engagement in Wabash, Arkansas. It was Sunday. Still the public response was swift and widespread. "My phone like to rang off the wall tryin' to get that thing straightened out. But it was somebody else that got hurt, it wasn't them." The incident, he added, showed "how popular they got right quick." [27]

As had been Jack L. Cooper's experience in Chicago and was to be the experience of many in other cities, black listeners enthusiastically supported this first attempt to appeal to them. W. C. Handy with his blues and Perry Bradford with his race records had similar responses. [28] The novelty of appeal and the progress such attention symbolized contributed greatly to these overnight successes. But what kept people tuned in to "King Biscuit Time" was the quality of the sponsor's product and Sonny Boy's music.

Williamson was the key to success. After long years of playing in roadhouses and juke joints, he was a master of performance and composition within the blues idiom. His lyrics spoke to the concerns of his audience, either treating them satirically or offering them advice. Few songs had the sorrowful message that people tend to equate with blues.

"One Way Out" is a good example. Playing the role of the backdoor man (an illicit lover), Sonny is trapped with his paramour in her room. A man stands outside. Who is it? Her husband? Uncertain of the person's identity but sure of the potential for danger, Williamson asks the woman to open the window so he can slip out and away. His wailing harmonica backed by a strong, rollicking beat heightens the tense mood. But is Sonny repentant? Of course not. If he escapes, next time he will make certain not to be caught. [29] Both through his inventive recreation of the scene and the uptempo musical accompaniment, Williamson defused a dangerous situation with wit and humor.

When not amusing the audience, Williamson offered advice. Passing on lessons taught by his own father in "Don't Lose Your Eye" he counsels listeners to be fair to friends and to treat neighbors correctly. But the song's main theme was to think before you act; don't spite your face by losing an eye. [30]

Some listeners even heard veiled commentary on race relations in his music. Commenting on his big hit "Eyesight to the Blind," one delta resident told folklorist William Ferris, Jr.:

You know what comes up again? Black. White. When you say 'I declare you pretty and the whole state know you fine,' that go for you and me. And you know what that do when he say that? That brings eyesight back to blind.[31]

The music accompanying these words also proved appealing and was perfectly suited for radio. The Williamson-Lockwood duo quickly expanded into a full-complement blues band featuring James "Peck" Curtis on drums, Robert "Dud Low" Taylor on the piano, and Joe Willie Wilkins replacing Lockwood. Another guitar player was added, along with bass and horns.

The delta tradition provided the musical foundation, but Williamson soon expanded his style. Unlike the heavy strumming and droning beat so characteristic of delta blues guitar, Lockwood and later his pupil Wilkins played in a modern, swinging single-string style that showed jazz influences. The piano was played in similar fashion, accentuating the uptempo, light jump blues Sonny Boy favored. The bass and drums however stood in marked contrast, adding a strong, often chaotic beat that propelled the songs. This raucous and rollicking combination stressed the good-time nature of the songs and provided listeners with a touch of something familiar yet at the same time profoundly new and different. Basically, Sonny merged the old-time string band with the new hot combo sounds that were becoming popular with the blacks to create a very popular blues style.[32]

An integral aspect of the music's development was Helena's rising status as a blues capital with KFFA acting as its center. Blues singer and guitarist Jimmy Rogers summarized the appeal of the town and KFFA, saying, "You'd get airplay and you could play gigs in that area . . . for blues that was the spot. That was the headquarters of radio."[33] KFFA became a testing and training ground for black musicians, amply supplying the station with new talent and inspiration. Bluesmen of note who played at KFFA included Muddy Waters, Little Walter, and Rogers, who together helped create the electric Chicago blues sound of the late 1940s and 1950s. Robert Nighthawk had his own show, as did Robert Jr. Lockwood. Sammy Lawhorn, a long-time member of Waters's band, was a Little Rock teenager recruited for the King Biscuit Boys Band, as they were called. James Cotton, of course, was another alumnus. The list goes on, but these examples show how fertile the Helena blues scene was.[34]

As the creation of the band demonstrates, all concerned with "King Biscuit Time" sought to fully capitalize on its success. Moore, for example, expanded his market developing a new brand of corn meal for blacks aptly called Sonny Boy Meal. The blues singer's picture was featured on the label exploiting the appeal of Helena's rising star. The meal "went over just as good as the flour did," Moore said.[35] KFFA disc jockey Carter aptly summed up its acceptance, claiming, "Sonny Boy made that meal famous."[36]

Williamson probably received no payment for this endorsement, but as with the radio show he reaped substantial benefits from it. His face greeted blacks not only on the stage but on grocery store shelves and in home cupboards. The name recognition such advertising provided far outweighed any meager remuneration Moore would have provided. Max was, to be polite, a frugal person.

Promotional appearances heightened the group's visibility. The band also became a regular attraction at festivals and parades. Several photographs show Sonny Boy and the King Biscuit Boys playing at such affairs. But the most blatant promotional effort occurred in the early 1950s. It was apparently Max Moore who conceived of the idea of making weekend tours throughout the countryside. First a truck and then a bus were outfitted with sound equipment. During the week the itinerary was advertised on the air. At each town and country store, hundreds of people crowded around to hear a free concert by the King Biscuit Boys starring Sonny Boy Williamson. Afterward, there was a drawing for free prizes, and refreshments were served. Moore recalls laughingly that these trips were "more like a circus than anything else."[37]

But the entertainment could not mask the promotional and marketing successes of the tours. "'Cause everywhere they would play, well, that was a new set of listeners," explains Jesse Carter. "They was gonna listen to them on the air."[38] So Anderson benefited by building his audience, Williamson acquired new fans and new engagements, and Moore expanded the market for his products. Not only did the black consumers buy his flour and meal but the country store owner hosting the gala profited from the advertising and the added revenue the concerts provided. As a result, these owners were likely to carry Interstate Grocer products. And the audience got to attend a party and hear a free concert by a prominent musician.

Though the tours ended after two or three years, "King Biscuit Time" remained a KFFA mainstay. A decade after he started performing on the air, Williamson finally placed his songs on record. Trumpet Records out of Jackson, Mississippi, gave him his start with several sessions in 1951 and 1952.[39] Later he recorded for Chess Records, a major independent label in Chicago. His rising popularity kept the blues singer on the road touring and away from KFFA. However, the show retained its listening audience during his long absences, and he always returned.

Williamson came back to Helena for the last time in 1965, after headlining a blues revue that toured Europe. Well into his sixties, if not his seventies, Williamson went to the Interstate Grocer offices to ask Max Moore if he could return one more time to the show that had launched his rise to national and international stardom. When Moore agreed, Williamson went out into the street and began playing his harmonica. The following of this favorite son had not diminished over the years. Such a crowd gathered to hear him play that "they had to block the highway and get the police down here to unblock it.''[40] Soon after returning to Helena, Sonny Boy Williamson died.[41]

Even though he had been away from Helena more than he had been in it, Williamson's death cast a pall over "King Biscuit Time." Moore considered changing the format to recorded music by various artists. "But after we got started into that thing we had so many complaints and so many requests for his numbers we decided to go ahead and play his records, which we did," he said in 1976. "And that's what we're doing today, playin' his old records.''[42]

BLACK-APPEAL ON KFFA

"King Biscuit Time" fostered other black-appeal programming on KFFA. Initially, Williamson's success spawned similar shows featuring live performances by blues musicians. Some were even sponsored by rival wholesale grocers and retail outlets. There were "Mother's Pride" and "Bright Star" flour shows as well as a program sponsored by Cat Clothiers.[43] None of these lasted long on the air.

By 1954, 35 hours of KFFA's schedule were devoted to black-appeal programming. Disc jockey and religious formats dominated. "In The Groove" was a morning show hosted by Jesse "Hot Rod" Carter; it featured blues and other black music. He also hosted the black religious programs. "I work with all kinds of religious groups—ministers and the deacons of the church on the different programs," says Carter.[44]

It is an understatement to say that "King Biscuit Time" filled a programming void. What is most remarkable, and this would be true throughout the rural South, is that black-appeal boomed at a time when mechanization and migration were draining the delta of much of its black population. Between 1940 and 1950 the number of Phillips County's black residents declined from 30,626 to 13,516.[45] That "King Biscuit Time" and other black shows were aired successfully indicates the sharp rise in the status of the blacks who found work (though many did not) and their strong support of such efforts.

But unlike that of Chicago and as the next chapter shows, of Memphis, KFFA's black-appeal programming never strayed from the entertainment and religious format. There was no public service component, and evidently little, if any, racially designed news or sports coverage. Black participation was strictly limited to announcing, performing, and the playing of black records. No blacks achieved management status, and none sold ad time.

The black disc jockeys did sell products on the air and some even wrote ad copy, though this was rare. "Hot Rod" Carter recalls that one sponsor, an automotive dealer, would not let anyone else write his commercials. "Just let him ad lib it," said Carter, imitating the sponsor. "Said he sounds better ad libbing. I ad libbed fifteen minutes for almost a year." Noting that it "was the hardest thing in the world to do,'' Carter also had to research the prices, because they were never provided.[46]

''King Biscuit Time'' went off the air temporarily, but renewed interest in the blues and a Helena Blues Festival led to its return to KFFA. As of Spring 1988, listeners still tune their radio dials to 1360 AM at 12:15 p.m. and hear Sonny Payne say those familiar words: ''Pass the biscuits, cause it's King Biscuit Time.''[47]

NOTES

1. See Chapter 2, pp. 105–106.

2. Interview, Joseph F. Ellis, Jr., Clarksdale, Miss., July, 1976.

3. James H. Street, *The New Revolution in the Cotton Economy* (Chapel Hill: University of North Carolina Press, 1957) p. 9.

4. Street, *New Revolution in the Cotton Economy*, p. 10.

5. *Ibid.*, p. 9.

6. *Ibid.*, p. 29.

7. W. E. B. DuBois, ''The Negro Farmer,'' ''Negroes in the United States,'' U.S. Bureau of the Census *Bulletin*, no. 8, 1904, p. 81.

8. Interview, Max Moore, Helena, Ark., July 1976.

9. On New Deal agricultural policies and their effects, see Arthur M, Schlesinger, Jr., *The Age of Roosevelt: The Coming of the New Deal* (Boston: Houghton Mifflin, 1958), pp. 27–28; Edwin G. Nourse, Joseph S. Davis, and John D. Black, *Three Years of the Agricultural Adjustment Administration* (Washington, DC.: The Brookings Institution, 1937); Holley, Winston, and Woofter, *The Plantation South;* E. L. Langsford and B. H. Thibodeaux, ''Plantation Organization and Operation in the Yazoo-Mississippi Delta Area,'' U.S. Department of Agriculture Technical Bulletin no. 682 (May 1939); Gove Hambidge, ''Soils and Men—A Summary,'' *Yearbook of Agriculture, 1938* (Washington, D.C.: U.S. Government Printing Office, 1938).

10. Street, *New Revolution in the Cotton Economy*, passim.

11. See pp. 169–171.

12. U.S. Bureau of the Census, *Sixteenth Census of the United States:* Vol. 1: *Agriculture, Third Series State Reports,* pt. 2: *The Southern States: Statistics for Counties* (Washington, D.C.: U.S. Government Printing Office, 1942), p. 35; ibid., vol. 1: *Agriculture, First and Second Series State Reports,* pt. 5: *West South Central Statistics for Counties* (Washington, D.C.: U.S. Government Printing Office, 1942), p. 35.

13. Interview, Max Moore.

14. ''King Biscuit Time,'' radio program transcript, July 8, 1976.

15. Interview, Max Moore.

16. Ray Poindexter, *Arkansas Airwaves* (North Little Rock: Ray Poindexter, 1974), p. 290.

17. Ibid.

18. Interview, Sam Anderson, Helena, Ark., July 1976.

19. See the comments of blues singer Johnny Shines in Peter Guralnick, *Feel Like Goin' Home* (New York: Vintage Books, 1971), pp. 100–1.

20. Interviews, Sam Anderson; Max Moore.

21. See Czitrom, *Media and the American Mind,* p. 73, for an interesting example of how radio exposure could boost a career.

22. Interview, Max Moore.

23. Interview, Jesse "Hot Rod" Carter, Helena, Ark., July 1976.

24. Interview, B. B. King, Nashville, Tenn., July 1976.

25. Interview, James Cotton, Monterey, Calif., September 1976.

26. Interview, J. C. Danley, West Helena, Ark., July 1976.

27. Interview, Max Moore.

28. See Chapter 1.

29. Sonny Boy Williamson, "One Way Out," Checker 1003 (1961).

30. Sonny Boy Williamson, "Don't Lose Your Eye," *Sonny Boy Williamson,* Chess 2ACM-206, originally recorded 1955.

31. William Ferris, *Blues From the Delta* (London: Studio Vista, 1970), p. 90; Sonny Boy Williamson, "Eyesight to the Blind," Trumpet 129 (1951).

32. The best recorded examples of Williamson's late 1940s and early 1950s music are on Sonny Boy Williamson, *King Biscuit Time,* Arhoolie 2020.

33. Jim O'Neal and Bill Goldsmith, "Living Blues Interview: Jimmy Rogers," *Living Blues,* no. 14 (Autumn 1973), p. 12.

34. Ibid.; interviews, Sammy Lawhorn, Arthur "Kansas City Red" Stevenson, Chicago, Ill., July–August 1976; James Cotton, Monterey, Calif., September 1976.

35. Interview, Max Moore.

36. Interview, Jesse "Hot Rod" Carter.

37. Interview, Max Moore.

38. Interview, Jesse "Hot Rod" Carter.

39. For a discography of these sessions, see Mike Leadbitter and Neil Slaven, eds., *Blues Records: January, 1943 to December, 1966* (New York: Oak Publications, 1968), pp. 295–6.

40. Interview, John Rogers, Helena, Ark., July 1976. Rogers was general manager of Interstate Grocer in 1976 and had been a salesman in the 1950s.

41. Williamson died on May 26, 1965. He was scheduled to appear on the radio that day.

42. Interview, Max Moore.

43. Giles Oakley, *The Devil's Music: A History of the Blues* (London: British Broadcasting Corporation, 1976), p. 223; O'Neal and Goldsmith, "Living Blues Interview," p. 12.

44. Interview, Jesse "Hot Rod" Carter.

45. U.S. Bureau of the Census, *U.S. Census of the Population: 1950,* vol. 2: *Characteristics of the Population, pt.5: Arkansas* (Washington, D.C.: U.S. Government Printing Office, 1952), pp. 4–81.

46. Ibid.

47. "King Biscuit Time," radio program transcript, July 8, 1976.

6

WDIA: THE MID-SOUTH GIANT

Because of the local nature of black-appeal entrepreneurship, the experience of each city and sometimes each station was unique in its specifics. But general similarities and basic patterns of development are readily apparent. A combination of personal motivation and market realities guided black-appeal radio ventures. Desire for wealth and race progress motivated Jack L. Cooper, and the Chicago ethnic radio market dictated how he fulfilled his aspirations. At KFFA, new career and business goals brought Max Moore, Sam Anderson, and Sonny Boy Williamson together to exploit the new market opportunities that the agricultural revolution had produced. In both these instances, though for very different reasons, black-appeal was, more or less, a freely made decision, a matter of choice rather than force. Before and after World War II, a different mix of motivation and markets stimulated black-appeal in Memphis, Tennessee: survival in the face of highly competitive or rapidly changing market conditions. Here necessity mothered black-appeal invention.

The pattern of development in Memphis was typical and representative of other southern cities. Black-appeal provided independent stations with a market niche similar to that supplied by ethnic programming in Chicago and other large metropolises. The same analogy, though conditions differed greatly, applies to small southern towns such as Helena. In every instance, the critical determinant of black-appeal was recognition of its viability. Many new stations, such as KFFA, quickly integrated black shows into their schedules because it was a logical move. Others, old and new, were forced to program black to survive. The Memphis experience exemplifies both these trends. But it also was unique because of the status attained by WDIA after World War II and the fact that it was the culmination of two prewar efforts.

BOB ALBURTY'S EXPERIMENT AT WHBQ

In 1926 Bob Alburty left his native Kansas City for a job as a singer and joke writer on WREC in the Memphis suburb of Whitehaven, Tennessee. The following year the station moved to Memphis's famed Peabody Hotel and later became a CBS affiliate. In the early 1930s, WREC's owner Hoyt Whooten expanded his business by buying a small, 100-watt station, WHBQ, and installing Alburty as manager. Given a weekly salary of $25, his task was to make the new acquisition profitable.

In 1978, when I talked with Alburty about the job he faced in building WHBQ, he was still laughing over its sorry state at the time. "It was a bootstrap operation," he said, with offices located "in the basement of an office building right next to the waste paper baler." Even the operating equipment was used. In addition, Whooten concentrated all his money and attention on WREC, so Alburty had only the station's meager income to use for upgrading it. "We sold our advertising by the week and we'd go out Saturday morning to collect," he continued. "And if we were lucky we'd collect enough to meet our small payroll. If there was anything left over, then I could get that."

Beyond lack of capital, the most serious problem was lack of recognition among listeners and sponsors. The solution, he explained, was that "You had to build an audience." But WHBQ was the smallest and least known of Memphis's four radio stations. Polls conducted in the 1930s, Alburty recalled, seldom even mentioned WHBQ because of its miniscule audience share. Such results were not likely to attract listeners or sponsors, particularly the latter, who often looked askance at radio. "Advertisers in those days, they didn't feel that radio was particularly good—and [they] certainly [felt] that a non–network station would have no audience."

Alburty used promotional gimmicks to capture the radio industry and the public's attention. When the two network outlets in Memphis engaged in a ratings war using newspaper ads to promote their victories, he countered with his own ad. "I'd been saving religiously for it," he said. "I wrote across the top: 'Hooray now we're a first! A survey of all radio stations shows we were the first station never to win a radio station survey. A survey conducted by other radio stations. We do not have coverage. We have audience. We have people. We have listeners.' " This ploy made radio executives and advertisers aware of WHBQ because it "was published all over the United States in the trade journals."

The next problem was making the public aware that WHBQ was on the radio dial. An amateur announcer's contest helped. Local people appeared on the air—meaning that they, their families, and their friends all learned to tune in the station. But this was a Pyhrric victory. Alburty had to use the desperately needed ad revenues the contest produced to pay for the announcing prizes.

Simultaneously working to improve the programming and facilities, Bob Alburty used the only commodity at his disposal, air time. He bartered "radio advertising for the use of some records"—not the sale but the rental of discs. He traded time for space in the Claridge Hotel, placing WHBQ in a more respectable and visible location. He also obtained a plate glass window for the studio through trade.[1]

Still the prime task of building an audience eluded him. The city's whites were locked up by the two network affiliates with whom he could not compete. They had the big advertising revenues, and the national programming featuring big stars. The population of Memphis did not include a large diverse ethnic component of immigrants, so foreign-language programming was not an option. Alburty's only hope lay in airing shows that were noncompetitive with the networks and that focused on specific program types for targeted audiences. In other words, he became an entrepreneur seeking to move to a higher level of productivity through programming innovation, not in format but in direction.

WHBQ began narrowcasting with the airing of religious services from a local church. In return for a one-year contract, Alburty gave a small discount for cash payment in advance. But religious narrowcasting only kept the station on the air, it did not produce the profits needed.

Further innovation—a greater switch to higher levels of productivity and more entrepreneurship—was needed if Bob Alburty was to successfully build a radio station. That, of course, was his aim. The white audience offered meager opportunities, but he noticed there was a void in the radio market. "I realized that, at that time, about thirty-five to thirty-seven percent of our population was black. There was no audience [sic] for blacks. So I converted our entire afternoon schedule to what was called jitterbug music in those days. And we had a young announcer quite well-versed in the vernacular of the jitterbugs." John Poorhall, a white disc jockey, hosted the "Jitterbug Johnny Show" Monday through Friday from 1:00 to 6:00 p.m. He played the swing music popular at that time: Benny Goodman, Duke Ellington, Jimmy Lunceford, and others.

Memphis blacks responded enthusiastically. "When you walked in the black areas of Memphis you could hear it [Jitterbug Johnny's show] all over," claims Alburty. He had also unexpectedly tapped a hidden advertising market. "Well, all the dollar down, dollar a week clothing stores and jewelry stores and furniture stores wanted to buy all across the board in the afternoon. Our afternoon was sold solid to reach the Negro audience." Since advertising was sold in 15-minute chunks, this was quite a feat.

Black-appeal entrepreneurship then involved moving to two higher levels of productivity through essentially one innovation: the decision to air shows to blacks. On one hand, a listening audience was exploited, and on the other, an advertising market of businesses catering to this audience was discovered. During the interview with Alburty it was obvious the advertising response had been a surprise.

Black-appeal was a perfect venue for a small independent station with limited range such as WHBQ. Alburty had a potential audience share of one in three Memphians. Similarly, the small businesses in the black areas could not afford to advertise on network shows. Even if they could there was no way to accurately gauge either listenership levels in the black community or the return at the cash register. Because this focus was so defined, narrowcasting to blacks provided greater returns on the advertising dollar. That, of course, is the point of narrowcasting. It does not reach as many people as broadcasting, it just reaches the right people. At least this is true of black-appeal, particularly when no competition exists, as was the case with WHBQ.

Having identified his market niche, Alburty expanded his black-appeal programming. The Le Moyne College chorus was signed to air a 30-minute weekly show. Bishop Mason of the Memphis-based Church of God in Christ contracted to air segments of its annual convocation. But not all ventures worked. A young, black female singer/pianist quit three weeks after she was hired to perform on a live music show. She felt the program's name, "Black and Blues," was offensive. At that time, *black* was considered a derogatory term; *Negro* was preferred. Here again the subtle working of the color line and black response to white ignorance is evident.

The most important black-appeal addition to WHBQ's schedule was "Amateur Night on Beale." This talent show was started in 1935 by Nat D. Williams, a graduate of Agriculture and Industry College, who taught high school history, wrote columns for the local black newspaper, and was a Beale Street personality. Earlier he had helped organize the first Cotton Makers Jubilee. Williams described the talent show as "a real wild affair. I'd do a little singing, dancing and joke telling—then the other people would come on."[2]

An irony of the color line put the show on radio. One night a week the audience was restricted to whites. Alburty shrewdly arranged to air a weekly segment on that night. The performers remained black, as did the announcer, Nat D. Williams, and, of course, the radio audience, although it is possible that whites also tuned in the show. A maker of pomade and other black beauty products, the Gottfreud Manufacturing Company of St. Louis, sponsored "Amateur Night on Beale."[3] It was 1937 and Williams's appearance probably made him the first black radio announcer in the South.

The significance of the show lay not in Williams's groundbreaking role or in the irony of the presentation. Instead, it acted as a training ground for later development, bringing together two of the three pivotal figures who would develop black-appeal radio in Memphis after World War II: Nat D. Williams and Bert Ferguson, then a college student working at WHBQ.

Alburty eventually bought WHBQ, where black-appeal shows were aired to the early 1940s. When war reduced advertising revenues he dropped the black-appeal component. It was resumed in the late 1940s but not with the success enjoyed in the 1930s.

In many respects WHBQ stands at an extreme end of the black-appeal spectrum, even further to the white side than KFFA. The idea for the shows came from a white man and they were produced by whites. The initial success was hosted by a white man who played white and black music. White businesses supplied the advertising. There was little, if any, direct black input in the programming; one woman quit as a result. Otherwise, the black perspective was solely at the microphone and even here it was often indirect, in that white announcers introduced entertainers or segments of religious services were aired. Only Nat Williams spoke directly to black audiences, who comprised the other black component. Still there is no denying the pioneering role WHBQ played in proving the viability of the concept of programming black.

The station served as the wellspring for future developments and not just in bringing Nat D. and Bert Ferguson together. In 1939 another link was forged. After founding radio station WJPR in Greenville, Mississippi, John Pepper returned to his native Memphis and, with Alburty's knowledge and possibly his blessing, hired Bert Ferguson as program director.[4]

BLACK-APPEAL AT WJPR

WJPR, John Pepper explains, "was a local full-time station with 250 watts. That's a very good area for coverage down there. You could reach out with a very good signal about 50 miles in the day time." The station was on the air about 18 hours daily. Pepper claims it "was the basis of WDIA ultimately ending up into black programming. Because in Greenville, which is in the Mississippi delta with over 50 percent black population, they supplied us with a good bit of programming. Because this was an independent station. It was not a network station."[5] Pepper obviously overstated his case, but in certain respects he was right. The station did succeed with black-appeal and it did cement the relationship between Ferguson and himself.

The black programming was varied, featuring live performances by local talent and sometimes prominent stars. "They had religious singing and popular singing. There would be blues. Some instrumental," continues Pepper. "Mostly just people who come and go, nobody of any national or regional importance." But the area did attract some big names. "Duke Ellington and some of the best black entertainers and musicians made a circuit through this part of the United States. At that time entertainers like Fats Waller would come through town, even small towns like Greenville." WJPR would feature these stars.

In addition, the station aired local sports coverage, with Ferguson acting as announcer. Working as program director on this small outlet meant he "had to do alot of jobs as everybody does." WJPR also used "the old INS news service."

When World War II broke out, first Pepper and then Ferguson went into the navy. Their affiliation with WJPR ceased, but the short experience is instructive. It both fits in with the general trends leading to black-appeal and stands out as being unique. WJPR was a small, independent station with limited capital. The demography of its signal area dictated black programming, something Pepper intimates was always part of the schedule. Logic not necessity was behind black-appeal. Live popular music and religious performances by local and national talent predominated. The sports and news coverage had general local rather than specific racial appeal.

WDIA: THE MID-SOUTH GIANT

The WJPR experience was analogous to that of KFFA, with one significant difference. Ferguson's experiences with black narrowcasting made the WJPR black-appeal programming unique. He knew the black audience was viable, an awareness Pepper came to share. But the war curtailed their operations. When peace came and they returned to Memphis, both were well-suited to profit from the black-appeal boom. However, they faced radically different conditions that were transforming both the black population and the radio industry, as shown in Chapter 4.[6]

Throughout the history of black migration, Memphis acted as a depot and sometimes the terminus of the mass population movement. "The big out-migration brought on immediately followin' the war from this area was first to Memphis," Joseph F. Ellis, Jr., editor of the Clarksdale, Mississippi, *Press Register,* explained. "Just as a way stop because everybody knew Memphis and regarded it almost as a second home. I mean it was the cotton market; it was where they took their crops to sell. Such entertainment as we had was there, for both blacks and whites. So Memphis was a way station and then they would move on."[7] The city also possessed the transportation links to the North and West that made it a logical departure point.

A continuous influx and outpouring of migrants became part of Memphis life. But not all who came to the city left, and even those who did leave may have stayed for an indefinite period of time. Between 1940 and 1950, the Tennessee city's total population grew by over 100,000. The number of blacks increased by 25,000. A similar rise had been recorded in the 1930s.[8]

Most important, there were jobs to be had in Memphis. Black men found work in construction, lumber mills, wholesale and retail trade, personal services, and the professions, earning an average wage of $1,565 annually. Concentrated in domestic service, women had an average yearly income of $560.[9] The black consumer class in the city was growing in numbers and buying power, but the initial postwar years witnessed no attempts by radio to appeal to them.

The radio industry emerged from the war seemingly stronger than ever. In Memphis and the nation, networks remained the dominant force on the radio dial, with independent stations that followed the comprehensive programming format dictated by the broadcasting philosophy. John Pepper explains the situation:

The radio audience at that time wasn't segmented the way it is today. You had just general, independent musical programming, and if you had different programming you had what we called at that time block programming. You had a block of country and western. You might have a block of ethnic programming. You didn't have stations as you do today that are just 100 percent devoted to one type of programming.[10]

Narrowcasting was largely defined by audience rather than programming type. Within each audience format there was a more comprehensive approach. Even black-appeal at this time followed this broadcasting in a narrowcast block format, dividing time into popular music, religion, news, and service. Specific types of programs aired at regular times so that different audience segments could tune in the shows they desired. Jack L. Cooper's schedule in Chicago followed this format design and "King Biscuit Time" on KFFA always appeared during the noon hour.

The advent of television quickly changed the nature of radio, bringing narrowcasting more to the fore and providing independents with a market edge. Many network affiliates had no studio facilities or sales staffs. They had merely thrown a switch and beamed programs into homes. This kept costs low and allowed network affiliates to present the shows the people wanted, but it also meant that changing to a different method of operation would take time. In the meantime well-organized, more flexible, and better equipped independent stations were encroaching on formerly untouchable territory. As John Pepper notes, just to survive, these independents had created "other types of programming."[11]

The age of narrowcasting had arrived. Television assumed radio's mantle as the broadcasting medium. The mass American audience sought a new diet from radio just as the number of stations on the air exploded. Formats became more diverse and experimental as stations designed specific types of programming for the populations targeted as their audience. In part, the black-appeal boom arose because of these new conditions. Often adoption of a programming/advertising strategy was dictated more by necessity than choice. The birth of WDIA in Memphis is a good example.

Following their discharges from the navy, John Pepper and Bert Ferguson came home to Memphis to resurrect their radio careers. The signs of change in the radio industry were not yet truly evident. "There were three networks in here that dominated the stations they were on," explains Pepper. "Well, you really had four counting Mutual because Mutual had a pretty active operation at that time. There were very few stations in the market at that time."[12] None was programming black and the two men initially did not try to fill this void. Instead they pursued a new idea, founding a radio station that would air only classical and "good" music. In other words, they experimented with the theme station concept very early in its development.

After forming the Bluff City Broadcasting Company, Pepper and Ferguson bought a 250-watt, daytime outlet with the call letters WDIA. It opened for business on June 7, 1947. But they soon realized, as Pepper says, that this "idea was ahead of its time." [13] In other words, neither the audience nor the advertisers supported the airing of high culture. The struggling station needed a new, more appealing format if it was to survive. They decided to return to black-appeal. "And so country-western hadn't hit this area because it was such a predominately black area," John Pepper explains. "There has always been a place for Negro music in this area among white people as well as blacks. There's always been a certain acceptance. And it's had a place in this general area due to the large black population." [14] More important, both men knew that the black community contained a strength hidden from whites. Their previous experiences at WJPR and WHBQ had shown, Pepper affirms, that "listener response in the black community is higher than it is in the white community, not only to advertising, but also to programming. That was really one reason we had confidence it would work." [15]

Bert Ferguson put some impressive numbers behind this belief in a 1952 *Sponsor* article. An advertiser, he claimed, "could very conceivably get 20% of his sales volume from the 10% Negro population of the United States. And he should get it at a lower cost-per-1,000, making it produce even more than 20% of his net profit." He concluded that "A good Negro-audience station puts your message directly into the ears of the people you are trying to convince with very little seeding of barren ground." [16] No other statement so succinctly shows that black-appeal radio was a classic entrepreneurial exercise.

Another key point in Ferguson's comments is the phrase "Negro-audience station." By 1952 radio narrowcasting had evolved to a point where stations adhered to a single format, talk or recorded popular music, for example, or devoted their entire schedules to one segment of the audience, such as blacks. In this development, WDIA was a leader, becoming the first 100 percent black-appeal station.

At WDIA Pepper handled the business end of the operations and Ferguson managed the programming. Ferguson's first task was recruiting on-the-air talent. Here the WHBQ connection proved invaluable. "The reason I went to Nat Williams," Ferguson says, "is because he had ten years before done an amateur show with all together black talent on WHBQ radio when I was with them. And I remembered him and his ability and searched him out to be the first disc jockey on WDIA." [17]

Or as the irrepressible Nat D. put it in summarizing the early history of WDIA:

Mr. Bert Ferguson, who was out there at WDIA at that time, had worked with me at 'Amateur Night on Beale Street.' So he thought perhaps I'd be useful on the radio. And

I think the big idea was that there wasn't enough people comin' in to get those ads and things so he figured, 'Well, now I'll do somethin' that nobody else has done and maybe that'll attract somebody.' So he decided to venture up with Negroes. And I was the first Negro he saw that he would work with . . . and he figured that I ought to be representative of all of 'em since I looked so much like 'em. Since he offered to pay me I thought I'd be useful, too.[18]

Ferguson's seeking out Nat Williams was a stroke of genius. He knew Nat D. could handle the microphone and that Williams was a universally known, well-respected leader who could draw people.

Williams' comments on being hired provide a wry commentary on image and race relations, mocking the white misconceptions of blacks. Saying he looked so much like them plays on the old stereotype that all blacks look alike. Similarly, Nat D. notes that their prior relationship prompted Ferguson to recruit him as the first black announcer on WDIA. Here the implication goes two ways. On the blackface image side, Williams could be commenting on another stereotypical reaction that led whites to consider blacks they knew personally to be different from the race as a whole. Or he could be citing a prime law of hiring evident throughout the world, namely, that being known and having your abilities known is the best way to get a job. Again it depends upon who was saying what to whom and why.

These three men started the WDIA black-appeal experiment with a 15-minute show scheduled around Williams's full-time teaching duties. The spontaneity of the debut deserves mention because it further illuminates the personality of Nat D. and because it provided him with a trademark. "My first radio program was a very, very serious situation," Williams recalled. "I had practiced for about two weeks gettin' ready to what I was goin' to say when the man pointed his finger at me to start talking'." Nat D. was representing his race on the radio. Both for him personally and as a matter of race pride his initial appearance was pivotal.

And of course that day came. And when he pointed his finger at me I forgot everything I was supposed to say. So I just did what became typical of me. I laid out for dead. I just started laughing 'cause I was laughin' my way away. And the man said, "the people seem to like that thing" and they told me to make it standard. . . . So ever since then . . . Nat has started his program laughin' and closed his program laughin'.[19]

Not surprisingly, Nat D. Williams's infectious laugh and his winning personality hit a common chord among black listeners. Listener and advertising response was swift and supportive as black programming "was expanded to a two hour segment as it sold out." During this period John Pepper traveled to New York City where he received some surprising but welcome news.

I went by to see a man named Mr. Hooper. The Hooper system was the top rating system used at that time. And it was, I would say, a pretty accurate system. We didn't subscribe to it. And much to my surprise I found out we were number two in the market audience particularly in the segments of the day when our black programming was.[20]

The decision was made after Pepper returned to Memphis. WDIA would break new ground. "From that time on," Pepper continued, "we gradually expanded and decided to make it a 100 percent operation."[21] The programming switch took 16 months and brought WDIA the distinction of being the first all-black radio station in the country. In this process Williams played a pivotal role, helping to develop the programming so that it would appeal to blacks and recruiting other air personalities, in addition to hosting his own shows. And he continued to teach history.

Initially, WDIA's programming format was popular recorded music. Nat D.'s first show featured records. He played a crucial role in developing programming of appeal but recalled there was some dispute over what selections to play because of different racially defined tastes. "I didn't have any blues records to play. I didn't have anything but a copy of records by white artists." One disc featured "Stompin' at the Savoy," which Williams found "a little too fast for me." He suggested some blues but, Williams continues,

They said, "we can't put this on the air." I said, "why?" He said, "it might be censored or against the law." Well, there wasn't anything all that wrong with the blues from my point of view. It was just a case where they thought it wouldn't be so polite to give it to a general audience of people consistin' of all kinds of people. . . . So the result was I had to take a turn with startin' a new type of program.

As he said later in the interview, the shows "had to appeal to black audiences and at the same time not offend white audiences."[22] Williams scoured the black shops looking for blues records more acceptable to whites and obviously found some.

In consultation with Nat D. and programming manager David James, Ferguson constructed a broadcastlike format for Memphis's black community. By June 1952, WDIA had established a well-rounded schedule of information, entertainment, and public service beamed daily to listeners between 4:45 a.m. and 7:15 p.m. "News That's Live at .55" was aired hourly between 6:55 and 8:55 a.m. and between 11:55 a.m. and 3:55 p.m. "Sports Round Up" was featured at 4:55 p.m. Monday through Fridays. Interestingly, the weekday schedule between ten in the morning and one in the afternoon was segmented into 15-minutes slots with 30-minute or hour programs being aired before or after those times.

Entertainment programming focused on live and recorded music with some talk shows in the comedy vein. Nat D. hosted the morning wake-up show, "Tan Town Coffee Club," and the afternoon drive show, "Tan Town Jamboree." On weekday mornings, religious offerings featured both live performances and records. Among the groups performing were the Spirit of Memphis and the Golden Gate Quartet. Ford Nelson acted as the religious disc jockey. Every morning the station went on the air with gospel records. Weekends, Sunday in particular, featured a wide range of religious programming including church remotes, gospel records, and live performances.

Secular entertainment predominated in the weekday afternoons, and of course the two drive shows (the programs aired in the morning and afternoon when people commute to work). Again there was a mix of live and recorded music. "Teen Town Singers" was beamed to young people at 10:00 a.m. on Saturday. There was also a Saturday afternoon music and comedy show starring Nat D. and Rufus Thomas called "Slim and Stumpy." The two men interspersed comedy routines with the playing of records.[23] In 1952 blues music dominated the secular schedule, with such artists as B. B. King, Joe Hill Louis, and Roscoe Gordon playing live.

Public service programming formed the last segment of the schedule and there were all sorts of helpful shows. "Workers Wanted" aired twice weekly on Tuesday and Thursday at 10:45 a.m. Willa Monroe, touted as the first black woman broadcaster (inaccurately, since Jack L. Cooper had employed women much earlier), hosted "Tan Town Homemaker" weekday mornings at nine. The Memphis Park Commission sponsored "Playground Parade." Other service venues included "Hi Neighbor," "Farm Show," and a program sponsored by the U.S. Treasury. "Brown America Speaks," hosted by Nat D. Williams, was a news discussion show along the lines of Jack Cooper's "Listen Chicago." "Call for Action" provided assistance in dealing with government agencies, landlords, and so forth.[24]

Such a comprehensive and extensive schedule required intensive staff development, which was both a planned process and a spontaneous one. Again Nat D. played the pivotal role, using his extensive school and entertainment contacts to recruit personnel. The public school system, in particular, proved a fertile ground for talent. Nat Williams was instrumental in recruiting former student A. C. Williams, then a biology teacher at Manassas High, and Maurice "Hot Rod" Hulbert, who produced ballets at Washington High. Another WDIA mainstay was Rufus Thomas, whom Nat knew as a former student and as an entertainer. Thomas succeeded Nat D. as host of "Amateur Night on Beale." Present in the studio for Nat's premiere on WDIA, Rufus Thomas was hired as an air personality in 1951.[25]

The station also attracted high caliber talent. In some instances, performers literally walked into the studios and a job. Theo "Bless My Bones" Wade came to WDIA's studios as leader of the "Spirit of Memphis" gospel group. His performance so impressed Ferguson that Wade was hired on the spot.[26] The most famous walk-in employee was blues singer B. B. King. The tale of his hiring is a major component of the voluminous folklore surrounding the Memphis outlet. Most interesting is the connection with Sonny Boy Williamson.

In 1947, Riley King tired of trying to convince other members of his spiritual group to leave Mississippi and go on tour. So he left Indianola, Mississippi, and hitchhiked to Memphis, where he stayed with his cousin blues singer Bukka White. During the day, King worked at the Newberry Equipment Company. At night, he competed at "Amateur Night on Beale," typically winning first prize.[27]

One day he tuned in the radio to KWEM and heard Sonny Boy Williamson singing. "But at this time he was not in Helena, Arkansas," King explained, "he was in West Memphis [Arkansas], right there near where I was. So I had listened to him for so long I thought I really knew him but I didn't. So I went over to West Memphis this particular day and begged him to let me do a tune." Sonny Boy let King play a song on the air. The audition was heard by a club owner who regularly employed Sonny Boy. Williamson had a better paying job that night and successfully offered King as his replacement.

"And the lady was payin' me $12 a night," King continued. "And she said, 'Well, like if you gets you a job on the radio as Sonny Boy have, then I will pay you $12 a night and give you one day off plus room and board.' " The club owner wanted King to advertise her place on the air. "I'd never heard of that kinda money." he recalled during a 1976 interview. "I couldn't even believe it. So that's how I went to WDIA."

The station was switching to an all-black format and was on the lookout for air personalities. King hopped a bus to Memphis and then started walking the mile from the bus station to the radio station. "I remember it started to rain." King slung his guitar on his back with the strings against his body so it wouldn't get too wet. When he reached the WDIA studios, he looked through the plate glass window at Nat D., who was on the air. "And I was frightened, wet, still frightened, and I'd knock on the door an' Mr. Williams came to the door and said, 'What can I do for you, young fella'?'" King made his request, asking to play on the air. Nat called David James and Bert Ferguson and "that very day they put me on the air," said King.[28]

An irony of the story is that Riley King was hired to advertise a new product called Pepticon, which competed with Hadacol, Sonny Boy's sponsor on KWEM. King played ten minutes a day, performing two songs. He received no pay and used the time to promote his appearances at the night club. Eventually he became so popular that he got more time, and when Maurice "Hot Rod" Hulbert left, King got his job as disc jockey. During this time he adopted the nickname the "Beale Street Blues Boy," which was shortened to B. B. By 1951, B. B. King was appearing two hours daily on the air.[29]

King's story shows how radio supplied a new employment opportunity that attracted high quality black talent, particularly performers who learned to use radio as a career stepping stone. Sonny Boy paved the way at KFFA and personally helped B. B. King follow in his path. Among those who traveled similar roads at WDIA were Bobby "Blue" Bland, Junior Parker, Johnny Ace, and Roscoe Gordon.

As a result, WDIA built up a superior black staff that, John Pepper indicates, "attracted others. They were high class, respectable people and they attracted people like that. And through them we gradually built the staff up until we had a good beginning, a real good well-rounded staff." [30]

This well-rounded staff was employed under conditions that differed greatly from those in Chicago, where time brokerage and sales commission positions predominated. These conditions influenced WDIA's growth and development. Nat D. Williams was hired as a salaried employee with no commission involved. He never sold air time to sponsors, nor did any other black personalities. Advertising sales were handled by a professional sales staff composed of whites. During the years that it was owned by Ferguson and Pepper, only one black salesman was employed by WDIA to sell the largely white advertising market. This decision had distinct racial overtones. "Most of the sales staff was white because they were dealing with white customers," explained Pepper. "At that time I don't think a black salesman would be as successful and effective in being able to make sales as he would be today, for instance." In addition, Pepper suggests that contact with out-of-town ad agencies required a white man. [31]

Unlike other stations, however, WDIA would not hire white air personalities. Only blacks appeared behind the microphone and although they didn't sell time, their employment did depend upon their selling the goods and services advertised. This reverse color line followed station policy and strategy, which Ferguson elucidated in *Sponsor:*

To a great extent, their speech is idiomatic to the extent that nobody sells a Negro like another Negro *who knows how to sell.* . . . Many sales messages intended for the ears of Negroes have fallen far short of their goal. But once that sales message is phrased in his kind of talk and voiced by a friend of his in whom he has confidence and pride, he'll buy more quickly and he'll buy more. [32]

Disc jockey Robert Thomas supported Ferguson's contention in profiling fellow WDIA announcer Theo "Bless My Bones" Wade, who hosted religious shows. "He wasn't the polished dj you look for," Thomas said, "but he's just down home, earthy and quite a salesman. And there's nobody else, I've been to quite a few places and it includes jocks in Memphis, wherever you want to go, can outsell Theo "Bless My Bones" Wade. Because when he decides he wants to sell a product, which is 99 and 29 tenths, or 99.29 percent of the time, he's going to sell." [33]

In 1952, WDIA furthered its advertising efforts by naming A. C. Williams promotion consultant. His job was "to do public relations, contact work, and merchandising among the half million Negroes in the counties reached by WDIA." Another service to advertisers was the blanketing of "grocery and drug outlets in its area with monthly lists of advertisers, reminding them that advertised products are easier for the merchant to sell." [34] In other words, WDIA reached out to both consumers and retailers to help their sponsors.

Not surprisingly, the Memphis outlet regularly sold out its advertising. *Time* observed that there was one advertiser for every five minutes of air time, including some national accounts.[35] The first black-appeal program sponsored by Lucky Strike cigarettes was B. B. King's WDIA program. Arrid deodorant, Bayer aspirin, Camel cigarettes, Cheer detergent, Crisco, Gulf Oil, Shell Oil, and Maxwell House coffee also bought time.[36]

What made WDIA so attractive to advertisers was the audience's response to the station. Service again was the touchstone of success. Though the comprehensive schedule appealed to all segments of the black population, it was little different from that of other black-appeal outlets, such as WSBC in Chicago, for example. WDIA differed and was unique because its public service function extended far beyond airing shows of public interest. The station actually became integrated into the black community, much to the surprise of its owners. "The station grew, you know, just from a little beginning up to where it kinda became more than just an entertainment medium," John Pepper explains. "It became sort of a spokesman, a part of the black community." He believed this evolution "just developed."[37] But it was less a spontaneous development than a logical culmination of events.

WDIA's integration into the black community was less spontaneous than a natural evolution for reasons that can be traced back to three basic circumstances. First, there were the prevailing institutional practices employed by WDIA, which barred blacks from selling time. Air personalities did not have to devote much of their time to survival by selling sponsors. But they did concentrate on selling consumers, and that activity necessitated a strong and regular presence in the black community in order to become known and to gain the trust of listeners. That many were already known and respected before going on the air helped in this regard.

The second source is the initial lack of competition that gave WDIA the opportunity to capture the black market. By the time the Memphis station opened its doors, the Chicago market was becoming extremely competitive. Jack L. Cooper had shows on at least four stations and faced heavy competition from newcomer Al Benson, among others.[38]

The combination of these institutional and marketing factors in Memphis created conditions conducive to WDIA's increasing community involvement. Human forces then took advantage of these conditions to achieve the goal of community integration. Spearheading this effort were the race-conscious black disc jockeys who had the employment security and time to pursue what was an obvious interest on the air and off. Nat D. was with WDIA for two decades. A. C. Williams was with the station for over 30 years. Rufus Thomas logged over 20 years on the air, as did Robert Thomas.[39] Longevity increased familiarity and trust.

WDIA followed two paths to community integration. One one hand, it acted as a spokesman and communications network for the black community. Shows such as "Brown America Speaks" allowed the black perspective on news events to be aired while the news and sportscasts kept blacks informed. Public service venues both educated and counseled blacks. The station brought people together, often solving problems for individuals, from locating a lost relative to mediating a listener's problem with a government agency. WDIA's missing person bureau "broadcasts more than 15,000 appeals for missing persons and articles each year—and locates an average of 90 percent of those missing persons."[40] *Time* magazine reported in detail on a unique late night feature that aired everything from distress calls to pleas for blood donors.[41]

The outreach activities opened up and maintained channels of communication within Memphis's black community and that of the surrounding metropolitan area. The corps of disc jockeys that had been recruited aided this process because they had their own personal communication networks. And their influence on program development certainly led WDIA to assume the posture it did.

The second avenue of community integration was direct service. As the 1971 public relations pamphlet put it, "Listeners have remained loyal to WDIA and have given it dominance in the Mid-South because the station is loyal to them in its response to their personal and community needs." The station boasted of its commitment, claiming that "WDIA's record of service to its listeners is unmatched in media. . . . It puts its support—financial and physical—where its mike is, contributing thousands of man hours and tens-of-thousands in funds."[42]

WDIA personalities made themselves available for all sorts of public appearances, ranging from store openings to participation in the two annual fundraisers sponsored by the station. The Starlite Revue and the Goodwill Revue acted as the major philanthropic events, showcasing the talents of black entertainers and the black disc jockeys. The combined gross for the shows, according to the 1971 pamphlet, "runs in the neighborhood of $60,000." This money, dispensed by the WDIA Goodwill Fund, Inc., supported a large number of projects, including a WDIA scholarship program, WDIA goodwill homes for children, and boys' clubs.[43] Writing about the station's service accomplishment in *Successful Television and Radio Advertising,* Gene Seehafer and Jack Laemmar listed some other WDIA activities. "The station constantly promotes a number of public service activities for the community—supports Little League baseball teams, participates in fund-raising activities, owns and operates buses for crippled school children, supports a hospital."[44]

In playing an integral role in the black community, WDIA reaped substantial rewards. Bert Ferguson saw responding to the needs of the black community as the keystone of his success. "The lack of this approach will cause the weakness or failure of many an operator who thinks that the key to the mint in the Negro market is a few blues and gospel records, and a Negro face at the mike."[45]

Listener support kept the station at the top of the ratings for decades. A 1957 *Time* magazine article reported that "WDIA tops every station in the mid-South in ratings and advertisers."[46] Not surprisingly, the Memphis outlet served as the model of black-appeal station development in the 1950s. Those examining its progress could see how service combined with programming could result in substantial growth. In 1954 Ferguson and Pepper applied for and received an FCC license for a clear 50,000-watt channel, making it the only station of its size "programming exclusively to the Negro market."[47] As a result, WDIA became a mid-South giant not only of black-appeal but of radio generally in the region and the nation.

Throughout the years the station garnered many honors. In 1969 it was awarded the *Billboard* magazine Station of the Year Award. The following year it received the National Association of Television and Radio Announcers Radio Station of the Year Award.[48]

In January 1957, WDIA was sold to the Sonderling Broadcasting Corporation for $1 million. The practices instituted by Pepper and Ferguson were continued, with the latter remaining on as executive vice president and general manager until 1970. In the mid-1970s, Viacom bought WDIA and again the operational philosophy and practices remained in force. As *Time* said, "the station's strongest pitch is not to the ear but the heart."[49]

NOTES

1. The WHBQ story is taken from an interview with Bob Alburty conducted in Memphis, Tenn., in July 1978, except when otherwise indicated.

2. Nat D. Williams, cited in Jerome Wright, "Beale Street Panorama Recalled," Memphis *Commercial Appeal,* July 14, 1974.

3. Interview, Bob Alburty.

4. Interview, John Pepper, Memphis Tenn., July 1978.

5. Ibid. The following quotes are from the Pepper interview.

6. See p. 81.

7. Interview, Joseph F. Ellis, Jr.

8. U.S. Bureau of the Census, *Census of the Population: 1950,* vol. 2: *Characteristics of the Population,* pt. 42: *Tennessee* (Washington, D.C.: U.S. Government Printing Office, 1953), p. 56; *Sixteenth Census of the United States: 1940, Characteristics of the Population,* vol. 2, pt. 2: *Florida-Iowa* (Washington, D.C.: U. S. Government Printing Office, 1943), p. 709.

9. U.S. Bureau of the Census, *U.S. Census of the Population: 1960,* vol. 1: *Characteristics of the Population,* pt. 44: *Tennessee* (Washington, D.C., U.S. Government Printing Office, 1963), p. 56.

10. Interview, John Pepper.

11. Ibid.

12. Ibid.

13. Ibid..

14. Ibid.

15. Ibid.

16. Cited in "Mr. Sponsor Asks . . .," *Sponsor,* vol. 6, no. 15 (July 28, 1952), p. 42.

17. Interview, Bert Ferguson, Memphis, Tenn., July 1978.

18. Interview, Nat D. Williams.

19. Ibid.

20. Interview, John Pepper.

21. Ibid..

22. Interview, Nat D. Williams.

23. WDIA Program Schedule, June 1952; interview, Robert Thomas, Memphis Tenn., July 1978.

24. WDIA Program Schedule, June 1952.

25. Interviews, Nat D. Williams; Rufus Thomas, Memphis, Tenn., July 1978.

26. Interview Robert Thomas, Memphis, Tenn., July 1976.

27. Interviews, B. B. King; Rufus Thomas.

28. Interview, B. B. King.

29. Ibid.

30. Interview, John Pepper.

31. Ibid.

32. "Mr. Sponsor Asks . . .," p. 42.

33. Interview, Robert Thomas, July 1976.

34. "Negro Radio: 200-Plus Special Stations," p. 79.

35. "Biggest Negro Station," *Time,* vol. 70, no. 20 (November 11, 1957), p. 86.

36. Interview, Robert Thomas, July 1976; WDIA advertisement in *Sponsor,* vol. 7, no. 17 (August 24, 1953), p. 79.

37. Interview, John Pepper.

38. See Chapter 4.

39. Interviews, Nat D. Williams; Rufus Thomas; Robert Thomas, July 1976.

40. "Goodwill at Work in Memphis: WDIA," WDIA public relations pamphlet (1977).

41. "Biggest Negro Station," p. 86.

42. "Goodwill at Work in Memphis: WDIA."

43. Ibid.

44. Gene F. Seehafer and Jack W. Laemmar, *Successful Television and Radio Advertising* (New York: McGraw-Hill Book Company, Inc., 1959), p. 501.

45. "Negro Radio: 200-Plus Special Stations," p. 79.

46. "Biggest Negro Station," p. 86.

47. Seehafer and Laemmar, *Successful Television and Radio Advertising,* p. 512.

48. "Goodwill at Work In Memphis: WDIA."

49. "Biggest Negro Station," p. 86.

PART III

CONSCIOUSNESS
AND CULTURE

INTRODUCTION

The study of history revolves around answering the same basic questions asked in the field of communications, though in historical study these queries are seldom strung together in a formula. Moreover, the study of history places primary importance on discovering why. Finding out the who, where, when, what, and how provides the data to be used in probing for the reasons why. In the previous chapters, the development of black-appeal radio is analyzed using the method of inquiry described above. But, again, historical study seldom distinguishes or separates the answers, merging them into a comprehensive whole that facilitates discussion and understanding.

In Part 3, we move to the effect radio had on blacks. The same questions apply, but the thrust is on how and why black-appeal affected racial consciousness and culture to produce the concept of soul—the what that resulted.

Identifying the how is easy since radio is a medium of communication. But comprehending the way in which this integral aspect of human interaction works requires some further investigation of the study of communications, a field of very recent origin and considerable flux.

Wilbur Schramm writes that "communication is the fundamental social process." It is "a relationship, an act of sharing rather than something someone does to someone else."[1] But sharing rather than doing was not always considered the act of communicating, particularly in regard to media. Initially, the propaganda of World War I, and that of the Nazis in Germany and the Communists in the Soviet Union during the 1930s gave rise to the "bullet theory." The audience was conceived as a sitting target that could be controlled, changed, and converted by "the insidious forces of propaganda carried by the mighty power of the mass media."[2]

This view of the media as controllers of human thought remained dominant until it was proved false by researchers Eunice Cooper and Marie Jahoda in the late 1940s. Their Mr. Biggott studies attempted to overturn prejudiced views of test subjects by using cartoons that portrayed the absurdity of bigotry. But the results contradicted the study's goal of having the participants reject their prejudices. "Prejudiced respondents . . . went to such lengths to extricate themselves from their identification with Mr. Biggott that in the end they misunderstood the point of the cartoon."[3] Far from being controlled by the media, they rejected its message. What Cooper and Jahoda did show is that propaganda and exposure to other mass media do not always influence the thought and beliefs of the receivers.

The negative reactions of blacks to the blackface image stereotypes they were constantly bombarded with also proves the "bullet theory" wrong. And this example demonstrates the limits of the media's powers of persuasion. Regarding blackface's influence on white racial perceptions, Chapter 1 indicates that it reinforced feelings of superiority rather than creating them.

Communication is based not on doing but on sharing, on creating a relationship between medium and respondent. Radio, for example, facilitates communication by providing something special to share. Without that something special, communication is at best flawed and most likely nonexistent. Tuning out is as integral an aspect of human interaction with, for example, radio and television, as tuning in.

Ideas and thoughts are not sent from communicator to receiver, messages are; and they are accepted, rejected, or altered depending upon the past experiences and such sociopsychological factors as the receiver's personal taste and beliefs. As Wilbur Schramm concluded, communication is "the sharing of an orientation toward a set of informational signs" (defining information in the broadest sense)." The success of communications depends on both parties "being 'in tune' with each other."[4]

Black-appeal radio was "in tune" with the black listener. Yet this compatible dialogue was not solely determined by the content of programming and advertising. Equally important was the process of communicating. During a 1978 interview, WDIA disc jockey Robert Thomas explained how he related to the audience and had related to it successfully for over 20 years. Early in his career, Thomas developed a routine to introduce himself during station breaks, to explain what he was doing and show how he felt about his work.

Using his nickname, Thomas said, "This is Honeyboy in the hive keepin' you alive. Here we have discs and data with a little bit of listening matter for those who live it, for those who love it, and for those who make a living of it." His message to listeners was "I'm a disc jockey just spinnin' your records and doing' a little rap with you, and this is my living. This is what I do for a living but I love it."[5]

Phrased according to the who was saying what in which channel to whom and with what effect formula, Robert Thomas, born and raised in Memphis, told those listening in the Memphis area that he was like them. He had a job to do. But he also said he was there to serve them and that he loved his work. The radio acted as the channel of communication with Thomas's enthusiasm and sincerity in delivering this message—plus his active public service which proved his point—forging a relationship with the audience that facilitated communication.

A professional communicator speaking the language of racial pride, Thomas symbolized progress every day on and off his show. The programming of WDIA, the advertising, and the high profile of the station in the black community all contributed to creating strong bonds of communication. These bonds were the how of black-appeal radio's effect on racial consciousness and culture. The why and the what, the when and the where are examined in the next two chapters.

NOTES

1. Wilbur Schramm and Donald F. Roberts, eds., *The Process and Effects of Mass Communications,* rev. ed. (Urbana: University of Illinois Press, 1971), pp. 5–6, 8.

2. Ibid., p. 40.

3. Eunice Cooper and Marie Jahoda, "The Evasion of Propaganda: How Prejudiced People Respond to Anti-Prejudice Propaganda," *Journal of Psychology,* vol. 45 (January 1947), p. 17.

4. Schramm and Roberts, *Mass Communications,* p. 13.

5. Interview, Robert Thomas, July 1978.

7 *BLACK-APPEAL RADIO AND SOUL CONSCIOUSNESS*

"Language is an organ of perception, not simply a means of communication," writes Julian Jaynes in *The Origins of Consciousness in the Breakdown of the Bicameral Mind*.[1] Black-appeal radio is a means of mass communication of language; thus it is also an organ of perception, on individual and mass levels.

During the boom years of the late 1940s and early 1950s, the language of black-appeal was communicated nationwide to blacks and whites. But this language was open to differing perceptions, since blacks and whites delivered and received various messages that were interpreted in the words and symbols of their own racially defined realities and consciousnesses. For blacks the result was the development of a new racial consciousness called "soul." For whites it was the fulfillment of their business interests.

Here the primary focus is on understanding how and why black-appeal contributed to soul's development and dissemination; such understanding implies, first of all, being certain of what consciousness means. Soul will be defined later. According to the *Compact Oxford English Dictionary*, consciousness is the state of knowing something in oneself that is known with others.[2] Jaynes delves deeper, defining it as the "subjective conscious mind" that provides a model of the real world that is "at every point generated by" and "constructed from" what is known about the real world. It is "built up with a vocabulary or lexical field whose terms are all metaphors or analogs [a model "at every point generated by the thing it is an analog of," such as a map, for example] of behavior in the physical world."[3]

Racial consciousness is that part of the "subjective conscious mind" that focuses specifically on the racial aspects of the real world, providing a model generated by and constructed from what blacks and whites know of these racial aspects. During and after World War II, the vocabulary of race changed because the black situation was dramatically altered. The switch to wage labor, urban migration, and the sharing of prosperity after 1945 created new analogs, new perceptions of black America centering around change, growth, progress, movement, and recognition.

WORLD WAR II, BLACKS, AND THE MILITARY

The changes that came about can be attributed directly to the Second World War. This global conflict stimulated the economy, set in motion the socioeconomic alteration of American life that came to full fruition with peace, and opened new vistas of experience and opportunity for blacks. The impact of the war was particularly pivotal for those serving in the armed forces.

Whether they saw action or not, blacks in the military were exposed to experiences, people, and environments far different from any they had met with on city streets or in farm fields. The tour of duty "was the first exposure most of these people had ever had to anything more than fifty miles away from home."[4] They faced the irony of fighting a war against prejudice under Jim Crow conditions. "The army was an experience unlike anything I've had in my life," said black realtor and author Dempsey Travis, a Chicago black who served at Camp Shenango in Pennsylvania. "I think of two armies, one black and one white. I saw German prisoners free to move around the camp, unlike black soldiers, who were restricted."[5]

For Travis and other blacks, the color line meant segregated units and more. "It seems the army always arranged to have black soldiers back up against the woods someplace. Isolated. We were never near the main gate," says Travis. At Camp Shenango, blacks could not use the PX, the camp store. There was no black servicemen's club and all five movie theaters in camp were off-limits.

An unexplained attack by white GIs on the black soldiers placed Travis in the hospital with three bullet wounds. When he recovered and returned to duty, "They had built a major service center for the black servicemen. They had opened up the main theater and blacks were permitted to go." Wryly, Travis concluded, "It appears you had to kill some guys" to achieve progress.

Yet military service proved a boon for Dempsey Travis. His psychological testing revealed a 135+ IQ. He rapidly advanced through the ranks, becoming the first black manager of an integrated PX in the state of Maryland. His rise was aided by a white mentor, an ex-Texas Ranger named Sloan, who unsuccessfully tried to convince Travis to stay in the army and go to Officer Candidate School. Sloan also singled out Dempsey for special duty, such as having him study the Bretton Woods Reports and then explain them to the troops. "I, who could hardly read. . . . How can I ever forget this experience and this man."

Military service in World War II was the nexus in the lives of many black soldiers like Travis. "Those four years in the army are the turning point in my life," he says. "I learned something about men. I learned something about racism. I learned something about values. I learned something about myself. I don't think I'd have that experience any other place or time. Under no other circumstance would I have seen so many men in one setting, where I could evaluate them and myself."

This evaluation led to a surprising conclusion. "The most sympathetic men in the army were actually southerners. . . . If they decided they're gonna go with you, they go all the damn way. And no forked tongue." He later found this "to be true in civilian life as well. The best breaks I've got as a business-man have come from guys out of Alabama and Georgia."

Travis also learned about dreams. Studs Terkel's book *The Good War* is full of examples of how World War II, the second war fought for democracy, inspired hope in Americans. Blacks, too, looked to the return of peace with great optimism. Travis recalls his bunkmates musing about their plans. "The lying and dreaming that soldiers do among themselves is unbelievable. . . . They were gonna do this, they were gonna do that."[6]

Peace made partial realization of these dreams possible. Prosperity and mi-gration created new, more lucrative employment opportunities for blacks. The triumph of the United States in the war fought to outlaw prejudice furthered the civil rights cause, fostering greater determination in blacks. Freedom was in reach. Equality under the law would be achieved. Black consciousness was changing.

One very prominent symbol of progress was the new white recognition of the black radio audience. Decades of neglect, scorn, and mistreatment slowly gave way to a new solicitude. Radio finally provided blacks with something special to share. They enjoyed the medium as whites did, and radio became a major channel for the generation and distribution of what we call soul con-sciousness. At the core of this development were two dialogues: one between white industry figures and blacks and one between blacks in radio and the black audience.

THE BLACK-WHITE DIALOGUE

Meaningful communications opened up between the races because black-appeal radio was a biracial cooperative endeavor. White station owners pro-vided the airtime and often the idea for the concept. Or blacks provided the idea for programming and whites again supplied the outlet. Program funding generally came from advertising sales to white-owned retailers or wholesalers catering to the black consumer. The initial sponsors were familiar with the black consumer market and were later followed by national advertisers who learned the value of media marketing to the black consumer. Black sponsors were in the minority.

Blacks provided the voice behind the microphone, often the selling expertise, program consulting, and the programming itself. In computer terminology, blacks supplied the software that was run on the white-owned hardware. They also provided the financial support to demonstrate the concept's viability to advertisers and stations. In other words, blacks were the customers.

Success in black-appeal therefore rested upon whites and blacks communicating with each other to learn and understand their respective wants and needs. The context of the communication was largely educational because of the racial separation the color line imposed and the persistence of long-engrained stereotypes among both races. Whites needed to learn more about blacks than vice versa because blacks were the customers.

The language used by both was similar and was guided by the perquisites of the radio industry: the black-white dialogue centered around business, marketing in particular. There was, however, a subtle difference in context. Whites were interested solely in profits, whereas blacks added the perspective of pride to the bottom line. Black entrepreneur Leonard Evans underscored the business imperative when he explained the motive behind his short-lived, mid-1950s National Negro Network: "This is not a crusade for the intermingling of races. . . . We're out to move tonnage, to sell merchandise. If we do help race relations, it's incidental." Yet Evans also explained that shows in the blackface minstrelsy vein would be unacceptable.[7]

White support of black-appeal depended upon blacks recognizing that radio was first and foremost a business run according to the profit motive, not for any altruistic reasons. If blacks bought the products of the sponsors, then advertising revenues to fund black-appeal programming would continue to flow to the stations airing the shows, insuring survival and perhaps dictating expansion.

Support, however, was a two-way street. To capture the hearts, minds, and dollars of black customers for their programming and products, whites had to respond to their needs and wants. America's foremost management expert, Peter Drucker, writes that there is "only one valid definition of business purpose: to create a customer." To Drucker, "Marketing is the distinguishing, the unique function of business. . . . The customer is the foundation of a business and keeps it in existence. He alone gives employment. And it is to supply the consumer that society entrusts wealth-producing resources to the business enterprise." As a result, he continues, "Marketing is not only much broader than selling, it is not a specialized activity at all. It encompasses the entire business. It is the whole business seen from the point of view of its final result, that is, from the customer's point of view."[8]

The task of black-appeal entrepreneurs, black and white, was to create the black customer by developing shows and commercials that would lure him and her to listen and to buy the products advertised. Whites had to learn about blacks to know and understand what appealed to them and what did not. The black-white dialogue occurred largely in this educational context.

The process of learning took place in a classic market research exercise revolving around surveys, statistics from the government and other sources, personal listener responses to various programming and advertising ventures, and, of course, consultations with blacks.

"When the radio stations began to present more black programs," explained Nat D. Williams, putting the whole learning process in perspective, "they had to stop and think about what kind they're going to do."[9] As Bert Ferguson explained, many a black-appeal failure was due to the false impression "that the key to the mint in the Negro market is a few blues and gospel records, and a Negro face at the mike."[10] Much more was involved in successful operations. The same rule held true for commercials.

For whites, the dialogue centered around certain key concepts, watchwords of the language of learning, so to speak: pride, respect, equality, and quality. First, however, came recognition. The message was delivered initially by blacks and later by members of both races to other untutored whites. In particular, the *Sponsor* black radio annuals exposed wary whites to the potential contained in black progress. The 1952 edition starts with the headline: "The Negro Market: $15,000,000,000 to Spend." The first line of this first article, set up in question-and-answer format, asks: "Is there really such a thing as 'the Negro market'?" The second inquires as to "the scope of the U.S. Negro market?"[11]

In the "Mr. Sponsor Asks . . ." column, Madeline Allison, media director of the Herschel Z. Deutsch advertising agency in New York City in 1952, succinctly answered the question: "Why is it worthwhile for a national advertiser to plan a special radio campaign geared to the Negro market?" She said, "Our actual experience has proved beyond question that the Negro market is definitely worthwhile . . . very profitable."[12]

Having recognized the value of black-appeal, whites learned the importance of racial pride and how it could have an impact on their business. "To a degree," writes Bert Ferguson, blacks "buy what our WDIA personalities sell because they are proud of them as symbols of progress. They are eager to cooperate with them for the good of all Negroes."[13] Blacks supported black-appeal because it was a source not only of entertainment, information, and public service but also of pride and progress, and for those working in the industry, income. Whites learned that promoting pride and progress resulted in greater profits.

Closely related to the pride factor was respect. A representative of WLIB in New York City writes, "The most important factor in approaching the Negro through air advertising is considering the Negro consumer a human being of dignity and self-respect—one who does not want to be talked down to, or catered to blatantly."[14]

Without doubt, the first step in building respect was eliminating any minstrelsy-inspired images from both programming and advertising. *Sponsor* published several such examples in each black radio annual to instruct its readers. In 1953 a top bakery company decided to air "a series of transcribed announcements'' on a black-appeal outlet in a Gulf of Mexico coast city. ''One of the announcements was to be a transcribed jingle which went 'Mammy's little baby likes Tip Top, Tip Top' to the tune of 'Shortnin' Bread,' '' explained an executive of the station, who had apparently rejected the commercial. ''Can you think of a better way to alienate the Negro listener who is on the lookout for so-called 'Uncle Tom-ing' anyway?'' he asked.[15]

A similar minstrelsy-inspired problem arose when advertising efforts sought to simulate black speech. In offering seven ''Tips on selling via Negro radio,'' *Sponsor* counseled that ''Attempts by advertisers to produce a synthetic 'Negro speech' in agency copy usually don't work out.'' Blacks desired ad copy that appealed to them by having radio announcers talk in their ''own style.'' The best results came from ''commercials . . . done live by Negro artists.'' [16]

Black-appeal dictated that programming feature black talent and music, though not exclusively. At WDIA, B. B. King played white artists such as French jazz violinist Django Reinhardt, Frank Sinatra's ''Three Coins in a Fountain,'' Vaughn Monroe's ''Ghost Riders in the Sky,'' and Tony Bennett's ''Rags to Riches.'' Richard Stams recalled playing Elvis Presley to black listeners who were amazed that Presley was white.[17] But primarily the record playlist was black. Nat Williams's problems with the records WDIA provided him are noted in Chapter 6. As was true on all record stations, the most popular songs were the ones played. Whites had to learn what was ''in'' with blacks. Record sales helped in this process.

Blacks also demanded other forms of programming. To learn about these wants, stations conducted surveys. Two California stations, KGFJ in Hollywood and KWBR in Oakland, reported that their surveys indicated a marked audience preference for ''personality disc jockey shows featuring rhythm and blues music.''[18] Other stations, such as WHOD in Pittsburgh, discovered that '' 'Rhythm and Blues' music is not catnip for all Negroes.''[19] A 1951 survey conducted by WAAA in Winston-Salem, North Carolina, polled 2,000 black families as to their listening preferences. Spiritual music was named as the number one choice by 736 families, and 459 cited blues. Soap operas were the choice of 212 families, 193 chose housewife shows, 193, contest programs, and 66, dramas. The last three first-choice preferences were swing, classical, and hillbilly music in that order.[20]

White education extended into news operations. ''We have learned to do newscasts that answer the question, 'How is this news going to affect me as a Negro?' '' Leonard Walk of WHOD Pittsburgh stated.[21] This need resulted in shows such as Cooper's ''Listen Chicago'' and WDIA's ''Brown America Speaks,'' which complemented news reportage with analysis of issues concerning blacks. Airing local news of interest was another essential part of programming. Walk continues, ''We have learned that church and social news deserves a unique place of importance in our daily Negro programming.''[22] Richard Stams said that reporting church events was a major public component at WGES.[23] The lesson learned was, Leonard Walk concluded, that ''you cannot generalize about Negro likes and dislikes any more than you can generalize about 'American' taste." [24] His statement deserves some scrutiny because his analogy explicitly raises blacks to the same level as whites. Saying the black population does not lend itself to facile generalizations represents a complete turn around from the blackface-image position. Blacks are no longer seen as caricatures all cut out of the same cloth. They are perceived as individuals with differing personalities. Certainly such changes in attitude and the actions that accompanied them did much to increase black self-respect.

Walk's conclusion indicates, too, that equality was a component of black-appeal and a major communication from black-appeal station executives to those buying advertising time on such stations. A WDIA spokesman, probably Bert Ferguson, expressed his opinion: "What sells a white person will sell the Negro listener in almost every instance. He needs and buys a home, food, clothes, and little luxuries. He needs respect in the community, recreation, a good job, just as white people do." [25]

Just as white people do. The implication here is clear and surely was evident to both whites and blacks. In the marketplace the same general principles that applied to white people applied to blacks. They were equals as customers, and blacks deserved respectful treatment just as whites did. A corollary was that whites were championing the black cause of marketing equality, which fact in itself was significant.

Equality equaled quality. The programming had to be high quality entertainment, information, or public service. The advertising had to feature high quality products and be phrased correctly. The treatment accorded the black listener and consumer had to be top quality. *Sponsor* is replete with comments on and examples of this point.

"They insist upon quality," writes D. Courtenay Jamison, advertising adviser to WERD, Atlanta, Georgia, "and will not stop at any sacrifice of price to get it." [26] The opportunity Max Moore of Interstate Grocer had recognized in 1938 when he marketed a high quality flour, "King Biscuit," to Arkansas delta blacks was evident nationwide. "Negroes buy Ivory soap and Camel cigarettes and many other top products in abundance when they hear these products advertised through Negro radio," writes Jim Vaughn, manager of Miami, Florida, black-appeal station WMBM. [27] Given the opportunity, blacks chose the best products and services their money could buy.

Conversely, ad appeals for low quality products aroused the anger of the black consumer, as is shown by the following: "Anxious to stimulate weekend sales in its meat department," a large supermarket in Philadelphia, Pennsylvania, decided to advertise a special on black-appeal outlet WDAS. The disc jockey "didn't like the look of the copy. But he read it anyway. . . . 'Say, folks . . . want some good ol' Southern eating? Well, just get a load of some of these weekend meat specials just waitin' for you to come in and buy 'em.' " The specials included "Pig knuckles. Ham hocks. Chitlins. Plate Beef. Kidneys. And other meat cuts in the lowest price bracket." The response to the ad was swift and furious as black listeners called in their protests. "I wouldn't feed that kind of stuff to my poodle," said one caller.[28]

As WDAS station manager Bob Klein explained, "Negro listeners will blow their tops at the 'condescending' commercial." The good old Southern eating "was exactly the kind of thing Negroes don't look back to with any fond remembrance."[29]

This ad campaign violated the first rule of appealing to blacks over radio. "Never use Negro-appeal radio to sell a second-rate product. . . . Negroes today earn good wages, prefer to buy premium-priced and top-quality merchandise." Or as one black woman said in response to another ad campaign involving free perfume, a low-priced brand, "when I buy perfume I buy Chanel Number Five."[30]

Having come to this realization, station owners took steps to insure that the ad messages reaching blacks were correctly phrased. Referring to the meat commercial aired on WDAS, *Sponsor* explained. "Things like this don't happen too often in Negro Radio today. Advertisers and their commercials are carefully screened. Many stations have firm policies about advertising acceptability."[31]

In New York City, WLIB instituted a rigorous screening policy. "We test out new products and get a reaction to advertising claims from a panel of Negro editors and community leaders before we accept them on the station," writes station manager Harry Novik. "In fact, it's safe to say that Negro Radio is generally more cautious in accepting advertisers than are print media slanted to Negroes."[32]

This cautiousness reflected another aspect of black life that whites learned about or probably already knew about, but in a very different context. Equality for blacks implied something special. Nat D. Williams puts much of this racial specialness in perspective, explaining, "We talked a little different. We used the language a little different. And we expressed a little bit different feelings. However, they were basically the same feelings that all human beings have."[33]

The feelings of blacks were the same as whites, their humanity was the same. But blacks were separate and they were different from the white majority. "Generally, you can say that as long as there is a distinction between 'white' and 'non-white,' there will be a Negro market," writes Joseph Wootton, a black marketing specialist. "As long as there is racial segregation or racial prejudice in this country, Negroes will continue to turn to their own news and entertainment media for everything from the interpretation of new legislation to the enjoyment of performing artists of their own race."[34]

Appealing to blacks meant doing so on their side of the color line without sacrificing quality or equal treatment. It meant stating this racial difference in a positive light rather than implying negativity, as was true in so many other facets of society. Blackface minstrelsy influences were eliminated in favor of the newly perceived pride/respect/equality/quality formula.

Airing programs of appeal and guarding against misdirected and offensive commercials created strong trust in blacks. Joseph Wootton, a black man who headed the radio division of Interstate United Newspapers explains, "Often, the Negro with an improved income is cautious, relying on the advertising that's aimed squarely at him in his own media to help him decide how he's going to spend that money."[35]

The result was the creation of a loyal, dependable, and supportive audience on one hand, and the development of a true black-appeal medium on the other. Even today, except for the cable television Black Entertainment Network, which reaches relatively small numbers of people, radio remains the only electronic mass medium regularly appealing to blacks.

Just how pivotal the correct appeal was is shown by examining the black reaction to television. "Is television a factor in reaching the Negro market?" asked *Sponsor*. "It goes without saying that Negro families own and enjoy TV sets," the magazine answered. By 1952, an estimated 850,000 black homes had television sets. Two years later, a survey placed black television set ownership at 27.2 percent. In northern cities, the figures ranged from 60 percent in Boston up to 75 percent in New York City. In the South, the range was from 1 percent in Hattiesburg, Mississippi, to 52 percent in Charlotte, North Carolina.[36]

But the figures showed that "television has not penetrated the Negro audience to the same degree as the white audience," explained Robert Lyons, manager of radio station WRAP in Norfolk, Virginia. "This is not due to lower buying power but to the fact that a Negro seeking entertainment is more apt to find it in listening to a program of specific Negro interest than in viewing a television program composed of white actors dealing with a white family situation."[37] The old problem that blacks faced in all the other media inhibited their acceptance of television: hardly any of the programming appealed to them, and there was little reassurance in the advertising that blacks were a market of appeal.

The white/black dialogue surrounding black-appeal radio obviously had a strong impact on black consciousness. It helped revise the analog of the black world. A major factor was that the dialogue itself was something new, as were its results. By recognizing black progress and saying that they were learning from blacks about blacks to exploit this new opportunity, whites communicated something new and different. Also new and different was approaching blacks as equals in the marketplace, deserving of the same respectful consideration accorded whites.

The language of the dialogue produced new metaphors in the black analog in addition to progress, recognition and learning, such as pride and respect, equality, quality, and whites championing the black cause. The impact of these communications was greatly enhanced by the fact that they were aired every day and every night. It became habitual for blacks to hear that being black was positive. Being black made one special. Blacks, like whites, were a proud people deserving of respect. Blacks needed their own radio stations. They needed their own commercials that advertised the same high quality goods offered whites. As consumers blacks were an important market, the equal of whites, if not superior to them.

Blacks exercised their freedom of choice in the marketplace, an option quite new to many raised under tenancy. The message sent to whites was that the black consumer dollar and black patronage could no longer be taken for granted. Action combined with words was the language used to send this message.

The white reply was that blacks held the reins of power. They dictated how black-appeal radio would develop, and what role it would play in their community. As Bert Ferguson said, "We have put ourselves at the disposal of the Negro community in every way we could think of."[38]

The irony was that in an age when integration was the watchword of the civil rights movement, black-appeal moved in the opposite direction. The concept of narrowcasting combined with the parameters of appealing to blacks effectively segregated radio. The reasons for this explain away the contradiction. The color line had exposed blacks to negatives for so long that separation was the only means of achieving a positive image. The color line also eliminated the black perspective from mainstream programming, news, and so forth. The best way to gain this racially focused insight was through a separate medium. Being equal, therefore, meant being separate.

By isolating black-appeal from mainstream programming and making the medium separate but truly equal, radio heightened the racial awareness of blacks. It placed blackness in a positive light. Black-appeal meant that the programming was strictly designed for blacks. Its very name intensified racial identification. So did the dialogue that developed between the people behind the microphone and those tuning in the shows.

Blacks considered the employment of black air personalities a prime criterion of black-appeal, though not an absolute one. Blacks behind the microphone provided the most audible proof of appeal, pride, and progress. It was good business to hire black air personalities but the benefits extended beyond selling. Black employees acted as channels of communication between the stations and the advertisers and the listening audience. They served as consultants in the development of programming and advertising. And they were strong spokespeople for blacks. What they said, how and why they said it had a strong impact on soul consciousness.

THE BLACK/BLACK DIALOGUE

As a class, black disc jockeys can be viewed as the first soul men and women. No, they did not necessarily invent soul. Nor did they overtly recognize the rise of soul consciousness. Rather they acted as producers and purveyors of soul consciousness, and were at the same time consumers of the new analog of the black subjective mind. Their position behind the microphone allowed their message to reach instantaneously hundreds of thousands of people at the same time. The mass impact they had on blacks cannot be refuted, but it has not yet been recognized, let alone analyzed.

A major aspect of the black radio personality's influence, at least in the initial years of black-appeal, has to do with who these personalities were. Even before appearing on the air, many had achieved success in varying fields. Jack L. Cooper was a well-known and respected entertainer and journalist who advocated morality, righteousness, and progress both in his performances and his writings. He was an archetypal New Negro of the 1920s who actually realized the dream of the Black Metropolis architects. Nat D. Williams was cut from the same mold but was more street-oriented. Unlike Cooper, Williams was college-educated and a teacher, but he too was an entertainer and a journalist. Both men were strongly motivated to support race progress in words and actions.

But what of others who entered radio? A composite profile drawn from information collected from interviews and various print sources indicates who the first- and, to a certain extent, second-generation black disc jockeys were.[39] The sampling totals 34 black air personalities, predominantly from Chicago and Memphis, but representing 15 cities from Brooklyn to Seattle. Cooper and Williams are included. Although this sample is not extensive or definitive, it is indicative. It illustrates the quality of personnel that radio attracted.

The most striking characteristic of those sampled is their high educational attainment. Nineteen had attended college or earned a degree. Mannie Mauldin, who worked for Jack L. Cooper, was a graduate of Northwestern University, as was Sam Evans of WGES.[40] Although data on WDIA personalities Maurice Hulbert and A. C. Williams are missing, their tenure as high school teachers indicates that they, too, probably attended college. In other words, 21 of the total 34 men had some higher education. This figure may be low, since data on the educational backgrounds of five others are missing.

Another dominant trait of these men is their experience in entertainment. Fifteen had performed professionally or been involved in musical productions.[41] Maurice Hulbert and A. C. Williams had both staged high school productions, and Jesse "Hot Rod" Carter of KFFA, Helena, Arkansas, was a former nightclub owner.[42]

Well-educated and well-qualified to entertain, the early black disc jockeys, by what they had already accomplished, signified progress. Most important in their role as race heroes was a prime requisite of radio employment: they could sell. No disc jockey lasted long on the air unless he or she forged a bond with the audience and gained its trust with respect to the products advertised. Success depended upon selling oneself as well as the goods of sponsors to the listeners. In black-appeal it also depended on selling race pride and progress. To a certain extent, the three were interconnected.

The intimate nature of radio communication, the one-to-one bond the voice behind the microphone creates with each individual listener, dictates a certain kind of style and a certain mind set. "If the jock is to relate to his audience he has to be part of his audience," says Robert Thomas of WDIA, Memphis. "The only way to be part of it is to mingle with them. You have to be where they are and they will show you where the happening spots are."[43]

Being with the audience provides exposure and keeps the radio personality in touch with popular tastes and trends. But there is another aspect of being part of the audience and relating to them. It involves, Thomas points out, "speaking their language." He explains one half of this process:

If you are there with them you pick up alot of tidbits of information unknowingly. It sticks with you and you are not aware of it until it's time for you to say something on the air, and you remember what you heard last night or last week that somebody said and you think, "This fits in right here. I can use this right here." At the same time your listener says, "Yeah, he's hip. He's what's happening 'cause he's speaking our language. You know, we were talkin' about this just the other day." To which another listener responds, "Yeah, I remember he was over here last week. We were rappin'."

The personal contact reinforced by the use of bits of information or of certain phrases touches a chord with the listener. It creates that special communication that McLuhan sees at the heart of radio's appeal. The man or woman behind the microphone and the listener are one. They have points in common. But Thomas adds a proviso to this communication link: "You should never talk at your audience. You need to talk to them. And there's a difference."[44]

The other half of this communication is the disc jockey's use of a phrase or rhyme that gains popularity among the audience and comes into common use. In this way the dialogue begins, and it continues with the playing of records popular among the listeners. The combination of speech and programming acts as the means by which a disc jockey gains a following and secures the trust and affection of the audience.

In the post–World War II era, this forging of bonds between the black radio personality and the black audience was something new, something not experienced before, except by those listening to Jack L. Cooper and a few isolated others. The early black disc jockeys were pioneers in radio. They had broken through the color line and were very visible and audible examples of race progress. They were heroes with a mission: to make radio appeal to blacks. By building an audience and selling sponsor products, black radio personalities insured that radio would appeal to blacks. The audience recognized this need and responded accordingly. Profits and progress were interconnected. One determined the success of the other.

Once this goal was reached, or even while achieving it, blacks labored to make radio work for blacks. They did this in two ways: as advocates of race progress and through community service. Advocating race progress involved a number of things, including keeping black-appeal programming on the air. It also entailed looking out for the black consumer, as noted above.[45]

Blacks demanded polite, respectful treatment at the stores where they purchased these advertised goods. Racial discrimination at the retail counter had long vexed black customers. Black disc jockeys such as Al Benson in Chicago provided this reassurance. His continual use of the phrase "And that's for sure" was "picked up by the Black community to symbolize something that was good *and for them,*" writes Norman Spaulding in his thesis on black radio in Chicago. "He often used this remark to assure his listeners that the product he was selling was for them and that the merchant would accept their patronage."[46]

In the late 1940s and 1950s, this question of patronage was important to blacks. Even after the Supreme Court outlawed segregation, the color line continued in effect. Blacks were not welcome everywhere. In Chicago, they often were refused service in downtown restaurants, and the treatment they received in certain stores hardly demonstrated concern for their patronage. The reassurance offered by Al Benson helped black consumers avoid embarrassment, anger, and frustration because it directed them to retailers who had demonstrated that they wanted black patronage by buying commercial time on the radio. Benson's "that's for sure" indicated that he was guaranteeing quality service and would redress any grievances, a claim he could make good on because of his selling power and the appeal he had in the community.

The black analog of the world was changed by this channeling into certain commercial outlets because it helped eliminate the negative aspects of shopping. The buyer protection that black disc jockeys provided—this was done to a certain extent through advertising reviews—expanded the concept of black-appeal from the radio dial to the marketplace. Just as black-appeal radio provided an alternative to network programming and its negativity so the same was true here. And the fact that blacks were exercising the power to insure quality goods and service symbolized another gain.

Similarly, the sales success of black disc jockeys indicated progress and competency. It reinforced the equality, if not superiority, of the black consumer market, along with the obviously greater sales ability of blacks in comparison to whites. Earlier in this book statistics were cited regarding a survey done in Chicago on listeners to Jack L. Cooper's shows.[47] It showed that 85.5 percent of those surveyed bought most or some of the products advertised on Cooper's shows. The *Sponsor* market tests cited above demonstrated, too, the power of black-appeal, of black radio personalities to sell.[48]

If black disc jockeys could sell their sponsors' products to black consumers then certainly they could sell race pride. Beyond the potent symbolism of just being on the air, their actions and words furthered black pride. The first step was cementing their status as race heroes through community service. By demonstrating real concern for community development and by producing results, the black personality's status in the community was enhanced. Service also expanded the bounds of radio far beyond that enjoyed by whites.

As has been true throughout this work, the starting point is Jack L. Cooper. His public service programming ventures aside, and beyond his strong crusade for black rights in radio, Cooper actively promoted community service. "He was interested in almost any proposition that black people came to him with, something to better the race," says Bob Roberts, Cooper's brother-in-law and long-time employee. "He would put time and money and energy into it. He helped sponsor several improvement organizations."[49]

Like many others in radio, Cooper focused his attention, though not exclusively, on youth. "He was instrumental in the South Side Boys' Club having many of the things that they had. He furnished money and time and helped youngsters with the baseball team," recalls Roberts.[50] A January 1, 1947, Chicago *Defender* article applauded Cooper's contributions to the boys' club, noting that "he has provided children with basketball and softball uniforms, bats, balls, and other sports items." He chaired the 1948 fund-raising drive for the South Side Boys' Club and extended his efforts to other youth organizations, such as the Morgan Park Youth Association. He received the Bud Billiken Award for his service to youth.[51]

Cooper became involved in a wide range of projects and was even cited for working in the World War II war bond drives. Governor Adlai Stevenson named him vice-chairman of the Interracial Commission. The Negro Labor Relations League declared February 21, 1948, Jack L. Cooper day for his contributions to labor, which included his direct action to have Dean's Milk hire black drivers. In 1949, the NAACP cited him for meritorious service.[52]

Outside radio Cooper was intimately involved with the betterment of the community he served. Inside radio he also worked for progress. Over one-third of his weekly air time, totaling 40 hours in 1948, was service-oriented. As the *Defender* explained, Cooper "is particularly interested in radio as a means of promoting the business and cultural life of the race."[53]

The above quotation is significant because it illuminates several facts. The first is that blacks recognized the value of using radio for race progress and did so actively. Second is the acknowledgement that the success of black-appeal itself served to promote the business aspects of race progress. Third is the role radio played in black cultural life, a topic that deserves scrutiny on its own and is covered in the next chapter. Finally, the conclusion that becomes readily apparent, especially when the service function is included, is that radio acted as a comprehensive vehicle for race pride and progress as used by such black radio personalities as Jack L. Cooper.

Whereas many of the actions of black radio personalities seemed tangential to the mounting postwar civil rights movement, some like Al Benson and Sam Evans in Chicago used the medium to further racial progress. Usually they functioned outside the normal political channels. As Norman Spaulding writes of Benson, "he never openly engaged in politics or endorsed political candidates."[54] Obviously, such advocacy would have been beyond the bounds of radio propriety. But this restriction did not apply to racial injustice and progress.

"I can truthfully say that I as an individual worked on my own. I was guaranteed freedom of speech. Nobody told me what to do or what to say," explains Benson. "What I said was never questioned. And I had a lot to say about the injustices that were going on back then." He claimed that the FBI was called in to guard WGES three or four times because of statements Benson had made over the air. "I remember the Harvey Clark incident," Benson told Norman Spaulding, "when the whites burned their apartment when they moved into Cicero [a Chicago suburb]. I spoke out about this on the radio and received numerous threats against my life." One evening Benson took a large party of blacks to Chicago's fashionable nightclub, the Chez Paree, and broke their policy of segregation. "I would do this with many other downtown and north-side clubs." In 1950, Benson received national attention by hiring an airplane to drop pamphlets protesting the treatment of blacks on the state capitol building in Jackson, Mississippi.[55]

Sam Evans worked with Benson at WGES and was second in popularity. He, too, had an active race posture. Evans's thrust, according to his widow, was to stress the positive aspects of being black.

Sam was in the Black history bag a long time before it became popular. . . . But more than that, Sam started talking about the things the Black folk were doing like it was something to be proud of. I think he was the first person to mention the expression 'soul food.' He would say over the air that he had some 'soul food' for dinner like ham hocks and beans, and greens. . . .[56]

What made Evans stand out was that this was a period when the black civil rights movement centered on integration: according to Evans' wife, on doing things that whites were doing. "But Sam brought it out into the open and made the audience feel as though Black things were good and that we should be proud of them."[57]

Each black radio personality had a different thrust. Cooper stressed community involvement and service, though he, too, was active in civil rights. Benson was more overt in his civil rights crusade while Evans emphasized the "black is good" theme that was so dominant in black-appeal radio. These three men are examples of how black disc jockeys used the radio to further the race on several fronts. Black disc jockeys were race heroes, not just because of their status behind the radio microphone but because of what they said and did.

In Memphis, the full-time status of black-appeal programming allowed WDIA a unique opportunity. A major factor in WDIA's rise was its service function. Again, the spark came from the station's community-minded black employees, many of whom came from the Memphis school system. "Working with young people is my mission in life," declared A. C. Williams, who also recognized the role service played in building the station. "And it's the most important thing we do in the way of public relations at WDIA. These kids remain our most faithful followers."[58] Whether it was presenting "Teen Town Singers," which gave black youth the chance to appear and perform on the air, or providing uniforms for black little league teams, or funding buses for black handicapped children so they could go to school, WDIA cultivated its listening audience by serving them.

The service WDIA offered expanded black consciousness not only for the reasons cited above in connection with Cooper, Benson, and Evans, but because blacks recognized that whites were involved in this service. The white-owned and operated station itself served the black community, becoming part of it. In becoming an integral part of black Memphis, WDIA added a new component to the black analog of life.

Bob Roberts provided some very poignant and striking comments on the black situation and the black radio personality as race hero. Asked if he thought Cooper was a race hero, Roberts replied:

He never thought of himself as a race hero but he was. He was because his influence was along racial lines. Because first and foremost in black people's minds especially years ago was, "I am black. What am I limited to? What can I do? How can I overcome this racial thing because it's something that you're born with and you live with." Yes, Jack Cooper was a race hero.[59]

Roberts's comments put this entire chapter into perspective. Black consciousness was based upon three essential facts: being black, facing limits, and overcoming the limits that one was born with. The very fact of being born black placed people at a disadvantage. Their skin color and ethnicity cast them in an inferior light, thus depriving them of the advantages of whites. At the same time, the democratic credo of the United States provided for equal opportunity for all and the right to life, liberty, and the pursuit of happiness, along with other rights under the law. Blacks did not enjoy many of these rights because of legal restrictions and racial etiquette, that is, racism.

The black world was proscribed by the color line. There were two Americas: one for whites and one for blacks. Dividing these worlds was the doctrine of separate but equal, which translated into separate but unequal and decidedly inferior for blacks. Even a simple thing like appealing radio programming was long denied blacks. The struggle to overcome the limitations imposed on them centered on removing the differences between the two worlds so that equality and integration could be achieved. At least this was the thrust of the civil rights movement during and after World War II. As black life changed and progress was made, the yawning racial gap became narrower. Limits were being overcome.

The widespread appearance of radio programming for blacks was one indicator of positive change. Radio posited a different racial consciousness that reflected and accentuated the changing black condition. New terms were added to the black lexicon: recognition; equality; blackness as a positive; and freedom of choice.

Using radio as the example, the profound alteration in the black consciousness is illustrated. Blacks came to share the radio dial with whites. They were thus recognized as equals by the medium. The concept of black-appeal demanded replacement of the negative blackface image with one more positive. Similarly, the positive aspects of race were reinforced by the very appearance of racially designed programming. Black-appeal also gave blacks freedom of choice. It did not eliminate the negative from life or from radio, but it did provide an alternative, a means to shut out the negative and accentuate the positive. All one had to do was switch the dial and a new world was brought into being.

The new world radio created for blacks was based on two very prominent features. Black men and women behind the microphone served as symbols of progress and actively espoused this progress in words and actions. Their manner and their actions helped define a new black style. As Gloria Evans said of her husband and Al Benson, "One thing that I can say is that neither Benson or Sam were ever Uncle Toms. They might have sounded black, but there was nothing in their manner on the air or off the air that was Uncle Tom." [60] The same was true of Jack Cooper, Nat Williams, Robert Thomas, and all the other black-appeal radio personalities.

The second feature was programming. It adhered to the same dictates and the same thrust that the black personalities did. Most important, radio changed black culture, bringing to the forefront new forms of expression more in tune with the changing situation of the black community. This alteration is graphically shown in the decline of the blues and the rise of soul music examined in the following chapter.

NOTES

1. Julian Jaynes, *The Origins of Consciousness in the Breakdown of the Bicameral Mind* (Boston: Houghton Mifflin Company, 1976), p. 50.

2. *The Compact Edition of the Oxford English Dictionary*, vol. 1, p. 522.

3. Jaynes, *Origins of Consciousness*, pp. 54–55.

4. Interview, Joseph F. Ellis, Jr.

5. Dempsey Travis in Studs Terkel, *"The Good War": An Oral History of World War Two* (New York: Pantheon Books, 1984), p. 151.

6. Ibid., pp. 152–57.

7. "Away from the Blues," *Newsweek*, vol. 42 (January 18, 1954), p. 51.

8. Peter F. Drucker, *Management: Tasks, Responsibilities, Practices* (New York: Harper & Row, Publishers, 1973), p. 61.

9. Interview, Nat D. Williams.

10. "Negro Radio: 200-Plus Special Stations—More Coming," p. 79.

11. "The Negro Market: $15,000,000,000," p. 30.

12. "Mr. Sponsor Asks . . .," p. 42.

13. Ibid.

14. "Selling to Negroes: Don't Talk Down," *Sponsor*, vol. 6, no. 15 (July 28, 1952), p. 37.

15. "4. Tips on How to Get the Most out of Negro Radio," *Sponsor,* vol. 7, no. 17 (August 24, 1953), p. 76.

16. Ibid., p. 77. A significant exception in Chicago was white disc jockey Marty Faye who aired shows on the jazz-oriented station WAAF for over 20 years beginning in 1952. James Maloney was another white disc jockey who gained black acceptance in Chicago. Spaulding, "Black-Oriented Radio in Chicago," pp. 60, 64–65.

17. Interviews, B. B. King; Richard Stams.

18. "Tips on Selling via Negro Radio," *Sponsor,* vol. 8, no. 19 (September 20, 1954), p. 147.

19. "Negro Radio Comes of Age," *Sponsor,* vol. 8, no. 19 (September 20, 1954), p. 149.

20. "2. Negro Radio: Keystone of Community Life," *Sponsor,* vol. 7, no. 17 (August 24, 1953), pp. 78–79.

21. "Negro Radio Comes of Age," p. 149.

22. Ibid.

23. Interview, Richard Stams.

24. "Negro Radio Comes of Age," p. 149.

25. "Selling to Negroes: Don't Talk Down," p. 37.

26. "1. The Negro Market: $15 Billion Annually," p. 67.

27. "4. Tips on How to Get the Most out of Negro Radio," p. 56.

28. "Tips on Selling via Negro Radio," p. 56.

29. Ibid.

30. Ibid.; "4. Tips on How to Get the Most out of Negro Radio," p. 76.

31. "Tips on Selling via Negro Radio," p. 56.

32. Ibid.

33. Interview, Nat D. Williams.

34. "The Negro Market: $15,000,000,000 to Spend," p. 30.

35. Ibid.

36. "Negro Radio: 200-Plus Special Stations," pp. 78, 161.

37. Ibid.

38. Interviews, Gertrude Cooper, Nat D. Williams, Robert Thomas; "Disc Jockeys," pp. 44–49; Spaulding, "Black-Oriented Radio in Chicago," passim.

39. Spaulding, "Black-Oriented Radio in Chicago," pp. 32, 47.

40. Interviews, Gertrude Cooper, Nat D. Williams, Robert Thomas, Rufus Thomas; "Disc Jockeys," pp. 44–49; Spaulding, "Black-Oriented Radio in Chicago," passim.

41. Interview, Robert Thomas; Jesse "Hot Rod" Carter.

42. Interview, Robert Thomas.

43. Ibid.

44. Ibid.

45. Spaulding, "Black-Oriented Radio in Chicago," p. 37.

46. See Chapter 4, p. 134.

47. Advertising circular, Jack L. Cooper Radio Presentations (1948). JLC Files.

48. See Chapter 4.

49. Interview, Bob Roberts.

50. Ibid.

51. Undated Chicago *Defender* article, JLC Files.

52. Chicago *Defender,* May 28, 1949, JLC Files.

53. Undated Chicago *Defender* article, JLC Files.

54. Spaulding, "Black-Oriented Radio in Chicago," p. 39.
55. Ibid., pp. 43, 44.
56. Ibid., p. 47.
57. Ibid.
58. "Goodwill at Work: WDIA."
59. Interview, Bob Roberts.
60. Spaulding, "Black-Oriented Radio in Chicago," p. 48.

8

BLUES TO SOUL

"I don't think anything stays the same except change, and that wouldn't be if it weren't for the name, change," commented B. B. King following a 1976 performance in Nashville, Tennessee. "I think that it should change because people today don't think as they did when I was a kid. It's quite a bit different from then until now."[1]

Born Riley King in a sharecropper cabin outside Itta Bena, Mississippi, on September 16, 1925, B. B. King is recognized as the foremost bluesman of the post–World War II era. Between 1950 and 1971, he had 18 top ten hits on the Rhythm and Blues record charts. Four of his songs cracked the top 50 on the pop charts, including "The Thrill is Gone," which hit number 15 in 1970. A multiple Grammy Award winner with over 50 albums to his credit, King performs regularly in Las Vegas and Lake Tahoe and on "The Tonight Show." Yet he retains a large following in the black community.[2] He is perhaps the first black blues singer to attain true crossover status to white audiences while maintaining black appeal.

Though his entertainment career and phenomenal success are unique, King's experience mirrors that of hundreds of thousands of other blacks born in rural poverty who migrated to the city. They, too, have lived through deep-rooted, revolutionary change, particularly in the post–World War II era, that has profoundly altered their consciousness and their culture.

A prime example is the shift in terms blacks use in referring to themselves. "Look how we went from 'nigger' to 'colored.' And then to 'Negro.' And now 'black,' " said soul singer James Brown, putting this name-change business into perspective.

A colored is a frightened to death Afro-American. A Negro is one who makes it in the system, and he wants to be white. A nigger, he's loud and boisterous, wants to be seen. Nobody likes a nigger. A black man has pride. He wants to build, he wants to make his race mean something. Wants to have culture and art forms. And he's not prejudiced. I am a black American man.[3]

Nat D. Williams endorsed James Brown's assertion regarding names, noting, "We used to refer to Negroes. We don't use the word Negro too much now. We say black."[4] Negro, as Brown said, is now considered a somewhat derogatory term harkening back to an earlier era when the word *black* held greater opprobrium. Blues singer Johnny Shines, who was born in Mississippi in 1915, recalled, "We was taught if you was Black, you was wrong. This got to the place where we would put all different kinds of stuff on our faces, trying to lighten our skin. We hated Black."[5] By contrast, soul singer James Brown touched a common nerve with his highly popular and influential 1968 song, "Say It Loud—I'm Black and I'm Proud."[6]

The ramifications of change are evident culturally, too. The irony of B. B. King's success is that it came during a period when blues was on the decline, when soul music was germinating and spreading over the black neighborhoods. As a result, King found himself crusading for the music he loved. "I really began to fight for the blues. The things people used to say about those I thought of as the greats in the business, the blues singers, used to hurt me." To King it seemed that in trying to progress blacks "just didn't want to be associated with the blues, because it was something still back *there*."[7]

THE DECLINE OF THE BLUES

One who disassociated himself from blues culture was soul singer Isaac Hayes. "As a kid in the fifties I was taught to be *ashamed* of the blues," Hayes recalled. "We thought of it as plantation darkie stuff. And that was miles away from where *we* wanted to be."[8] The image of the blues revolved around its rural, farm origins. When the migrants went to the city, they left this music behind in the country. As late as 1976, blues guitarist Sammy Lawhorn who had no rural background still said, "The Negro's blues is blues from the cotton patch."[9]

No matter what the evolving reality of blues was, for Isaac Hayes and his generation *soul* became both the music of choice and the term denoting the black, not the Negro, experience.[10]

Time and change played a crucial role in the decline of blues and the rise of soul.[11] In the words of disc jockey Reggie Lavong of WWRL, New York, "Soul music is an expression of how we feel today, blues was how we felt yesterday.''[12] Perhaps the most important reason behind these feelings lies in the opposing messages of the two music forms.

Blues scholar Dave Evans summed up its message: "blues simply reflect an attitude that despite all of one's efforts things are not likely to get better in the long run.''[13] This philosophy accurately reflected life on the tenant plantation, and to a lesser extent in the inner city ghetto during the age of segregation between 1890 and 1954. The role of the blues was to provide release from life's frustrations.

During a 1960 interview with Mississippi farmworker-blues singer Robert Curtis Smith, British blues expert Paul Oliver learned first-hand about blues, life and release in song. "The most reason I sing the blues is because most things in my life and coming up was so difficult, it seemed like I had a harder time than most people," Smith explained. He sang the blues because it "is the only thing that gives me relief when it seems like everything go wrong.''[14]

Following this line of thought, Mississippi farmer Jack Owens succinctly stated the blues philosophy. "I ain't going no higher, no lower down," he sang for Dave Evans.[15] Not surprisingly, this status quo message fell on deaf ears during the upwardly mobile 1940s and 1950s. Isaac Hayes bluntly expressed the feelings of his generation when he said, "The blues weren't going to help you advance." Motown soul singer Smokey Robinson was even more disparaging, declaring that "The blues is torment or some degrading type of thing.''[16]

In addition, blues style was considered passé by younger blacks, indicating another reason for decline: generational change. Perhaps the most lyrical and durable of soul singer-composers, with a career spanning three decades, Smokey Robinson seldom listened to his mother's records while growing up in Detroit in the 1950s.

More convincing proof of the switch in generational taste came from folklorist William Ferris. In the early 1960s, while researching blues in the Mississippi delta, Ferris discovered that "blues records are appreciated by adults in their thirties and older." In Leland, teenager Earlier Mae Thomas told Ferris, "I'm not just talking about my daddy's music, but it's *old folk's* music. . . . Soul music is more popular and that's mostly what the teenagers dig. The old folks dig blues to dance off but I can't.''[17]

WDIA disc jockey Robert Thomas experienced this aversion to blues early in his career. In the mid-1950s he noticed that the teenagers preferred the rich, complex group vocal harmonies and lush band accompaniment of the rhythm and blues groups like the Eldorados and the Spaniels. "You start playin' blues and the youngsters would call up and ask when would you play some music," he recalled. "Youngsters couldn't relate to blues. And I think mainly the reason is they were more music-minded. Blues was just simple. They used a simple instrument, maybe a guitar and a guitar wasn't popular then with youngsters as it has become now."

Thomas noted that the blues players' lack of sophistication extended into the performance realm. "Most of the blues singers weren't polished musicians. The blues groups weren't polished musicians and didn't really play what we call music," Thomas said. "It was just plunkey-plunk and then somebody sing a verse and that turned the youngsters off." [18]

Neither Sonny Boy Williamson nor B. B. King's music was this simple or old-time, but since the rejection of blues was multifaceted, focusing on one aspect can be misleading. The connection of blues with an older generation on a visceral level related to listening pleasure and danceability. But on a deeper level there was a strong resentment of the blues among the black youth coming of age after World War II. They rejected the music not only because it appealed to their parents but because its origins and message were alien.

Yet the essence of both words, their intrinsic meaning and expression in song, their role in the black community, are the same. Speaking of blues, singer James Cotton says, "It's a feeling you have to have." [19] Wilson Pickett, a top soul artist of the 1960s, commented that "Soul ain't nothing but a feeling." [20] In either case, the feeling itself is rooted in deep expression of emotion. Cotton continues, "When I hear the blues I think it has happened to somebody somewhere down the line. They're singing what they feel and they mean it." [21] Milt Jackson, a jazz vibraphonist who recorded "Plenty, Plenty Soul" in 1957 echoed Cotton's description, but the application was different. Soul "is what comes from within; it's what happens when the inner part of you comes out." [22]

The similarities between blues and soul regarding the meaning of the words and their function as vehicles of cultural expression through music are obvious. And the fact that both achieved great commercial success certainly influenced their popularity and longevity. Blues, as has been shown above, was the black-appeal spearhead in the publishing of black music on paper, recording black music on disc, and airing black-appeal programming on radio. It is a catchall term originally denoting a specific style of folk music that was swiftly applied to various forms of music—black-appeal, black crossover, and white—that arose out of the original twelve-bar, three-chord blues core. Accepted and known by blacks and whites, blues provided the common entertainment ground upon which black-appeal media as business ventures were launched.

Classic blue singers such as Lovie Austin and Ethel Waters were Jack L. Cooper's programming favorites in his first years on the air. Austin even appeared on one of his shows. In Helena, the blues of Sonny Boy Williamson was *the* music of "King Biscuit Time." Later shows on KFFA also mined blues popularity in the locale, making the Arkansas city a blues center. In Memphis, Nat D. Williams requested blues records to play on his pioneer black-appeal show on WDIA. B. B. King's blues show on the same station was the first black-appeal program sponsored by Lucky Strike cigarettes.

Soul music followed a similar course of commercial development, building on the foundation laid by the blues in record and radio industries. It, too, is a catchall term describing various musical forms delineated by time and the synthesis of rhythm and blues, popular music, big band jazz, and gospel elements. Like blues, soul has become integrated into the American mainstream on both sides of the color line. Compelling reminders of this fact are seen and heard on television everyday. In 1987, the Queen of Soul, Aretha Franklin, hawked gasoline on television commercials. The 1985 television summer season included a 60-minute, prime time Friday evening music show produced by Motown, a major purveyor of soul music. And, of course, there are the white, or blue-eyed soul, musicians, ranging from the Righteous Brothers of the 1960s to the Average White Band of the 1970s to Boy George and Culture Club in the 1980s.

Still, the world of the blues and the world of soul differed vastly both in the minds of blacks and in reality. They are separate chapters in an experiential and musical continuum that perpetuated the traditional roles played by music in black communities. The change in name and attitude reflected the deep alteration in black life during the twentieth century.

Put in the context of Afro-American history, the blues is black folk music of the segregation era, whereas soul is black popular music of the years of integration, at least constitutionally mandated if not realized, and later black power. Blues is the music of cotton fields and plantations, of tenant farmers and unskilled city workers—of the lower classes. Soul is the music of the city and of workers of all classes. Blues is the expression of an individual voicing community themes and concerns. Soul is the community expression of the group. Blues is the devil's music situated on the secular side of life, while soul is more a popular musical adaptation of gospel that straddles the line between secular and sacred in the black community. Blues is the music of despair and acceptance; soul is the music of inspiration. As a musical form, blues is low-down and dirty, and soul is clean.

The decline of blues and the rise of soul focus on time, place, and image revolving around differences in origins, style, and message. A strong contributing factor was the increasing importance radio played in determining music popularity. Lack of airplay could literally kill a record. Some blues singers claim this was what killed the blues but that explanation skews the facts.[23]

THE RISE OF SOUL

Paul Oliver discovered the change in black attitudes in 1960 while talking to Alice Moore, a young black civil rights worker. She responded angrily to Oliver's suggestion that she was related to a blues singer of the same name. "I'm not an avid fan of blues singer or blues. As a Negro, I think that we have been stereotyped—that all Negroes like blues," she said. "I think that you might take a look at the noted Negro musicians, and those that have reached fame and fortune are not necessarily blues singers; I think the great majority are not." Moore concluded her outburst with this claim: "Among my friends I don't think I know of anyone who is a fan of . . . blues."[24]

Alice Moore's assumption that blacks had been stereotyped as blues lovers identifies another possible misconception: that all black music was similarly typed as blues. The term is hardly all encompassing. For one thing it leaves out the religious side of black song. Second it does not describe the totally new, vocally oriented music of teenagers who sang a capella (without musical accompaniment) on city street corners. Third, it omits the crossover, popular music of such groups as the Mills Brothers and the Ink Spots. Last, big band jazz played by whites and blacks, which achieved, perhaps, the first integration of the races in popular music performance, is left out. These four sources melded together to form soul music and, while even the blues contributed to soul, the major thrust was outside the blues tradition.

A 1951 survey by a North Carolina radio station showed religious music's popularity in the black community. Of the 2,000 black families polled, 736 respondents, over one in three, cast their vote for sacred music over the next choice, blues, which received 459 votes.[25]

In every black-appeal example studied in these pages the popularity and appeal of gospel, of all sacred music, in the black community is shown. During the 1930s Jack L. Cooper's programming mainstays were remote airings of church services, many of which featured choirs and musical accompaniment for gospel songs. By the late 1940s, his WSBC programming schedule included either church services or religious music shows Sunday through Saturday. Almost one in every three hours of Cooper's airtime on this station was devoted to such shows.[26]

In Memphis, too, sacred music was a programming mainstay. At WHBQ, Bob Alburty's first black-appeal effort was airing the services of a local church. Music, most likely, was featured. The LeMoyne College chorus sang spirituals on their 30-minute weekly show and there were other religious programs.[27] WDIA also fielded a strong religious segment. Every morning the station went on the air with gospel music. During the day at selected times live and recorded religious music was played. Sunday was almost exclusively devoted to religion, including a musical segment with the LeMoyne College chorus.[28] In Helena on KFFA where black-appeal was a minor programming aspect, Sunday featured religious shows for blacks.[29]

The narrowcasts of sacred music, church services, and other religious shows comprised one-third of the foundation upon which black-appeal radio was built. Popular music, especially blues in the formative years, and the information/ service sectors were the other two-thirds. Black churches were good customers for radio stations. They signed long-term contracts. Alburty signed his first church up for one year. Jack L. Cooper's church customers provided essential funding during his lean years. Most important, religion was a stable programming force much less affected by the trends that made other ventures wax and wane in popularity. It was not the hook that initially attracted listeners so much as the bait that kept a substantial number listening, and increasingly this bait was gospel music.

Gospel's formative years paralleled those of black-appeal radio and for that matter largely overlapped those of soul music. All three developed and reached peaks of popular acceptance and creativity between the 1940s and 1960s. In part, radio acted as the medium of exposure that brought religious and secular music together. Gospel singer Cissy Houston, a member of the Sweet Inspirations, commented on this fertile relationship: "You started to hear gospel in black popular music in the mid-fifties because that's what was going on in black *life*." This statement alone says much about gospel's role in the black community. "Everybody was getting crazy that R and B was making it big, crossing over for whites and all," she continues. "But gospel stations were just as exciting to listen to. Gospel was making folks jump in a big way."[30]

Houston's comments indicate some very important aspects of soul music. The obvious point is that gospel exerted as great an influence as the black popular—and secular—music known as R and B (rhythm and blues). Second is that the radio was featuring both types of music prominently, thereby promoting musical synthesis. Last is the crossover effect. In an era of integration, the 1950s, the ability of black music to cross over to white audiences without losing its racial essence implied much progress. Both black gospel and rhythm and blues had achieved this goal.

Any discussion of soul music's origins must begin with gospel. It stands as a pivotal point in a black music continuum that historian Lawrence Levine traces back to slavery but that has its beginnings in Africa. In *Black Culture and Black Consciousness,* Levine writes, "The antebellum songs of the praise house and field strongly influenced the work songs, blues, and jazz of the postbellum years which were incorporated into the gospel song that in turn helped shape the secular rhythm and blues, jazz, and soul music of the post World War II era."[31]

An important aspect of this continuum was the mixing of religious and secular music. In the black community a very real line exists between worldly and sacred music. The two are not supposed to mix. One sings for the Lord or one does not. It is that simple in theory.[32] In practice this line is continually crossed, as the development of gospel shows.

Though its roots date back before World War I, gospel is largely the creation of Thomas A. Dorsey, the man who coined its name. The son of a Baptist minister, Dorsey was born in 1896 in Georgia. He was a musical child prodigy whose early career was in blues and ragtime. In 1921 Dorsey was saved at a Baptist convention. During the 1920s, he continued his popular career as "Georgia Tom" but began writing religious songs. His career in popular entertainment reached its zenith in 1928 when he cowrote and recorded with guitarist Tampa Red a ribald song "It's Tight Like That." One year later, he forsook a popular career for one in gospel, but he never forgot his musical roots. "I was a blues singer and I carried that with me into the gospel songs," he explained. Blues influenced his piano playing and his composing, as did other styles of popular music. "I started putting a little of the beat into gospel that we had in jazz. I also put in what we call the riff, or repetitive (rhythmic) phrases.''

Though the music itself was influenced by blues, the inspiration for and the message of gospel was the opposite of that of the blues. Dorsey's creation was a child of the hard times of the 1930s and his goal was to give blacks "something to lift them out of that Depression." Gospel was intended, Dorsey says, "to strike a happy medium for the downtrodden. This music lifted people out of the muck and mire of poverty and loneliness, of being broke, and gave them some kind of hope anyway." He accentuates the positive feel and message: "Make it anything but good news, and it ceases to be gospel."[33]

The word *gospel* reinforces this "good news" theme. Derived from the Old English word *godspell* meaning "good tidings," the term mistakenly but more appropriately became identified with *God* rather than *good*. The *d* was dropped and the word *gospel* came to mean, among other things, "the glad tidings (of the kingdom of God) announced to the world by Jesus Christ."[34] This definition clearly applies to gospel music sung in church by Christians. The connection is strengthened by the dominance of New Testament themes in the lyrics and the promise of a better life to come, if not in this world then in the next.

Gospel lyrics stress the certainty of progress, of betterment. Lawrence Levine cites several examples including: "There's a crown at the end of the road" and "There'll be joy on tomorrow."[35] Unlike blues, which seemed mired in the past, gospel spoke only to the present and the future. There was no looking back. And the future will be glorious, say the gospel songs.[36]

The first gospel queen, Mahalia Jackson, commented on the message and philosophy of gospel, using the blues for contrast: "Blues are the songs of despair, but gospel songs are the songs of hope." Singing gospel instills "a feeling that there is a cure for what's wrong. It always gives me joy to sing gospel songs. I feel better right away."[37]

The positive and progressive message of gospel was born out by the real gains blacks experienced following World War II, of which black-appeal radio was a potent symbol. The instant catharsis that singing gospel brought was enhanced by radio's ability to communicate this message instantaneously to millions of blacks throughout the United States. Both these factors contributed to the present and future orientation of soul, as succinctly stated by the godfather of soul, James Brown: "Where I been is not where I am, no thank you."[38] It is who you are now, not where you come from or where you were in the past that defines the soul philosophy. It does not mean forgetting, it means not dwelling on the past.

Gospel's message is only half of its contribution to soul. The other half relates to the expression of this philosophy in song, to the style of performance. Above all else, gospel is the music of human voices singing in unison. The work of Rebert H. Harris exemplifies this emphasis on the human voice and the group and its influence on soul music's performance style.

Harris founded the Soul Stirrers during the formative years of gospel, the

1930s. The very name of the group reveals a soul music connection. Harris innovated two practices that profoundly affected vocal style and group composition. He claimed to be the first to use falsetto, long a blues performance trademark, in gospel group singing. This technique, which can be traced back to Africa, involves artificially raising one's voice to a higher register. He also changed the organization of the group by increasing the number of members from the standard gospel quartet. Harris moved the lead singer out in front of the group and then added a fifth member as second lead. This change altered the mode of performance from a strict group sound punctuated by brief solos to ones in which the lead singer was featured more prominently while at the same time retaining the four-part harmony.[39] Both these changes became regular stylistic features of soul, as evidenced in the music of the Temptations and Smokey Robinson and the Miracles, to name just two groups.

Harris's innovations underscored the vocal freedom that was an integral part first of gospel and later of soul. During an interview, composer Don Covay told writer Gerri Hirshey that soul implied total vocal freedom for the singer. Soul singer Wilson Pickett replied, "And that brings you right back to gospel."[40]

Covay's reference to total vocal freedom did not mean lack of control nor did it imply freeing one's voice from the melody or harmony of a song. It referred to the singer's ability to use the human voice as an instrument, stretching it to its physical and musical limits within the confines of the music to express honest, deep emotions. Descriptions of the singing of Sam Cooke, a top artist of the 1950s and early 1960s, show how this freedom was manifested in performance.

"Lost in a melody," writes Gerri Hirshey, "[Sam] had a way of slapping his thigh to bring himself back to the beat." In the words of Luigi Creatura, who coproduced many of Cooke's records:

You'd be listening intently, and on a certain note, he might come in on a place you initially thought was wrong. You'd look up through the glass and realize it was only the beginning. And he was gonna run, coming up to the note you're looking for on your chart. He'd reverse things, work changes you could never expect. But they always worked.[41]

Cooke's expressive vocals were predicated, the singer explained, on "making the audience feel what you feel." He traced the forging of this emotional bond back to the church. "If you have ever attended Baptist service, you well know what I mean. You have to stir up the emotion of the congregation and literally lift them from their chairs. To do this, you have to muster all the sincerity in your body and project it to every solitary person in the room."[42]

Sam Cooke was a cool performer whose emotionalism was not shown "in shouting or dynamic crying" as is typical of singers such as James Brown, Jackie Wilson, and Wilson Pickett. Instead, writes Arnold Shaw in *Honkers and Shouters,* he "seduced" his audience, displaying "a deep-down, gospel intensity—the intensity of a man so possessed by his feelings that his listeners could not help sharing them."[43]

Cooke strengthened the sharing between performer and audience by using certain vocal trademarks to reassure the audience that sacred or secular, group member or solo artist, he was still Sam Cooke. "Oh, we all heard it. In a lot of pop stuff he'd give you the high sign," explains singer Solomon Burke. Cooke would yodel or use some other vocal trademark that, "if you knew Sam from gospel, it was him saying, 'Hey, it's me.' "[44]

In the 1950s and 1960s—in fact until his untimely death in 1963—Sam Cooke was the archetypal soul star. He was born in Clarksdale, Mississippi, in 1931, the son of a preacher. His family migrated to Chicago, where Cooke began singing in church. While still in high school, he joined a gospel group called the Highway QCs. At the age of 20, in 1951, R. H. Harris recruited Cooke for the Soul Stirrers and he became an overnight gospel star. In 1956 Cooke switched to pop music with equal success among blacks and whites.[45]

His lean, sensual body and good looks combined with a sophisticated, and urbane yet warm, engaging manner made Sam Cooke an idol of black teens in the 1950s and 1960s. He epitomized the success story of the rural migrant making it big in the city. He was cool and he lived in the present, a man who had it all and had it his way. Isaac Hayes summed up this consummate star's appeal: "What was so important was that he was so sophisticated."[46] The fact that the soul singer drove a Ferrari certainly helped his image among car-conscious young blacks—and whites. For Cooke crossed over to white audiences without losing his black following, and his racial identity—his soul.

Success came to Sam Cooke not because of his singing talent but because he attended to business. He founded Sar/Derby Records to gain greater control over his career and to maximize his financial return. "Control was very important to Sam," Luigi Creatura said. "He was always looking for investments. . . . His record company was in the black from the start."[47]

What lay behind the appeal and stardom of this first soul king? The trail leads back to his roots in the church and gospel and indicates a major factor in gospel's influence on soul. Basically it provided a training ground for young performers, teaching them how to sing. Especially in the 1940s and 1950s, religious music was a major industry in the black community. The large radio airplay gospel commanded after World War II was basically a continuation of the situation in the 1920s and 1930s when recorded sermons and religious music were mainstays of race record catalogs. Those looking for a career opportunity beyond the bounds dictated by the color line could find it in gospel. The churches also provided the training ground for a number of blues singers, including Muddy Waters and B. B. King.[48]

The list of soul singers who started in church is even more impressive. Ray Charles recalls that as a boy growing up in Greenville, Florida, he "went to church *every* Sunday."[49] Years later, on November 19, 1954, Atlantic Records cut a disc by Ray Charles called "I Got a Woman" that fused "deep-chorded, churchy piano, a strong band, and a vocal that bounced between the bedroom and the blessed." It is considered the first soul song, as Atlantic Records co-founder Jerry Wexler explains. "Ray had the guts and the genius . . . to sing and play exactly what he *felt*. It's as simple as that. But in 1954, coming from a black man, that was a *revolution*. Later they called it soul."[50]

Wexler obviously overstates his case: blues singers had been singing and playing what they felt for decades. But there was a sharp difference in Ray Charles's music, and that was the gospel connection shown by blatant display of religious feeling in secular song. Though there were previous examples of this combination, they seem never to have captured the public's imagination as Ray Charles did. Nor did they prove as controversial. "I got a lot of criticism from the churches," Charles recalls, "and from musicians, too."[51] He also got a lot of airplay on the radio. In fact, the song was recorded in an Atlanta radio station and became his first number one hit.

The Ray Charles example gives credence to writer Charlie Gillette's claim that stylistically soul music is "the use of gospel singing style in popular music." Gillette, however, contends that gospel and religious feeling in secular music antedates both Charles's record and Sam Cooke's switch to pop music. He traces the first example of this crossover to 1950, "when a New York gospel singing instructor, Billy Ward, formed a rhythm and blues group, the Dominoes, with four of his students."[52] The group's leader was Clyde Mc-Phatter.

The son of a Baptist preacher, McPhatter's mother played the church organ. At the age of five Clyde was singing in the church choir. In high school he formed his first professional gospel quartet, the Mount Lebanon Singers. In 1950 he went pop and enjoyed success throughout the 1950s with various groups and as a solo performer.[53]

When McPhatter left the Dominoes his replacement was Jackie Wilson, who followed a similar career path. "I never studied music," he explained. "Didn't like instruments. But I sang in church . . . spirituals and gospel. Gave me good feelings."[54]

Consciously and unconsciously, gospel influenced black popular song as the experiences of these singers show. Perhaps the crowning comment came from Jerry Wexler, the white man who cofounded Atlantic Records, the label that helped put R and B as well as soul on disc. "I don't think there's much question that 'rhythm and blues' is a term that I coined when I was working at *Billboard*," he claims. "If I understood then what I know now, I would have called it rhythm and gospel."[55] Whether Wexler coined the term *rhythm and blues* is unimportant. What he and Gillette do is to identify rhythm and blues as the other major musical influence on soul.

Rhythm and blues is a catchall term that the music industry applied to black popular music after World War II. It replaced the worn and no longer relevant race records nickname. But *rhythm and blues* implies a certain style of music in which the accent was on rhythm, the beat, and therefore danceability. Arnold Shaw defines it as "good-time dance music" of the ghetto. He calls it "group and joy music" sung to "combo accompaniment and electrified instruments." Shaw also points out that R and B benefited from such technological developments as electrified instruments but more important, recording tape. It thrived because blacks enjoyed greater purchasing power and because it expressed the new freedom blacks experienced after World War II, "hemmed in though that freedom was by ghettos."[56]

R and B represents a transitional phase in black music that culminated in soul.[57] In one sense the only difference between the two was time and attitude. Musically rhythm and blues differs little from soul, but it appeared a few years before the term *soul* became current and before black popular music served as an expression of the new black consciousness.

Like gospel, rhythm and blues provided a training ground for young singers to practice their art. Typically, the sacred/secular chasm was bridged by these teenagers, producing the logical musical synthesis evident not only in soul but in gospel and R and B as well. For instance, Sam Cooke sang in church and on Chicago street corners. So did another early soul star, Ben E. King, who achieved fame as lead singer of the Drifters, a group he joined in 1959, and as a solo artist. His hits included "Spanish Harlem" and "Stand By Me." The latter enjoyed a new vogue of popularity in the mid-1980s.

Born in Henderson, North Carolina, King moved to Harlem and grew up there in the 1950s. He heard rhythm and blues on records and on the radio. "R and B was on the air nationally," he says, but for him "it all got started as a *neighborhood* thing. And if you came up, like so many of us did, from the South, singing could help you get it together. Turn you into a city boy, you know."

Like many other black teenagers at that time, King divided his singing between two groups. "I sang with an R and B one, but I stayed with the gospel. I mean, for us it was no blasphemy, that kind of garbage. For me the feeling I got was the same. If it was an old church song . . . or a new hit you'd been learning off the records, you took a song and made it your own."[58] An important point on the role of media, particularly the relationship between records and radio, is illustrated by King's comments. Because recorded music was the dominant programming for many black stations, and of course white music-oriented ones, too, radio played a pivotal role in determining the success of a record and therefore a song. It provided the needed exposure for introducing the music to teenagers such as Ben E. King. Records allowed them to learn the songs and to develop their styles through improvisation.

The process of reworking the songs was a group effort, one that emphasized solidarity and being in tune with one another. "And your buddies," King continues, "the guys who did it with you, they were your *heart*. You could get so in tune it seemed you all had but one heart between you. Man you knew when all the other guys were gonna *breathe*." Looking back, King told Gerri Hirshey that the street corner days were his best. "But listen, it's just real hard to describe now the feeling a quartet gave you. You never felt alone, is all."[59]

Singing in a group brought several rewards, including easing the assimilation to urban life. It instilled a feeling of fellowship, of being together. The loneliness of the blues singer lamenting his plight was replaced by the joy and celebration of creating something with others. There was also the emotional involvement that occurred because, as King put it, "it was a human voice you picked up on."[60] Finally there was the feeling of accomplishment when a song truly came together in perfect harmony.

The parallels between the group style of R and B and gospel are self-evident. The human voice—with several voices merging together to create a single sound or with one voice singing out front backed by the tight harmonies of others—was accompanied by an ensemble of instruments. The emotions generated were accentuated by positive feelings of joy and celebration that arose out of a philosophy of progress, freedom (symbolized by the expressiveness of the vocals), and living in the present to make a better future. The very fact of standing on a street corner or in a church and developing a performance right there and then also contributed to this present orientation.

The church and street corner served as focuses where rural migrants could find a hospitable environment that allowed assimilation into city life to proceed. People torn from their roots came together. Each fostered the brotherhood and comradeship, the sense of all being in it together and of succeeding that stand at the core of soul philosophy.

The two musics complemented each other. In fact, looked at from one perspective, the only difference between them was that one involved singing for the Lord and the other did not. They also shared time on the radio where the obvious connection would eventually produce the logical result.

The close relationship between gospel and rhythm and blues was complemented by another, older influence that completed the coalescence of soul. It came from a strikingly different spot in the music spectrum, black popular music of the 1930s and 1940s geared for whites. Ray Charles's major early pop influence was Nat "King" Cole, whose music showed little black influence. By the early 1950s, Cole had reached the height of popular music stardom, gaining, perhaps, a greater following among whites than blacks, though his success did make him a symbol of progress to blacks.[61] The same was true of the Mills Brothers and the Ink Spots, who were 1930s precursors of the group R and B style.

Both groups stressed multivoice harmonies and featured the sophisticated, plush arrangements that became standard on many R and B songs. Just as important, they achieved a measure of success that rivaled that of black actors such as Eddie Anderson, Rochester on the "Jack Benny Show." The Mills Brothers, in particular, attained the greatest crossover acceptance. They were featured artists on network radio shows. In 1935 they even hosted their own program.[62]

As indicated in Chapter 2, network radio of the 1920s and 1930s did feature blacks, and black musicians were much in demand. Although the venue was not black-appeal, the music certainly appealed to blacks who regularly tuned in the programs. The problem with network offerings centered on the black image presented in dramas and comedies and the fact that so little of the programming appealed to blacks. There was no concerted effort to reach them. But this does not mean nothing of appeal was aired. It was, and the prime beneficiaries in terms of this work were first the rhythm and blues groups and later the soul musicians.

The five Mills Brothers were sophisticated performers whose tight, effortless harmonies on such songs as "Glow Worm" provided younger groups with an example to follow. A straight line of development can be traced from the Mills Brothers and the Ink Spots to the seminal rhythm and blues group, the Ravens, to the 1950s Moonglows, a group much copied, to such soul groups as the Temptations and Smokey Robinson and the Miracles.[63] And the testaments to their influence are numerous.

The Clovers were an early R and B group who originally wanted to cross over into white pop music but were guided by Atlantic Records president Ahmet Ertegun into the black music market. They had two number one records on the R and B charts in 1951 and continued, in Arnold Shaw's words, to have "the most consistent record of delivering best-sellers of any R & B attraction of the time. . . . They became one of the first groups to serve as a bridge between R & B and pop."[64] Clyde McPhatter was recruited for the Dominoes because Billy Ward was looking for "a high tenor voice like that of Bill Kenny of the Ink Spots."[65] McPhatter's successor as lead singer for the Dominoes, Jackie Wilson, recalled: "I grew up listening to the Mills Brothers, Ink Spots, Louis Jordan, and Al Jolson."[66]

Instrumentally, the sophisticated arrangements of big band jazz served as the musical foundation. The emphasis was on a full-bodied orchestral sound. Saxophone, strings, piano, horns, the strong rhythm section of drums and bass all became standard, providing the creative and complex vocals with a rich music base. Ray Charles fronted a large band. In fact he served his apprenticeship writing arrangements for big bands. James Brown's back-up band was more of an orchestra. How important such orchestration was is shown by the above comment by WDIA disc jockey Robert Thomas regarding the popularity of blues vs. R and B among young blacks.[67]

THE SOUL SYNTHESIS

The four sources—gospel, street-corner rhythm and blues, its precursor, white crossover groups, and big band jazz—came together to form soul. For the purposes here, the first three are most important. Their respective differences and influences are best phrased in the communications formula guiding this work.

Gospel groups sang of the promise and reality of good news in churches, on records, and on radio to the black public, especially the religiously inclined, so as to inspire them with the feelings and knowledge that better times were possible in the present and in the future. Gospel obviously lent the good news philosophy expressed through honest, deep emotion that bound the audience together into one with the singers. It inspired blacks and fostered feelings of brotherhood.

Street-corner groups sang of the joy, freedom, and brotherhood of the black community to those within range of their hearing, those buying their records, and those listening to the radio. The rhythm and blues groups celebrated the same things as gospel, but outside church. They also contributed a growing sense of freedom and accomplishment.

The crossover groups sang also of joy and good times to whites and blacks, but to blacks they symbolized the ability of blacks to successfully compete with whites in the quest for stardom. These performers acted as symbols of success and sophistication, stressing that the ultimate triumph depended not only on black acceptance but on that of whites, too. This reflected the integrationist philosphy of the 1950s that was later replaced by the black nationalism of the 1960s. The need for white acceptance, however, was never lost, for both economic reasons and reasons of personal pride among performers.

Finally, all three music forms instilled pride and solidarity in blacks and enhanced feelings of freedom through the use of the human voice as an expressive instrument of that freedom. The resulting musical fusion added a new dimension to the white acceptance factor. The late music writer Ralph Gleason wrote, "The Mills Bros., like the Ink Spots, were really black men singing white songs." Or as Arnold Shaw put it, they "sugared their style for white palates."[68] Neither rhythm and blues groups nor soul performers made this concession. Their success and acceptance in the white community was made on their own terms. In fact, the criterion for ultimate success was reaching the white audience while retaining a large black following. Sam Cooke, for one, realized this goal. So did a record company in Detroit called Motown whose founder, Berry Gordy, purposely geared his black music products to the white market.[69]

There is one more aspect of soul. It centers on style, on being in touch with current trends, on being cool. Singing in a group, says Wilson Pickett, "could make you so cool you *smoked.*" Of his movement from gospel to rhythm and blues, Pickett explained that his friend had persuaded him "to do the group thing and be cool."[70]

To be cool, to be "in," was and is a high priority for teenagers. In the 1950s in the black neighborhoods, though styles changed rapidly, it meant having marcelled, processed hair. For singers, it meant wearing suits with wide lapels with trim in a contrasting color and pants tapered down so slim that putting your foot in was difficult.[71] Being cool and professional in a group also meant developing a choreographed routine that complemented the highly styled vocalizings. Ben E. King recalled that the Cadillacs, coached by tap dancing master Cholly Atkins, who later developed routines for many Motown groups, "were so sharp it hurt." They had "the best clothes, the best steps." The Cadillacs sang in tight harmony and had a hit record, "Gloria," which featured a plush arrangement.[72]

All these ingredients make up soul music, which developed into the most popular cultural expression of the new racial consciousness of change and progress. The word *soul* itself came to define the black experience of the post–World War II era. Once blacks had the blues. Later they had soul. The details of its parts changed over time to reflect the changing attitudes of blacks but certain fundamentals remained: the philosophy of progress and building a better life; the freedom to be black without feeling any insecurity, which in turn implies having racial and individual pride; and gaining the respect if not the acceptance of whites.

Music remains soul's most popular and most potent expression because it has fulfilled all the above requirements and more. Soul music is accepted on both sides of the color line as a major popular music form and soul musicians have earned the respect of the music industry and most segments of the public. The 1980s have witnessed a resurgence of popularity for many soul stars of the 1960s, such as Aretha Franklin, the Four Tops, and Smokey Robinson. The irony is that even black music performed in blackface was accorded high testimony; soul represents just one more step in this image continuum with one major exception. In the marketplace, through the establishment of such companies as Motown, soul has demonstrated that blacks can and will compete successfully with whites given the right circumstances, the right product, and the opportunity.

As a medium of creation, evolution, and dissemination, radio's role in soul's development was pivotal. Black radio personalities helped to define soul style and consciousness both symbolically by being on the air and in practice by their actions behind the microphone, one of which was playing the new music. They furthered this influence into areas of self-help through service to the community. They acted as role models to be followed and symbols of success.

Radio also allowed for mass, instantaneous delivery of soul consciousness and culture. It provided a medium—in a biological sense—for soul to germinate and grow. In a communications sense it accelerated the spread of soul music and consciousness. Radio bound the changing, disparate, and increasingly atomized black community together by providing a unified mass medium that reached virtually everybody with the same messages of progress, pride, solidarity, and racial positivity. As a result, the medium changed from black-appeal to radio soul.

NOTES

1. Interview, B. B. King.

2. Charles Sawyer, *The Arrival of B. B. King* (Garden City, N.Y.: Doubleday & Company, Inc., 1980), pp. 33–67.

3. Gerri Hirshey, *Nowhere To Run* (New York: Times Books, 1984), pp. 60, 265.

4. Interview, Nat D. Williams.

5. Robert Neff and Anthony Connor, *Blues* (Boston: David R. Godine, 1975), p. 6.

6. James Brown, "Say It Loud—I'm Black and I'm Proud," King 6187 (1968).

7. Oakley, *The Devil's Music*, p. 256.

8. Hirshey, *Nowhere to Run*, p. 5.

9. Interview, Sammy Lawhorn.

10. See Rowe, *Chicago Breakdown*, passim.

11. Interview, B. B. King; Sawyer, *Arrival of B. B. King*, pp. 152–57.

12. Michael Haralambos, *Right On: From Blues to Soul in Black America* (New York: Da Capo Press, 1979), p. 118.

13. David Evans, *Big Road Blues* (Los Angeles: University of California Press, 1982), pp. 19–20.

14. Paul Oliver, *Conversation with the Blues* (New York: Horizon Press, 1965), p. 23.

15. Evans, *Big Road Blues*, pp. 19–20.

16. Hirshey, *Nowhere to Run*, pp. 5, 352.

17. William Ferris, *Blues from the Delta* (Garden City, N.Y.: Anchor Press, 1978), p. 45

18. Interview, Robert Thomas, July 1978.

19. Interview, James Cotton, Monterey, Calif., September 1976.

20. Hirshey, *Nowhere to Run*, p. 51.

21. Interview, James Cotton.

22. Hirshey, *Nowhere to Run*, p. 77.

23. During our interview, James Cotton suggested this possibility. B. B. King also noted the lack of airplay for blues.

24. Oliver, *Conversation with the Blues*, p. 3.

25. "2. Negro Radio: Keystone of Community Life," p. 78.

26. See Chapter 3.

27. See Chapter 2.

28. See Chapter 6.

29. Interview, Jesse "Hot Rod" Carter.

30. Hirshey, *Nowhere to Run*, p. 26.

31. Lawrence Levine, *Black Culture and Black Consciousness* (New York: Oxford University Press, 1977), pp. 185–86.

32. Virtually every book or article on black music, particularly those dealing with blues, covers this dichotomy. See Evans, *Big Road Blues*, p. 22; Ferris, *Blues from the Delta*, pp. 84–85; Oakley, *The Devil's Music*, pp. 216–18.

33. Ibid., p. 177; Georgia Tom and Tampa Red, "It's Tight Like That," Vocalion 1216 (1928). See also Anthony Heilbut, *The Gospel Sound*, rev. ed. (New York: Limelight Editions, 1985), pp. 22–23, 27; Levine, *Black Culture*, p. 183.

34. *The Compact Edition of the Oxford English Dictionary*, vol. 1, p. 1178.

35. Levine, *Black Culture*, p. 174.

36. Heilbut, *Gospel Sound*, p. 61.

37. Cited in Levine, *Black Culture*, p. 174.

38. Hirshey, *Nowhere to Run*, p. 274.

39. Heilbut, *Gospel Sound*, pp. 78, 80.

40. Hirshey, *Nowhere to Run*, p. 51.

41. Ibid., pp. 48, 111.

42. Arnold Shaw, *Honkers and Shouters* (New York: Macmillan, 1978) pp. 270–71.

43. Ibid., p. 270.

44. Hirshey, *Nowhere to Run*, p. 110.

45. Ibid., p. 47.

46. Ibid., p. 351.

47. Hirshey, *Nowhere to Run*, p. 112.

48. James Rooney, *Bossmen: Bill Monroe & Muddy Waters* (New York: Hayden Book Company, 1971), p. 107; Sawyer, *Arrival of B. B. King*, pp. 39–40, passim.

49. Hirshey, *Nowhere to Run*, p. 49.

50. Ibid., pp. 50–51.

51. Ibid., p. 50.

52. Charlie Gillette, *The Sound of the City* (New York: Outerbridge & Dienstfrey, 1970), p. 179.

53. Arnold Shaw, *Honkers and Shouters*, (New York: Macmillan, 1978), pp. 381–84.

54. Ibid., p. 442.

55. Hirshey, *Nowhere to Run*, p. 23.

56. Shaw, *Honkers and Shouters*, p. 16.

57. The discussion here focuses on group sounds that represented just one R and B style, even though one with great influence.

58. Hirshey, *Nowhere to Run*, p. 36.

59. Ibid.

60. Ray Charles and David Ritz, *Brother Ray: Ray Charles' Own Story* (New York: Dial Press, 1978) passim; Hirshey, *Nowhere to Run*, p. 351.

61. MacDonald, *Don't Touch That Dial*, p. 335.

62. This line of development is most evident in the genealogy of the Fuqua family and the career of Harvey Fuqua, lead singer of the Moonglows. His uncle sang with the original Ink Spots and Harvey later worked as a producer for the Motown label. Gillette, *Sound of the City*, p. 185; Shaw, *Honkers and Shouters*, p. 134.

63. Ibid., p. 386.

64. Ibid., p. 282.

65. Ibid., p. 442.

66. Ibid., p. xvii.

67. See pp. 307–308.

68. For the story of Motown's development, see Jim Miller, ed., *The Rolling Stone Illustrated History of Rock and Roll* (New York: Rolling Stone Press & Random House, 1976) pp. 222–33.

69. Hirshey, *Nowhere To Run.*, p, 46.

70. Ibid.

71. Ibid., p. 34.

72. Ibid., p. 166.

CODA:
MONEY IS
THE MESSAGE

In 1960, Detroit songwriter Berry Gordy and singer Barrett Strong collaborated on an early soul hit called "Money." To paraphrase the lyrics, money was what Gordy wanted and money was what Gordy got. He founded Motown records, the first black-owned recording company that truly succeeded, and even made the Fortune 400 list of the wealthiest Americans.[1] Other black-appeal media entrepreneurs also wanted money.

W. C. Handy only turned to blues when he realized that people were paying for it. Perry Bradford touted race records because blacks would buy discs featuring their own music and musicians. Jack L. Cooper feared an old age of poverty and got them sold on black-appeal programming. Sonny Boy Williamson saw radio as the perfect vehicle to boost his career. Because he was getting paid, Nat D. Williams agreed to appear on WDIA. Joseph Silverstein, Max Moore, Sam Anderson, Bob Alburty, Bert Ferguson, and John Pepper all saw the dollar value in appealing to blacks. So did thousands of others who participated in black-appeal radio.

Perhaps the most disturbing and blatant pursuit of money occurred after World War II. As the recorded music format increasingly dominated the radio dial, a simultaneous explosion in music and records occurred. New styles of blues, gospel, rhythm and blues, and then soul hit first the streets and then the record stores. The major labels, like the radio networks, were too unwieldy to capitalize on this renaissance. Newly started record companies formed to take advantage of the entrepreneurial opportunity. Hit records were pivotal to their survival.[2]

A pernicious relationship evolved between the music, record, and radio industries because of the marketing role radio played in exposing the new discs to the buying public. The recorded music format provided virtually free advertising, and no other method could reach so many people in so many places at the same time. Radio became the arbiter of success for new songs. Airplay could zoom a song to the top. Lack of it could relegate a disc to the garbage can. Where Bob Alburty bartered airtime for the rental of records in the 1930s, two decades later record companies not only provided discs for free; they also paid disc jockeys to play the songs, to make them hits through heavy promotion, that is, repeated airplay. This illegal practice, known as payola, produced a nationwide scandal in both industries.[3]

The fact of payola demonstrates, in very exaggerated fashion, that money is the message of the medium. In one sense, the practice was just an aspect of advertising, no different from a sponsor buying time to hawk a product like milk, cigarettes, washing machines, or houses. Conversely, payola was bribery. Either way, its existence illustrates that money talked on radio, deciding what was said.

The profit imperative is far from alien to American life in general or the media in particular. The public accepts it as the mechanism of the market economy just as advertising is the basis of the media. In radio, advertising provided the funding for programming, community service, station operations—and profits. Because radio is a communications medium, the key to success was sharing messages between sponsors, disc jockeys, and the audience that were accepted and understood by all.

An ironic example of how radio communication worked was provided by Richard Stams. The Chicago disc jockey was prosecuted and found guilty in a payola scandal. During a 1978 interview he suggested that the money paid out little influenced playlists since the disc jockey had to play what the public wanted to stay on the air.[4] Although an obvious attempt at justifying his conduct, Stams' explanation illustrates the fact that profits depended upon successful communication just as communication was made possible by profits.

What the above discussion indicates, as do the previous pages of this book, is that black-appeal media depended upon the marketing of racial pride to secure profits. Pride connected the essential triad of radio operations—sponsor, station, black audience—allowing communication to be shared and understood. Chapter 7 contains many examples of how this communicating did and did not work—the rules of sharing appealing messages, so to speak.

The influence of money on the medium's message and communication is a subject little developed in scholarship. It seems a given, taken for granted as much as electricity. Both power the media. Its role in black-appeal radio was both paramount and pivotal.

In the preceding pages the reasons behind black disgust with radio was shown to center around the inability of the black population to overcome negative imagery. There were two sides to the image problem. First was the image aired by the media. Second was the image of the black listener-consumer as someone unable or unwilling to respond to media appeals. In other words, the black image of not having the money to merit appeal predicated neglect and influenced the continuation of the negative imagery aired by the networks. Broadcasting remained largely closed to blacks because of this perceived inability to respond at the cash register. If blacks could not afford to buy radio sets, how could they be expected to buy sponsor products?

Conversely, the airing of the imagery hardly prompted blacks to buy the goods and services advertised. To do so meant supporting the blackface image. In this way perceptions and the use of money inhibited communications, distorting the medium's message to blacks. They were unwilling to respond with purchases.

Yet the true sharing of meaningful communication was possible. The boom of black-appeal programming amply illustrated that blacks had the money to support the media. Jack L. Cooper's tenure on the air during the 1930s indicates that even in depressed times blacks had the means to fund shows. Money therefore acted as a message telling whites that blacks could afford sets and that they would tune in programs and buy sponsor products if the appeal was right. Pride turned on the black-owned sets and opened black wallets and purses, paving the way for clearly understood communication in the radio triad.

White recognition of the spending power and the faithfulness of blacks largely fueled the black-appeal boom. The greater the success of the concept, the larger the pride component became. Each fed the other, allowing race-conscious disc jockeys to move one step further in the progress continuum. These voices behind the microphone became race promoters both in words and actions, inside and outside the radio station. The ability to help create, develop, and instill a new consciousness among blacks depended upon money.

As Richard Stams aptly phrased it, you had "to cut the mustard."[5] You had to sell the advertised products to sell the race. And selling the race helped sell the products. But selling the race involved buying the culture the audience wanted, in this case the new music. Listeners tuned in to hear the new sounds that reflected their changing situation. Stations bought into this process, trying to keep up with the fast-changing taste of the black public. Blues no longer cut the mustard among the majority of blacks, so it declined on playlists, except in the case of a unique artist like B. B. King. Rhythm and blues and gospel became the choice, later merging into soul.

On all sides of the triad, communication developed in an open, comprehensible fashion around one general message: profits and pride. The listening public profited from hearing the programming they wanted, programming that instilled pride in them because of its message and appeal. Also at work here was the undeniable fact that they were the recipients of respectful, solicitous treatment.

In turn, the stations geared their playlists to audience wants, developing sophisticated polling techniques revolving around record sales and requests. They aired pride to receive profits. The sponsors followed in the same pattern, gearing the products advertised and the messages to the pride-profit formula.

For our purposes, the most important aspect was not the revenue generated but the black image the medium projected. It was the absolute reverse of the blackface minstrelsy stereotype and is best explained by defining the term that characterized this new imagery: *soul*. Norman Spaulding writes, "The word 'soul' (meaning the black experience) rather than being a thing to be ridiculed or ashamed of suddenly took on a new meaning. Black suddenly became beautiful and to be without soul was considered a fault."[6] This statement is indicative rather than definitive.

I suggest that soul means the black self-image of the 1950s and 1960s. It revolves around concepts like pride, progress, respect, and equality that merged to produce a mind set that stressed black was beautiful and being black was positive. It implied living in the present with a look toward further improvement in the future best realized by one's own efforts. Having soul meant being independent. Having soul meant being creative and expressive to the point where blacks and whites together accepted these cultural expressions.

Radio provided a very visible and audible example of soul. It was a symbol, a creator, and a purveyor of the concept. What started as a New Negro dream envisioned by Jack L. Cooper decades earlier in Chicago became the soul reality. And it fulfilled this dream by following the business dictates of the American marketplace, not through a racial crusade. The color of money not skin color was the message black-appeal entrepreneurs pitched to sponsors and listeners. But black not green made this message clearly understood. By 1960, the radio dial was fully integrated, appealing to blacks in a way no other medium ever has.

NOTES

1. On Berry Gordy and the Motown story, see Miller, pp. 222–33.
2. Shaw, *Honkers and Shouters,* passim; Rowe, *Chicago Breakdown,* passim.
3. Miller, *Rock and Roll,* pp. 102–3.
4. Interview, Richard Stams.
5. Ibid.
6. Spaulding, "Black-Oriented Radio in Chicago," p. 102.

BIBLIOGRAPHY

GOVERNMENT PUBLICATIONS

Books and Monographs

1. U.S. Bureau of the Census. *Negroes in the United States, 1920–1932.* Washington, D.C.: U.S. Government Printing Office, 1935.
2. ———. *Statistical Abstract of the United States: 1959.* Washington, D.C.: U.S. Government Printing Office, 1959.
3. ———. *Historical Statistics of the United States, Colonial Times to 1957.* Washington, D.C.: U.S. Government Printing Office, 1960.
4. U.S. Department of Commerce, Radio Division. *Commercial and Government Radio Stations of the United States: June 30, 1931.* Washington, D.C.: U.S. Government Printing Office, 1931.
5. DuBois, W. E. B. "The Black Farmer," "Negroes in the United States," U.S. Bureau of the Census *Bulletin,* no. 8 (1904).
6. Federal Writers' Project, Tennessee. *Tennessee: A Guide to the State.* New York: Hastings House, 1949, originally published 1939.
7. Hambidge, Gove. "Soils and Men—A Summary," *Yearbook of Agriculture: 1938.* Washington, D.C.: U.S. Government Printing Office, 1938.
8. Holley, William C., Ellen Winston, and T. J. Woofter, Jr. *The Plantation South, 1934–1937.* Works Project Administration, Division of Research, Research Monograph 22. Washington, D.C.: U.S. Government Printing Office, 1940.
9. Langsford, E. L. and B. H. Thibodeaux. "Plantation Organization and Operation in the Yazoo-Mississippi Delta Area," U.S. Department of Agriculture Technical Bulletin no. 683 (May 1939).

10. Woofter, T. J., Jr. *Landlord and Tenant on the Cotton Plantation*. Works Progress Administration, Division of Social Research, Research Monograph 5, Washington, D.C.: U.S. Government Printing Office, 1936.
11. Writer's Program of the Works Progress Administration, Arkansas. *Arkansas: A Guide to the State*. New York: Hastings House, 1941.

Decennial Census Reports

1. U.S. Bureau of the Census. *U.S. Twelfth Census, 1900: Special Reports: Occupations*. Washington, D.C.: U.S. Government Printing Office, 1902.
2. ——. *Fifteenth Census of the United States: 1930*, vol. 3: *Population*, p. 2: *Reports by States*. Washington, D.C.: U.S. Government Printing Office, 1932.
3. ——, *Sixteenth Census of the United States: 1940*, vol. 1: *Agriculture, First, Second and Third Series State Reports*, p. 2: *The Southern States: Statistics for Counties*, p. 5: *West South Central Statistics for Counties*. Washington, D.C.: U.S. Government Printing Office, 1942.
4. ——, *Sixteenth Census of the United States: 1940, Characteristics of the Population*, vol. 2, pt. 2: *Florida-Iowa*. Washington, D.C.: U.S. Government Printing Office, 1943.
5. ——, *U.S. Census of the Population: 1950*, vol. 2: *Characteristics of the Population*, pt. 5: *Arkansas*, pt. 42: *Tennessee*. Washington, D.C.: U.S. Government Printing Office, 1952.
6. ——, *U.S. Census of the Population: 1960*, vol. 1, *Characteristics of the Population*, pt. 44: *Tennessee*. Washington, D.C.: U.S. Government Printing Office, 1963.

RADIO STATION AND PRIVATE COLLECTIONS

Jack L. Cooper Collection (a portion of these files originally held by Gertrude Cooper are now housed in the Chicago Historical Society).
1. "The Two Black Diamonds of Radio," "All-Negro Hour" radio script (n.d.).
2. "I'll Never Try That Again," "All-Negro Hour" radio script (n.d.).
3. "Giggles and Grins with Jack and Billie," "All-Negro Hour" radio script (August 30, 1931).
4. "Luke and Timber," radio script (n.d.).
5. "Mush and Clorinda," radio script, episode 62 (n.d.).
6. "Listen Chicago," radio script (March 27, 1949).
7. "Tips and Tunes," featuring Jack L. and Gertrude "Trudy" Cooper, radio tape (c. late 1950s). Several shows are on one 90-minute tape cassette.
8. Advertising circular, Jack L. Cooper Radio Presentations (c. 1948).
9. Playbill, Belmont Theatre (January 8–9, 1923).

WSBC, Chicago, Illinois

1. Advertising mailer, World Battery Company (1926).
2. *You Can't Cover Chicago without WGES-WCBD-WSBC*, marketing pamphlet published by owner Gene T. Dyer, c. 1938.

3. WSBC Program Schedule (c. late 1940s).
4. *Tip-Top Advertising Is Tip-Top in Chicago.* Ward Baking Company marketing pamphlet, c. 1943.

WDIA, Memphis, Tennessee

1. WDIA Program Schedule (June 1952).
2. *Goodwill at Work in Memphis: WDIA.* WDIA public relations pamphlet, 1977.

BOOKS

1. Alicoate, Jack, ed. *The 1939 Radio Annual.* New York: Radio Daily, 1939.
2. Angelou, Maya. *I Know Why the Caged Bird Sings.* New York: Bantam Books, 1971.
3. ———. *Gather Together in My Name.* New York: Bantam Books, 1974.
4. Baker, Ray Stannard. *Following the Color Line.* New York: Harper & Row, 1964, originally published 1908.
5. Barnouw, Erik. *A Tower in Babel: A History of Broadcasting in the United States to 1933.* New York: Oxford University Press, 1966.
6. Blum, John Morton. *V Was for Victory.* New York: Harcourt Brace Jovanovich, 1976.
7. Bradford, Perry. *Born with the Blues.* New York: Oak Publications, 1965.
8. Broonzy, William, and Yannick Bruynoghe. *Big Bill's Blues.* New York: Oak Publications, 1955.
9. Bryson, Lyman, ed. *The Communication of Ideas.* New York: Institute for Religious and Social Studies, 1948.
10. Charles, Ray, and David Ritz. *Brother Ray: Ray Charles' Own Story.* New York: Dial Press, 1978.
11. Charters, Samuel. *The Poetry of the Blues.* New York: Avon Books, 1963.
12. Chicago Commission on Race Relations. *The Negro in Chicago: A Study of Race Relations and a Race Riot.* Chicago: University of Chicago Press, 1922.
13. Correll, Charles J., and Freeman F. Gosden. *All about Amos 'n' Andy.* New York: Rand McNally, 1929.
14. Cripps, Thomas. *Slow Fade to Black.* New York: Oxford University Press, 1977.
15. Czitrom, Daniel J. *Media and the American Mind: From Morse to McLuhan.* Chapel Hill: University of North Carolina Press, 1982.
16. Dollard, John. *Caste and Class in a Southern Town.* Garden City, N.Y.: Doubleday & Company, Inc., 1949, originally published 1937.
17. Doyle, Bertram. *The Etiquette of Race Relations in the South.* Chicago: University of Chicago Press, 1937.
18. Drake, St. Clair, and Horace Cayton. *Black Metropolis.* 2 vols., rev. ed., New York: Harper & Row, 1962.
19. Drucker, Peter F. *Management: Tasks, Responsibilities, Practices.* New York: Harper & Row, Publishers, 1973.
20. DuBois, W. E. B. *Black Reconstruction in America, 1865–1880.* New York: Atheneum Press, 1973, originally published 1935.
21. Evans, David. *Big Road Blues.* Los Angeles: University of California Press, 1982.

22. Ewen, David. *The Life and Times of Tin Pan Alley.* New York: Funk & Wagnall's, Inc., 1964.
23. Ferris, William. *Blues from the Delta.* Garden City, N.Y.: Anchor Press, 1978.
24. Fireman, Judy, ed. *TV Book: The Ultimate Television Book.* New York: Workman Publishing Company, Inc., 1977.
25. Frederickson, George. *The Black Image in the White Mind.* New York: Harper & Row, 1971.
26. Gelatt, Roland. *The Fabulous Phonograph, 1877–1977.* 2d rev. ed., New York: Macmillan, 1977.
27. Gillette, Charlie. *The Sound of the City.* New York: Outerbridge & Dienstfrey, 1970.
28. Guralnick, Peter. *Feel Like Goin' Home.* New York: Vintage Books, 1971.
29. Handy, W. C. *Father of the Blues: An Autobiography.* Edited by Arna Bontemps. New York: The Macmillan Company, 1941.
30. Haralambos, Michael. *Right On: From Blues to Soul in Black America.* New York: DaCapo Press, 1979
31. Harmon, Jim. *The Great Radio Comedians.* Garden City, N.Y.: Doubleday & Company, Inc., 1970.
32. Heilbut, Anthony. *The Gospel Sound.* Rev. ed., New York: Limelight Editions, 1985.
33. Henri, Florette. *Black Migration: Movement North, 1900–1920.* Garden City, N.Y.: Anchor Press, 1976.
34. Hirshey, Gerri. *Nowhere To Run.* New York: Times Books, 1984.
35. Huggins, Nathan. *Harlem Renaissance.* New York: Oxford University Press, 1977.
36. Hurst, Mont. *The Tip-Top Minstrel Book.* Syracuse, N.Y.: Willis N. Bugbee Company, 1931.
37. Jaynes, Julian. *The Origins of Consciousness in the Breakdown of the Bicameral Mind.* Boston: Houghton Mifflin Company, 1976.
38. Johnson, Charles. *Patterns of Negro Segregation.* New York: Harper & Brothers Publishers, 1943.
39. Keil, Charles. *Urban Blues.* Chicago: University of Chicago Press, 1965.
40. Kennedy, Louise V. *The Negro Peasant Turns Cityward.* New York: Columbia University Press, 1930.
41. Kirwan, Albert D. *Revolt of the Rednecks: Mississippi Politics, 1876–1925.* Magnolia, Miss.: P. Smith, 1964.
42. Kluger, Richard. *Simple Justice: The History of Brown v. Board of Education and Black America's Struggle for Equality.* New York: Alfred A. Knopf, 1976.
43. LaFeber, Walter and Richard Polenberg. *The American Century: A History of the United States Since the 1890s.* New York: John Wiley & Sons, Inc., 1975.
44. Leadbitter, Mike, and Neil Slaven, eds. *Blues Records: January, 1943 to December, 1966.* New York: Oak Publications, 1968.
45. Leadbitter, Mike, ed. *Nothing But the Blues.* New York: Oak Publications, 1971.
46. Levine, Lawrence. *Black Culture and Black Consciousness.* New York: Oxford University Press, 1977.
47. Link, Arthur S., and William B. Catton. *American Epoch: A History of the United States Since 1900.* Vol. 3: *1946–1973,* 4th ed. New York: Alfred A. Knopf, 1974.

48. Locke, Alain, ed. *The New Negro: An Interpretation*. New York: Albert & Charles Boni, 1925.

49. Mahoney, Dan, comp. *The Columbia 13/14000-D Series: A Numerical Listing*. Stanhope, N.J.: Walter C. Allen, 1961.

50. MacDonald, J. Fred. *Don't Touch That Dial: Radio Programming in American Life from 1920 to 1960*. Chicago: Nelson-Hall, 1979.

51. McIlwaine, Shields. *Memphis Down in Dixie*. New York: E. P. Dutton & Company, Inc., 1948.

52. McLuhan, Marshall. *Understanding Media*. New York: McGraw-Hill, 1964.

53. Mezzrow, Mezz, and Bernard Wolfe. *Really The Blues*. Garden City, N.Y.: Anchor Books, 1972, originally published 1946.

54. Miller, Jim, ed. *The Rolling Stone Illustrated History of Rock and Roll*. New York: Rolling Stone Press, 1976.

55. Mirken, Alan, ed. *1927 Edition of the Sears, Roebuck Catalog*. New York: Crown Publishing, Inc., 1970.

56. Mitz, Rick, ed. *The Great TV Sitcom Book*. New York: Richard Marek Publishers, 1980.

57. Nash, Gary B., ed. *The Private Side of American History*, vol. 1: *To 1877*. 2nd ed. New York: Harcourt Brace Jovanovich, 1979.

58. Neff, Robert, and Anthony Connor. *Blues*. Boston: David R. Godine, 1975.

59. Nourse, Edwin G., Joseph F. Davis, and John D. Black. *Three Years of the Agricultural Adjustment Administration*. Washington D.C.: The Brookings Institution, 1937.

60. Oakley, Giles. *The Devil's Music: A History of the Blues*. London: British Broadcasting Corporation, 1976.

61. Oliver, Paul. *Blues Fell This Morning*. New York: Horizon Press, 1960.

62. ———. *The Story of the Blues*. New York: Chilton Book Company, 1969.

63. ———. *Conversation with the Blues*. New York: Horizon Press, 1965.

64. O'Neal, Hank, comp. *A Vision Shared: A Classic Portrait of America and Its People, 1935–1943*. New York: St. Martin's Press, 1976.

65. Osofsky, Gilbert. *Harlem: The Making of a Ghetto*. New York: Harper & Row Publishers, 1963.

66. *The Compact Edition of the Oxford English Dictionary*, 2 vols., New York: Oxford University Press, 1971.

67. Passman, Arnold. *The Deejays*. New York: Macmillan, 1971.

68. Poindexter, Ray. *Arkansas Airwaves*. North Little Rock, Arkansas: Ray Poindexter, 1974.

69. Rawick, George P. *The American Slave: A Composite Autobiography*, multivol. Westport, Conn.: Greenwood Publishing Company, 1972.

70. Rice, Edward Leroy. *Monarchs of Minstrelsy from Daddy Rice to Date*. New York: Kenny Publishing Company, 1911.

71. Robertson, Ross M., and Gary M. Walton. *History of the American Economy*, 4th ed. New York: Harcourt Brace Jovanovich, Inc., 1979.

72. Rooney, James. *Bossmen: Bill Monroe & Muddy Waters*. New York: Hayden Book Company, 1971.

73. Rosenberg, Jerry M. *Dictionary of Business and Management*. New York: John Wiley & Sons, 1978.

74. Rowe, Mike. *Chicago Breakdown*. New York: Drake Publishers, Inc., 1969.
75. Sackheim, Eric, ed. *The Blues Line*. New York: Schirmer Books, 1975.
76. Sawyer, Charles. *The Arrival of B. B. King*. Garden City, N.Y.: Doubleday & Company, Inc., 1980.
77. Schlesinger, Arthur M., Jr. *The Age of Roosevelt: The Coming of the New Deal*. Boston: Houghton Mifflin, 1958.
78. Schramm, Wilbur, and Donald F. Roberts, eds. *The Process and Effects of Mass Communications*, rev. ed. Urbana: University of Illinois Press, 1971.
79. Seehafer Gene F., and Jack W. Laemmar. *Successful Television and Radio Advertising*. New York: McGraw-Hill Book Company, Inc., 1959.
80. Shapiro, Nat, and Nat Hentoff, eds. *Hear Me Talkin' to Ya*. New York: Dover Publications, Inc., 1955.
81. Shaw, Arnold. *Honkers and Shouters*. New York: Macmillan, 1978.
82. Southern, Eileen. *The Music of Black Americans: A History*. New York: W. W. Norton & Company, Inc., 1971.
83. Spear, Allan. *Black Chicago: The Making of a Negro Ghetto, 1890–1920*. Chicago: University of Chicago Press, 1967.
84. St. John, Robert. *Encyclopedia of Radio and Television Broadcasting*. Milwaukee: Cathedral Publishing Company, 1967.
85. Stewart-Baxter, Derrick. *Ma Rainey and the Classic Blues Singers*. New York: Stein & Day, 1970.
86. Street, James H. *The New Revolution in the Cotton Economy*. Chapel Hill: University of North Carolina Press, 1957.
87. Terkel, Studs. *"The Good War": An Oral History of World War Two*. New York: Pantheon Books, 1984.
88. Titon, Jeff. *Early Downhome Blues*. Urbana: University of Illinois Press, 1977.
89. Toll, Robert. *Blacking Up: The Minstrel Show in Nineteenth Century America*. New York: Oxford University Press, 1974.
90. Tucker, David M. *Lieutenant Lee of Beale Street*. Nashville, Tenn.: Vanderbilt University Press, 1971.
91. U.S. Bureau of the Census. *The Statistical History of the United States: From Colonial Times to the Present*. New York: Basic Books, Inc., 1976.
92. Vincent, Theodore G. *Black Power and the Garvey Movement*. San Francisco, Calif.: Ramparts Press, 1972.
93. *Walker Evans: Photographs for the Farm Security Administration, 1935–1938*. New York: DaCapo Press, Inc., 1973.
94. Waters, Ethel with Charles Samuels. *His Eye Is on the Sparrow*. Garden City, N.Y.: Doubleday, 1951.
95. *Webster's Third New International Dictionary*. Springfield, Mass.: G. & C. Merriam, 1976.
96. Wharton, Vernon. *The Negro in Mississippi, 1865–1890*. Chapel Hill: University of North Carolina Press, 1947.
97. Woodward, C. Vann. *Origins of the New South, 1877–1913*. Baton Rouge: Louisiana State University Press, 1971.

UNPUBLISHED WORKS

Dissertations and Theses

1. Edmerson, Estelle. "A Descriptive Study of the American Negro in the United States Professional Radio, 1922–1953." Unpublished M.A. thesis, UCLA, 1954.
2. Foreman, Ronald C., Jr. "Jazz and Race Records, 1920–1933: Their Origins and Their Significance for the Race Record Industry and Society." Unpublished Ph.D. diss., University of Illinois, 1968.
3. Spaulding, Norman. "History of Black-Oriented Radio in Chicago." Unpublished M.A. thesis, University of Illinois at Chicago, 1974.

Pamphlets

1. Bellavia, Ray J. "A Capsule History of Past and Present Radio Stations in the Chicagoland Area." Unpublished pamphlet, Chicago, 1978.

ARTICLES

Magazines and Journals

1. Beverly, Dick. "Black Radio and the Black Community," *The Black Collegian*, vol. 3 (January-February 1972).
2. Cooper, Eunice, and Marie Jahoda. "The Evasion of Propaganda: How Prejudiced People Respond to Anti-Prejudice Propaganda," *Journal of Psychology*, vol. 45 (January 1947).
3. DiMeglio, John E. "Black Pride and Protest: The 'Amos 'n' Andy' Crusade of 1931," *Journal of Popular Culture*, vol. 12, no. 2 (Fall 1979).
4. DuBois, W. E. B. editorial, *Crisis* (May 1919).
5. Gatewood, Willard P., Jr., ed. "Arkansas Negroes in the 1890s: Documents," *Arkansas Historical Quarterly*, vol. 33 (Winter 1974).
6. Goldberg, Dan. "Chicago's Negro Station," *Variety* (January 3, 1940).
7. Guralnick, Peter. "Rufus Thomas," *Living Blues*, no. 29 (September-October 1976, reprinted from Boston *Phoenix*).
8. House, Eddie "Son." "I Can Make My Own Songs," *Sing Out!*, vol. 15, no. 3 (July 1965).
9. Kahlenberg, Richard S. "Negro Radio," *Negro History Bulletin*, vol. 29 (March 1966).
10. Muhammed, Muslimah. "Chicago Black-Oriented Radio," *Dollars & $ense* (April/May 1979).
11. O'Neal, Jim, and Bill Goldsmith. "Living Blues Interview: Jimmy Rogers," *Living Blues*, no. 14 (Autumn 1973).
12. Pinkerton, Jane. "The Negro Market: Why Buyers Are Looking Twice," *Sponsor*, vol. 11, no. 19 (September 28, 1957).
13. Weinrott, Lester. "Chicago Radio: The Glory Days," *Chicago History*, vol. 3, no. 1 (Spring-Summer 1974).
14. "The Entrepreneur in You," *Across the Board*, vol. 21, nos. 7, 8 (July/August 1984).

15. Article, *Colliers,* vol. 101, no. 18 (April 30, 1938).
16. "Disc Jockeys," *Ebony,* vol. 11 (May 1957).
17. "Away From the Blues," *Newsweek,* vol. 43, no. 3 (January 18. 1954).
18. "Radio's Wacky Road to Profit," *Newsweek,* vol. 105, no. 12 (March 25, 1985).
19. "Black Radio," *Radio & Records* (February 16, 23, 1979).
20. "The Negro Market: $15,000,000,000 to Spend," *Sponsor,* vol. 6, no. 15 (July 18, 1952).
21. "Selling to Negroes: Don't Talk Down," *Sponsor,* vol. 6, no. 15 (July 28, 1952).
22. "Mr. Sponsor Asks . . .," *Sponsor,* vol. 6, no. 15 (July 28, 1952).
23. "Negro Radio: 200-Plus Special Stations, *Sponsor,* vol. 7, no. 17 (August 24, 1953).
24. "1. The Negro Market: $15 Billion Annually," *Sponsor,* vol. 7, no. 17 (August 24, 1953).
25. "4. Tips on How to Get the Most Out of Negro Radio," *Sponsor,* vol. 7, no. 17 (August 24, 1953).
26. "Negro Radio: Keystone of Community Life," *Sponsor,* vol. 7, no. 17 (August 24, 1953).
27. "Negro Radio Comes of Age," *Sponsor,* vol. 8, no. 19 (September 20, 1954).
28. "Negro Radio: Step-by-Step Analysis," *Sponsor,* vol. 8, no. 19 (September 20, 1954).
29. "Negro Radio Results," *Sponsor,* vol. 8, no. 19 (September 20, 1954).
30. "Tips on Selling via Negro Radio," *Sponsor,* vol. 8, no. 19 (September 20, 1954).
31. "3. Negro Radio: Over 600 Stations Strong Today," *Sponsor,* vol. 9, no. 19 (September 19, 1955).
32. "Biggest Negro Station," *Time,* vol. 70, no. 20 (November 11, 1957).

Newspapers

1. Chicago *Bee.* Article, August 17, 1930.
2. Wright, Wilbur. "Chicago's All-Colored Radio Hour," *The Bronzeman,* 1934(?)
3. Wright, Jerome. "Beale Street Panorama Recalled," Memphis *Commercial Appeal,* July 14, 1974.
4. Pittsburgh *Courier.* Article, May 22, 1930.
5. Chicago *Defender.* Article, November 24, 1924.
6. Chicago *Defender.* Article, July 27, 1930.
7. "Jack L. Cooper Opens Door of Radio to Negroes." Chicago *Defender,* 1946(?)
8. "Meet Jack L. Cooper." Chicago *Defender,* March 5, 1949.
9. Chicago *Defender.* Article, May 28, 1949.
10. Hunter, Bob. "74 and Blind, Jack L. Cooper First Negro Deejay, Still Airs Radio Show," Chicago *Defender* Magazine, May 14, 1963.
11. "Jack L. Cooper, 1st DJ, Is Dead." Chicago *Defender,* January 12, 1970.
12. Ottley, Roi. "From Poverty to 90 Suits—Saga of a Negro." Chicago *Tribune,* January 10, 1954.
13. Chicago *Tribune.* Obituary, September 8, 1980.
14. Beale, Lewis. "The Struggle, Sacrifice, and Hope behind 'Soldier's Story,'" Chicago *Tribune,* October 7, 1984.

DISCOGRAPHY

1. Brown, James, "Say It Loud—I'm Black and I'm Proud," King 6187 (1968).
2. Cooke, Sam, "Somebody Have Mercy"; "Having a Party," Sam Cooke, *Live at the Harlem Square Club, 1963,* RCA AFL-15181 (1985).
3. Georgia, Tom, and Tampa Red, "It's Tight Like That," Vocalion 1216 (1928).
4. House, Eddie "Son," "My Black Mama," Paramount 13042 (1930).
5. Hurt, Mississippi John, "Got the Blues, Can't Be Satisfied," (1928).
6. Jackson, Michael, and Paul McCartney, "This Girl Is Mine," Michael Jackson, *Thriller,* Epic Records QET38112 (1982).
7. King, B. B., "3 O'Clock Blues," RPM 339 (1952).
8. ———, "Sweet Sixteen," pts. 1 and 2, Kent 330 (1952).
9. ———, "Please Love Me," RPM 386 (1953).
10. ———, "Everyday I Have the Blues," RPM 421 (1954–1955).
11. Waters, Muddy, "I Can't Be Satisfied," Aristocrat 1305 (1948).
12. ———, "Long Distance Call," Chess 1452 (1951).
13. ———, "Hoochie Coochie Man," Chess 1560 (1954).
14. ———, "I Be's Troubled," Muddy Waters, *Down on Stovall's Plantation,* Testament Records T-2210, originally recorded 1941.
15. Williamson, Sonny Boy, "Too Close Together," Trumpet 212 (1951).
16. ———, "Keep It to Yourself," Checker 847.
17. ———, "Don't Lose Your Eye," *Sonny Boy Williamson,* Chess 2ACMB-206, originally recorded 1955.
18. ———, "One Way Out," Checker 1003 (1961).

INTERVIEWS

(unless otherwise noted, interviews conducted by author)

1. Alburty, Bob, Memphis, Tenn., July 1978.
2. Anderson, Sam, Helena, Ark., July 1976.
3. Carter, Jesse, "Hot Rod," Helena, Ark., July 1976.
4. Cooper, Gertrude, Chicago, Ill., June 1982.
5. ———, by Arnold Passman, Chicago, Ill., July 1983.
6. Cotton, James, Monterey, Calif., September 1976.
7. Danley, J. C., West Helena, Ark., July 1976.
8. Ellis, Joseph F., Jr., Clarksdale, Miss., July 1976.
9. Ferguson, Bert, Memphis, Tenn., July 1978.
10. Jaecker, Edward, Chicago, Ill., June 1982.
11. King, B. B., Nashville, Tenn., July 1976.
12. Lawhorn, Sammy, Chicago, Ill., August 1976.
13. Moore, Max, Helena, Ark., July 1976.
14. Pepper, John, Memphis, Tenn., July 1978.
15. Roberts, Bob, Chicago, Ill., July 1982.
16. Rogers, John, Helena, Ark., July 1976.
17. Schneider, Sam, Oak Park, Ill., August 1978.
18. Stams, Richard, Chicago, Ill., August 1978.
19. Stevenson, Arthur, "Kansas City Red," Chicago, Ill., July 1976.

20. Thomas, Robert, Memphis, Tenn., July 1976 and July 1978.
21. Thomas, Rufus, Memphis, Tenn., July 1978.
22. Wilkins, Joe Willie, Monterey, Calif., July 1976 and Memphis, Tenn., July 1978.
23. Williams, Nat D., Memphis, Tenn., July 1976.
24. Williams, Nat D., by Ronald Walter, Memphis, Tenn., September 1976 (typed transcript in Memphis Public Library).

INDEX

About the Author

MARK NEWMAN teaches at the University of Illinois at Chicago and Barat College. He co-produced a film documentary on black radio and has published articles on the subject.